GHOST CITIZENS

GHOST CITIZENS

Decolonial Apparitions of Stateless, Foreign and Wayward Figures in Law

Jamie Chai Yun Liew

Fernwood Publishing
Halifax & Winnipeg

Copyright © 2024 Jamie Chai Yun Liew

All rights reserved. No part of this book may be reproduced or transmitted in any form by any means without permission in writing from the publisher, except by a reviewer, who may quote brief passages in a review.

Copyediting: Amber Riaz
Cover illustration: Ophelia Liew
Cover design: Evan Marnoch
Text design: Brenda Conroy
Printed and bound in the UK

Published by Fernwood Publishing
Halifax and Winnipeg
2970 Oxford Street, Halifax, Nova Scotia, B3L 2W4
www.fernwoodpublishing.ca

This book has been published with the help of a grant from the Federation for the Humanities and Social Sciences, through the Awards to Scholarly Publications Program, using funds provided by the Social Sciences and Humanities Research Council of Canada.

Fernwood Publishing Company Limited gratefully acknowledges the financial support of the Government of Canada through the Canada Book Fund and the Canada Council for the Arts. We acknowledge the Province of Manitoba for support through the Manitoba Publishers Marketing Assistance Program and the Book Publishing Tax Credit. We acknowledge the Nova Scotia Department of Communities, Culture and Heritage for support through the Publishers Assistance Fund.

Library and Archives Canada Cataloguing in Publication

Title: Ghost citizens: decolonial apparitions of stateless, foreign and wayward figures in law /
Jamie Chai Yun Liew.
Names: Liew, Jamie Chai Yun, author.
Description: Includes bibliographical references and index.
Identifiers: Canadiana (print) 20230558992 | Canadiana (ebook) 2023055900X | ISBN 9781773636665 (softcover) | ISBN 9781773636788 (EPUB)
| ISBN 9781773636795 (PDF)
Subjects: LCSH: Statelessness.
Classification: LCC K7128.S7 L54 2024 | DDC 341.4/86—dc23

CONTENTS

Acknowledgements i

1 **The Stateless:**
   Wayward Foreign Ghosts 1
   The Conjuring of Ghost Citizens 1
   A Preliminary Note on Statelessness and a Universal Case Study 3
   Defining Ghost Citizens 3
   Imagining Purgatory: Understanding Statelessness 8
   The Case Study of Malaysia 19
   Ghost Hunting: Outline of the Book 25

2 **The State:**
   Colonial Vestiges of Racial Citizens 27
   Malaysia, Truly Asia 27
   The Postcolonial Formation of the Malaysian State 29
   Membership in the State: Bumiputera, Indigeneity and Citizenship ...34
   A Contemporary Unitary Malay Identity 42
   Statelessness: Constructing Ghost Citizens and Non-Malaysians 42

3 **The Law:**
   The International Legal Construction of Ghost Citizens 44
   Law-as-Text Shrouding States 44
   International Law: The Definition of Stateless and
   the Right to Nationality 45
   The State Prerogative and the False Promise of International Law.....62

4 **The Citizen:**
   Domestic Legal Construction of Ghost Citizens 64
   Malaysia: A Universal Case Study 64
   A Thin Conception of Human Rights in Malaysia............................... 64
   Citizenship Law in Malaysia 65
   Ghost Citizens as Judicial Facts 69
   Children as Ghost Citizens..73
   Finding Ghost Citizenship: A Thin Evidentiary Foundation 84
   Ghost Citizens Via Discretion: The Alternative Remedy.......................85
   Ghost Citizens in Prison..88
   Ghost Citizens Outside the Courtroom 88
   State Practice Thinning of the Definition of Statelessness
   with Ghost Citizenships 92

5 **Our Kin:**
   Homegrown Stateless Persons 94
   Experiencing Statelessness 94
   The Identification of Six Categories of Statelessness 96
   Disturbing the Ghost Citizen Concept: Genuine
   and Effective Links and Legal Ideas of Kinship.. 104

6 **The Government Counter:**
   The Discretionary Creation of the Stateless Person 109
   At the Government Counter 109
   The Administrative State and Administrative Justice 111
   Administrative Work Versus Administrative Barriers............................113
   Challenges Stateless Persons Face Before Getting to the Counter .. 113
   Barriers at the Counter with Street-Level Bureaucracy 124
   Lack of Transparency in Discretionary Decision-Making 132
   Ghosting: Lack of Reasons 132
   Politicization of the Conferral of Citizenship... 132
   Time 133
   Conjuring Ghost Citizens at the Government Counter........................ 136

7 **The Spectacle:**
   Performing Citizenship and State Benevolence........................... 141
   The Performance 141
   Roisah's Loss of Citizenship 143
   Federal Court Hearing.. 145
   Roisah's Day Trip to Putrajaya 146
   Appeasing Roisah's Wilful Disobedience 150
   Roisah Granted Citizenship 151
   Registration Rally 159

8 **The Ghost Citizen:**
   Believe in Ghosts: Unsettling Narratives of the
   Foreign Stateless.. 165
   The Ghost Citizen... 165
   Implications of Recognizing Ghost Citizens 169
   Informing Theories and Conceptions of Citizenship 171
   Fuelling Innovation 174
   Rewriting Pontianak's Story 176

Appendix 177
Endnotes 192
Index 243

For my father who migrated because he was stateless,
For all those who shared their stories with me,
For all those who are stateless today, I see you.

ACKNOWLEDGEMENTS

This book was written on various Indigenous lands: the lands of the Orang Asli (Peninsular Malaysia), the Orang Ulu (Sarawak Malaysia), Algonquin Anishinaabe territory (Ottawa), and Treaty Seven (southern Alberta) territory. All these lands have been home to me and my family in different ways, and I recognize I have been a guest in all of them. I still have much to learn and I apologize if I did not acknowledge peoples or lands appropriately or at all.

I have so many people to thank for this book and I see so many people's works in it. First, the University of Ottawa, Vice President Research Seed Funding was instrumental in providing me the modest means to travel to Malaysia to conduct interviews for this book. It is amazing what a $10,000 budget can help you do. For their helpful feedback while I prepared my application, I have Cintia Quiroga and Peter Oliver, then Vice Dean Research, to thank. I am also grateful for financial support from the Canadian Bar Association, Law for the Future Fund which allowed me to hire research assistants in Canada.

In the field in Malaysia, I was lucky to find partners for this research. Eric Paulsen, who was then with Lawyers for Liberty in Malaysia, helped me design a project on statelessness after he heard about my personal connection (through my father's previous status as a stateless person) and my interest in researching in the region. I am privileged to have Eric as a partner in this research. Eric was instrumental in helping me connect with the various persons I interviewed on the ground, including many stateless persons, providing in-kind support such as a place in his office, and the invaluable support of a research assistant.

Special thank you to Nursyahirah Mohd Daud (Syaz), a stellar research assistant. Syaz did not just provide legal research and translation and interpretation services, she was an excellent driver, a great co-interviewer, and a friend. I always think fondly of the many food adventures we had when we ventured somewhere to conduct an interview.

Nursyahirah Mohd Daud (left), Amanda Cheong (right back), Jamie Liew (right front). Photo credit: Jamie Liew.

Immense gratitude for Amanda Cheong, who at the time was conducting her PhD research (Sociology and Social Policy, Princeton) in Malaysia on the same topic. Amanda, you feel like a long lost cousin to me with our common history of stateless parents from Brunei. I am privileged to have had your assistance in helping map out the context in Malaysia, introducing me to key persons to interview, and also co-conducting interviews. I have enjoyed our various conversations on the topics but most of all, the collaborative approach we took in sharing our research. Your insights can be found in this book too.

To the many lawyers and advocates I interviewed: You are many and remain anonymous in the body of the work to protect the identities of stateless persons I interviewed but I am so grateful for the time you took to share your insights and your stories of advocacy. I admire your work and hope you see parts of your work in this book.

To all the stateless persons I interviewed, your courage, bravery and resilience was inspiring. I think of you often and hope that you have been able to find the recognition you are seeking. I hope that this book conveys your stories in an honest and respectful way.

In Canada, I am grateful to participants in an Emerging Works Workshop held by the Public Law Group at the University of Ottawa, Faculty of Law in the spring of 2018 during which scholars from both Queens Law School and the University of Ottawa gave helpful feedback on early work included in one of the chapters in this book. I am grateful to the Migration Research Collective for providing such a great research community and particularly for providing feedback on one of my chapters. Specific thanks to Jenny Francis, Shauna Labman, Luna Vives, and Sarah Zell. To Tendayi Bloom and Lindsey Kingston: Thank you for creating a community of scholars researching statelessness and for providing space for me to workshop and publish early parts of this research.

I have had many research assistants over the years assist me in searching for resources. With warm gratitude to uOttawa Faculty of Law alumni: Peter Choi, Emily Cumbaa, Silvia Esteves Domingues, Tara Rose MacDonald, Seema Shafei, and Stephanie Nedoshytko.

I have a few cherished colleagues to thank. Thank you to my colleague Constance Backhouse. It was during lunch one day that I shared what I was working on, and Constance told me I had a book. Constance: You talked me through the project and gave me the warm, encouraging push to dive into a book project. I am so glad I did. This work would otherwise be in separate, divided pieces. I am grateful you helped me see the thread and the greater contribution I hope it makes through this woven piece.

Thank you to my colleague John Currie who also encouraged me to think big and put my work into book form. I am grateful for your steadfast, wise mentorship and career advice throughout the many years.

To my colleague, Jennifer Chandler, thank you for planting the seed in my head that I could go to Asia and conduct research there. I have enjoyed our food adventures and conversations.

Thank you to my friends and colleagues who, through fruitful conversations, helped me think through different pieces of this book and supported me on the publication journey: Natasha Bakht, Anne Baltazar, Roisah Binti Abdullah, Kristy Belton, Helen Brunt, Y.Y. Chen, Vivienne Chew, Aimée Craft, Paul Daly, Goh Siu Lin, Alok Gupta, Amrita Hari, Sathiya Kebajikan, Ummni Khan, Latheefa Koya, Samuel Leong, Tracey Lindberg, Graham Mayeda, Laura Madokoro, Raymond Mah, Rodziana Mohamed Razali, Petra Molnar, Sarah Morales, Michael Orsini, Maalini Ramalo, Melissa Sasidaran, Terry Skolnik, and Hartini Zainudin.

Thank you to Emily Andrew for your kind professional advice. To Fiona Jeffries and the Fernwood Publishing team, thank you for championing this work. I also thank the anonymous peer reviewers. Your time and feedback were appreciated.

Thank you to Yasmeen Abu-Laban, Renisa Mawani and Daiva Stasiulis for engaging with and reading this work and providing kind blurbs.

Finally, thank you to my family here in Canada but also in Southeast Asia for supporting me during my field work and in my research endeavours. Thank you to my sister, Ophelia, for the beautiful cover art and her support. Thank you to both my parents, Uncle Tahir, brother (Jeffrey) and my children (Maxym and Vera) who are some of the many reasons I strive to record and preserve our shared history.

Most of all, I have unending gratitude for my partner Roman for coming with me halfway across the world "back home" for this adventure and for doing the heavy lifting of caring for our family when I was off interviewing, conducting research, and writing. I know you understand the importance of the research given that your own family, in the past, have experienced statelessness and refugeehood. Thank you for being the equal and loving partner who allows me to thrive in my passions.

ONE

THE STATELESS
Wayward Foreign Ghosts

The Conjuring of Ghost Citizens

The Tale of the Ghost of Pontianak

When I was a little girl, I heard ghost stories. These were not the ghost stories you might have heard at summer camp around a fire. They were folk tales my aunties told that people feared and believed. They were told to teach lessons but to also instill a respect of the unknown, our ancestors, and of things that may affect our fate.

One of the most memorable stories told to me was of a woman ghost known as Pontianak. I remember this story because my auntie, visiting from Southeast Asia, was shocked to find a small banana tree as a plant flanking our bay window in the kitchen of my childhood home. She warned me that Pontianak likes to live in banana trees and that she is a vengeful spirit that can inflict bad luck on those around her. I never looked at that plant the same way again. Yuen Ben Lee Adrian, a scholar in communication and film studies, explains that

> The *pontianak* is widely recognised as the most dreaded supernatural being in Malay folklore and mythology. Often described as a fearsome mythical creature with vampire-like qualities, she is said to have fangs, possesses ghost-like traits and can only be subdued using a sharp object which is usually a nail struck to the back of her neck. She is also recognised through her high-pitched shrieks, long flowing hair and a fondness for the blood of children. Despite possessing such fearsome and horrifying characteristics, the *pontianak* peculiarly remains popular among Malaysian and Asian audiences …[1]

Pontianak's story has been retold in folklore as that of a beautiful woman who died shortly after giving birth. In some versions of the story, she died from the shock of hearing that her child was stillborn and then returns from the dead. She is the equivalent of the Western conception of the female vampire with her long black hair and long robe-like dress. Historical and modern sightings of Pontianak are frequent with attestations and videos shared on social media. The myth of how she died or why she has come back has evolved. She conjures fear with the bad luck she can bring, and the ways in which to avoid or kill this spirit in violent ways are frequently discussed.

Adrian explains that Pontianak is a figure that transcends traditional belief in folklore and popular culture, manifesting in cinematic representations in horror films.[2] He finds her popularity increasing because of social, cultural, and political anxieties. Adrian discusses how Pontianak emerged "as a form of 'living dead'" transgressing normative forms of proper behaviour but asking for repentance.[3] Adrian further notes that

> The *pontianak* is a nebulous figure not only because of her existence as a being neither dead nor alive but also because of her ambiguous role as it is not clear if she is a villain or hero … On one hand, she could be seen as a villain or antagonist due to the chaos, destruction and murder of those regardless of their innocence; on the other, she could be read as a hero or the protagonist as she seeks justice for those who are oppressed.[4]

Pontianak haunted me in Malaysia while I was conducting field research. Friends would send me videos where wispy apparitions would be seen to float on a dark highway. The superstitious side of me held a respect for the warnings and stories, but the scholar in me also started to see a parallel between the lived experiences of stateless persons and Pontianak. I began to believe again, like I did as a child, that ghosts, the living dead, were among us.

A Preliminary Note on Statelessness and a Universal Case Study

This book is about the existence and maintenance of statelessness, the condition of not having citizenship to any country whatsoever. Being without citizenship is not for the faint of heart, for it means, at the very least, an inconvenience in obtaining life sustaining benefits such as employment, education, health care and identification, but at its worst, it can also mean racist violence, genocide, and oppressive and indigent living conditions. The status of citizenship can shield you from criminalization, prison, a life of limbo, and deportation to unknown parts of the world. Citizenship allows you easier and greater access to things such as social services and legal venues. Statelessness often means hiding for fear of detection and mistreatment.

This book is grounded in research from a place I consider to be one of my homes: Malaysia. Studying statelessness in Malaysia is also not a remote exercise. Malaysia has a history of British colonization and a vibrant Indigenous population. It is multijuridical with a common law system; it has a large administrative state, making this is an apt case study. Much of the world's stateless populations reside in states that were colonized by the British with colonial legal vestiges scarring its citizenship laws and administration. What is gleaned from this seemingly remote jurisdiction is common and familiar in many places in the world.

Defining Ghost Citizens

This book is about ghosts, but more specifically about *ghost citizens*. Like Pontianak, stateless persons have a bifurcated reception; while many view stateless persons as illegals, cheaters, and foreigners, some view stateless persons as kin, citizens, and resilient advocates.

Ghost citizen is a term I use for stateless people in situ, or for stateless persons who reside in the state they consider their "own country."[5] Stateless persons are those that are without any citizenship whatsoever; no state has legally conferred citizenship to them. Ghost citizens are a subset of the millions of stateless people around the world; they live within the country with which they have genuine, long-standing, enduring, effective and thick links. Thus, it is not just the status of being stateless but the added condition that they *also* live within their home country that makes a person a ghost citizen. A stateless person is considered to live in their "own country" if they have deep links with the state. These links may include their birth on the territory; long-term or permanent residence; family, including generational links with parents, grandparents, and children in the territory; employment or business; and cultural and ethnic community and support networks. Ghost citizens are persons who are stateless but who are living in a country where they believe they are citizens, but for a variety of reasons, have no citizenship in the country they are in. More than that, ghost citizens contest their statelessness by identifying ties, bonds, relations with their home state.

The term ghost citizen is more than a descriptor of stateless persons within their home country. It is a term I use to describe *how* stateless people become and remain stateless. Ghost citizens denotes the manifestation of statelessness in two ways. First, stateless persons become stateless because they are ghosted by their home states. In other words, the state they have genuine and effective links to does not recognize or acknowledge them as a citizen; they are denied citizenship by their own state. The term ghost citizen traces the historical, colonial construction of race and citizenship to uncover how and why stateless persons are being ghosted, denied, or ignored by their home states.

Second, stateless persons are rendered a citizen of a foreign country by their home state. In other words, their own state confers ghost citizenship on them; they deem them a citizen of another foreign state even though the home state has no jurisdiction or power to do so. I use the term ghost citizenship to recognize that states are making factual findings that a person is a citizen of an alternative state despite the lack of evidence, documentary proof, or legal assurance that they are in fact a citizen of another foreign state. It is citizenship in absence of any concrete confirmation, corroboration, or substantiation, hence the use of the term ghost alongside citizen. It is citizenship without actual conferral and is seemingly conjured. Ghost citizenship reduces stateless persons to the Other, the foreign and, consequently, provides fodder or rationale for why the home state does not recognize the person as kin or citizen.

More than that, the factual finding of foreign citizenship without any evidence allows states to gaslight stateless persons and their lived experiences. It allows states to simultaneously cast doubt on claims that stateless persons are indeed citizens of their home country and denies them the status of being stateless. Ghost citizenships are used to deny that statelessness exists; they are used by states to counter a stateless person's narrative about their history with their home state and to manipulate perceptions of the stateless person's memory or place within their own country.

The term ghost citizen is grounded in the experiences of in situ stateless persons. In my conversations with stateless persons, they have communicated their feelings of invisibility in a variety of ways that invoke ghostlike imagery. For example, one stateless person told me, "I found out I was stateless when I was around 18 years old when I wanted to apply for a bank account, when I was sick and went to the hospital, and I realized this is statelessness. I can't go anywhere. I can't do anything. I'm invisible."[6] Another stateless person poignantly reflects: "It's been difficult without status. I'm still young. It feels like I am missing out; that I'm missing out on life. People are living and going on without me."[7]

Beyond people's lived experience, the term ghost citizen also exhibits the actions and activities by which persons come to live in a phantom-like state through the taking of documents at a government office, the denial of applications by a bureaucrat, the finding of fact by a court that a person has foreign citizenship without concrete evidence, for example. One stateless person provides, "When my documents were taken away, I felt lost. Missing the documents has meant I feel like I am a missing person."[8] Moreover, the term ghost citizen evokes a make-belief problem; the term explains the gaslighting of the stateless person's lived experience. One advocate for stateless persons told me that "Even the legal decisions are not there for us to see. A lot of decisions are not public. It's like this problem doesn't exist."[9] Another advocate told me that "Unfortunately, people do just give up. They are not in the records. They are nowhere. They just disappear."[10]

This book documents the duality of the term ghost citizen: the ghosting of persons by the denial of citizenship on the one hand, and the conferral of ghost or foreign citizenships without any evidence to substantiate any citizenship has been conferred by any state.

Further, creating ghost citizens in the ontology of how we discuss citizens or statelessness is helpful in recognizing the lived experiences of stateless persons. Like Pontianak, stateless persons live a phantom-like experience. They experience an administrative death in the denial of their citizenship but live among us, sometimes hiding and other times making appearances while invoking questions of the unknown. They are sometimes ignored, rendered invisible, and they hide in the crevices of our society because they themselves fear the consequences of interacting with those free to benefit from citizenship rights. These consequences include arbitrary and lengthy detention as well as deportation to a foreign country. Some live in poverty, unable to obtain legal work, relying on the goodwill of family or members of their community. Some work in unauthorized, exploitative, and abusive employment to survive. A large proportion of stateless persons are children, and many cannot access education, living in a purgatory waiting for their status to be resolved to begin their lives. Some never resolve their citizenship issues and lead a life drifting from one survival mechanism to another. Due to their structural exclusion from education, employment, and social services, some turn to informal means to survive and sometimes come into conflict with the law, which criminalizes them and further deems them deviant. Many cannot access health care and are forced to struggle with injuries and other ailments or simply perish due to neglect. The things we may take for granted such as opening a bank account, obtaining a cell phone, or signing up for a sports team sometimes requires identification that a stateless person cannot provide. Everything in a stateless person's life is difficult and requires overcoming a multitude of barriers. Sometimes stateless persons and their families simply abandon the pursuit to be a citizen.

Stateless persons also haunt and terrify people. The misunderstandings about who stateless people are and the narrative that states have crafted—where foreign persons are portrayed as taking advantage of the legal system—have instilled a fear in the national citizenry of a flood of alien figures invading the state, taking up precious space, resources, and jobs, muddying the national identity of the state. In some contexts, stateless persons are subjected to violence, discrimination, and oppression.

It is not a coincidence that Pontianak is female. This book chronicles the occurrences of statelessness among persons whose mother was a foreigner, a citizen of another state, and her connection to a child is seen as marring their perceived loyalty, identity, and ultimately chances of obtaining citizenship. While Pontianak represents the racist and misogynistic framework of citizenship law, a vestige of colonial British law, she also represents the vehicle by which citizenship denial is undertaken. She is the foreign citizen mother haunting the courtroom, the government counters, casting shadows on citizenship applications. The mother, whether known/present or not, is a legal device to deny citizenship and ghost persons that may otherwise have genuine, strong, and enduring links to the state. She is the proxy by which to mark a stateless person wayward, Other, or foreign.

As with sightings of Pontianak however, we should be wary of conclusions drawn from perceived apparitions and scrutinize the conception of reality told to us by others, especially that by the state. We should not place importance on an imagined citizenship, one that is not based on evidence or proof of actual conferral of such status. This book disturbs the narrative the state has crafted around stateless persons. It upsets the accounts conveyed through the factual findings in legal and administrative decisions where stateless persons are made to be citizens of other states but also non-citizens of their self-identified own state. The research here challenges the construction of ghost citizens by highlighting the erasure of the status of statelessness and by foregrounding the general gaslighting—that such persons are not necessarily kin or members of the community.

This book, however, also chronicles the survival work undertaken by stateless persons and traces the troubling paths ghost citizens float through to disrupt notions that they do not belong or are wayward Others. As well, during my time in Malaysia, I was searching for people who were hiding from the state, and was aided by guides, overseers or undertakers who ferried me to communities and persons to interview. This book, thus, also recounts courageous efforts by advocates to guide persons from purgatory back to life.

While this book uses the case study of Malaysia, I see ghost citizens in other contexts. Therefore, I argue that the ontological turn to ghost citizen is useful in not only identifying similar trends in a multitude of locales where stateless persons reside, but an important way to disturb narratives and stories about who are stateless. For example, in my examination of statelessness in Canada, I see administrative and judicial decision makers referring to "entitlement to foreign citizenship" as a reason to make factual findings that a person is not stateless, but a foreigner. This allows Canada to deny its obligation to confer refugee protection or to preserve citizenship for a particular person.[11]

Ultimately, this book attempts to make sense of what is happening to stateless people and to "imagine possible futures."[12] While documenting the administrative and legal construction of statelessness, I imagined stories of hope, where ghost citizens will be brought back to life. In some ways, I imagine the folktale ending this way: Pontianak died in childbirth but was mistakenly told that her baby died too. She stays in purgatory trying to right a wrong. In the end, even though the baby's new parents want to keep ghosts away, she is somehow able to meet her baby and tucks a passport or citizenship certificate in her baby's swaddle. Once she is able to do this one last task, she leaves the in-between and floats into the afterlife. She is ultimately a hero in a story of oppression.

Imagining Purgatory: Understanding Statelessness

A Preliminary Understanding of the State

Contemporary citizenship, whether we agree with the conceptual principle or not, rests on the notion of states as defined territories that are self-contained political units. The world is scarred with borders, even in contested forms, giving states the seemingly normative authority to govern activities, people, and institutions within such borders.[13]

The emergence of the state has been attributed by some to the end of the Thirty Years War, and the Peace of Westphalia in Europe (which encompasses a pair of treaties).[14] The peace treaties led to the demise of the overarching power of the Catholic Church and the Holy Roman Empire, both of which were sources of legal and moral authority. They also led to the advent of an international legal system where autonomous states became sovereign over their own domain.[15] It is important to understand that the treaties do not only address sovereignty over territory but also over a state's citizens, referring to "vassals," "subjects," "soldiers," "inhabitants," "servants," "people," and others. Passages referring to such citizens in the peace treaties were written with the intention to provide protection; that is, the state's sovereign right not only included unencumbered right to rule over people but the reciprocal responsibility of protecting citizens.

While this system of international law started in Europe, other states were folded into this new world order through the violent expansion of European colonial empires. States that were not colonized reluctantly adopted this European model. As a result, by the early twentieth century, the European model of international legal order was universalized.

At the core of this system was the principle of state sovereignty, albeit sovereignty that favoured colonial powers.

The necessary corollary of creating self-contained and sovereign states is the development of rules and procedures by which people can enter, stay in, and exit such states. Ultimately, sovereign states necessitate the creation of national communities where certain people are conferred membership and others are not.

The idea of citizenship is often cited as a consequence of the rise of the modern sovereign state. However, English common law reveals that there were early iterations of the concept of citizenship. Calvin's case is the earliest and most influential theoretical articulation of birthright citizenship by an English court. Robert Calvin, who was born in Scotland around 1606, had inherited estates in England but to claim his rights to the estates, he had to prove he was an English subject. The question was whether he was an English subject even though he was born in Scotland. The Court of King's Bench ruled that Calvin was an English subject since he was born in Scotland after the Union of the Crowns (Scottish and English) and entitled to the benefits of English law.

Despite this early pronouncement of the concept of birthright citizenship, Calvin's case does provide limitations. The court makes exceptions where ambassadors of foreign nations have children within England; they are not "natural-born subjects" of the king. Similarly, enemies that come into the kingdom, possessing hostility, are not loyal or obedient to the king, and therefore cannot be subject to the king. These exceptions, bounded in loyalty, are reflected in the modern legal conceptions of citizenship.

Throughout this book I use the term "state." This refers to the state in the Westphalian sense where the territorial boundaries that demarcate enclosed tracts of land are identified as countries and where persons within are at the behest of the governments managing those communities. There has been a plethora of research discussing how states should be studied in a "civic" or "ethnic" sense, but these approaches are outside of the scope of this book.[16] This book also does not reconcile the debate as to how nation-states are formed and does not propose how one would resolve contested claims of statehood.

In utilizing the term "state," I also refer to the government in both the administrative and legal senses. Since this book focuses on a case study that has a democratic context, the term state refers to not only the institutions that make laws, but the agents that embody those decision makers. Further, the state is evoked in the administrative sense and points to the administrative bodies that represent the state be they registrars and bureaucrats that implement and enforce law. As well, the state embodies the decisions flowing from the judiciary, one of the arms of government.

I acknowledge that at times, when using the term state, I may be attributing actions and decisions to the state writ large. I do this to contest narratives that occurrences of statelessness are one-off, isolated, or individual instances and instead challenge the reader to think about how state actions and decisions are masking more systemic and deliberate strategies to hide or deny the common experience of statelessness. Further, I invite readers to think about how state action, while manifested in one encounter with a bureaucrat, or a decision by one judge, may be part of a pattern and approach undertaken by the government to create ghost citizens by denying their citizenship and rendering them foreign citizens of other states. I argue that this design was a result of the racial categories created during British colonial rule and the postcolonial bargains undertaken between the racialized communities that formed during British colonial rule. The racial categories are now firmly entrenched in law, whether in the constitution as law-in-text, legislation, or administrative and judicial decisions.

I want to make clear that while this book acknowledges that the Westphalian model of states prevails, I recognize that this is a colonizing framework. I do not endorse this model. I see the colonial violence this model has created by destroying communities and denying their statehood and demands for self-determination. Indeed, part of the work of this book is to discuss the state's location as a product of colonialism. This book questions the focal point on "recognition by states,"[17] or a "state's monopoly over access, status and belonging"[18] and challenges the prevalent view that the nation-state in theory is a sanitized, neutral construct which we should not take for granted. As Rita Dhamoon and Andrea Smith point out, "the nation-state itself is a settler-colonial structure and form of governmentality" that is "governed through domination and coercion" and "based on control over territory."[19] This book acknowledges that statelessness is a product of migrations and the movement of people regulated by a system of nation-states, and furthers scholarly work that situates persons "in the service of settler colonial projects" and that understanding the "state-produced colonial hierarchies that privilege non-Indigenous peoples, including people of colour, at the expense of Indigenous peoples" is an "ongoing practice of ruling."[20] This book extends research that there are "uneven colonial processes of settler dominance" and that there are "differentials of power *among* marginalized peoples."[21] While I am working with the Westernized, colonizing definition of state, this book also, particularly through Chapter 2, utilizes the work of Jodi Byrd in presenting the "cacophony" of connections across different forms of racism and colonization illuminating the "multiple interactions among different colonialisms, arrivals and displacement at work" to understand the "multiple co-constituting" struggles of "colonizer-colonized and other minority oppressions."[22] Therefore, while I utilize the term state, make no mistake that this book is, in part, about disrupting the generative Eurocentric systems of creating and managing hierarchies, constructions, and categorizations of people. In fact, even though this is outside of the scope of this book, I recognize that different communities may conceive of communities and membership differently than that modelled in the world. This book aims to encourage more dialogue about how we might want to conceive of communities and membership differently than state-citizenship models that necessarily invoke borders as violent means of exclusion. I am also mindful of past erasures and renderings of Indigenous peoples and communities to the "mythic past or 'the dustbin of history'" and the reduction of "groups of racially and culturally defined and marginalized individuals" as "drowning in a sea of settlers."[23] I know that my work may not fully grapple with these conversations and for that, I acknowledge also that there may be shortcomings in how this is discussed in this book.

Worldwide Statelessness

There are over 10 million stateless persons in the world, persons without any citizenship whatsoever.[24] This number is an estimate since the counting relies on government data.[25] The problem of statelessness is often conflated with the plight of refugees and forced migrants, but in many cases, persons are stateless in situ, meaning that they were both born and continue to reside in countries to which they have genuine and deep connections.[26]

There is an urgency to understanding how persons are rendered stateless, especially within their own country. The International Court of Justice (ICJ) in The Gambia v Myanmar is currently assessing whether Myanmar has committed genocide against the Rohingya.[27] Since Myanmar gained independence from the British Empire in 1948, the Rohingya have been subjected to military-led violence, residential segregation, forced labour, and the deprivation of citizenship and basic rights including education, health care, freedom of movement, marriage, and reproductive autonomy.[28]

In the state of Assam in India, colonial- and postcolonial-era struggles' construction of Assamese indigeneity vis-à-vis Muslim Bengali foreignness have persisted and resulted most recently in the deletion of over 1.9 million residents from the 2019 version of the National Register of Citizens, rendering them at risk of statelessness and deportation.[29] In both cases, the stateless populations of the Rohingya and Muslim Assamese have long-standing connections and links to the impugned state spanning multiple generations.[30]

Malaysia, the focus of this study, shares a history of British colonial occupation and a significant in situ stateless population with the examples of the Rohingya and Muslim Assamese. This warrants further study because in Malaysia, the creation and maintenance of statelessness differs from that in Myanmar and India. That is, statelessness in Malaysia is produced mainly through administrative law rather than through executive orders (as is the case in Myanmar) or via legislation (as in India).

There is a rich body of research on statelessness. Political theorists have pointed out the exclusion of stateless persons from theory, discourse, and scholarship, rendering the stateless figure as leftover residue, invisible, forgotten, or ignored, calling for a more inclusive lens on theory.[31] Legal scholars have pointed out the historical perception that statelessness is a legal problem that requires tweaking or filling in gaps in the law[32] and also have turned to human rights as a mechanism to resolve statelessness.[33] Despite legal reform, some posit that the problem rests with legal interpretation or implementation.[34] Others have found that focusing on law reform masks the political, social, and cultural structures enabling statelessness.[35]

The occurrences of statelessness and the experiences of stateless persons are well documented in multiple places, for example, in the Caribbean,[36] Europe,[37] in member states of ASEAN (Association of Southeast Asian Nations),[38] Middle East (especially among Palestinians),[39] India,[40] Myanmar,[41] Nigeria,[42] Thailand,[43] Tibet,[44] and Vietnam.[45] This book contributes to the literature, but also discusses how statelessness is constructed through the material legacies of colonial administrative and legal mechanisms. The research herein disrupts state narratives that there are no stateless persons, that stateless persons are foreigners with citizenship elsewhere, and that stateless persons have no genuine links to the state they are claiming as their own. In doing so, this book proposes the conceptual device of the ghost citizen.

The Study of Statelessness

There is a plethora of work interrogating the state's treatment of migrant workers,[46] immigration detainees,[47] undocumented persons and/or "irregular" migrants,[48] and refugees[49] among others.[50] There is also research that questions the salience of citizenship[51] and work on the broader category of non-citizens.[52] Scholarship on statelessness, however, is an emerging area.[53] This book contributes to this developing body of research.

Theories of the state and citizenship typically begin with the dichotomous assumption that persons are either citizens (or subjects) or foreigners.[54] The republican model posits that a social contract exists between citizen and state[55] whereas the liberal model sees citizenship as ideally inclusive and indefinitely extensible.[56] Feminist critiques of the republican and liberal model point out that some citizens are more equal than others and discuss how laws structure personal circumstances.[57] As well, universalist conceptions contextualize perspectives to argue that citizenship rights should be extended to groups previously excluded (such as African Americans and women in the American context).[58] Critics of the universalist conception advocate for a differentiated citizenship to discourage generalizations, which, in turn, points to discussions on the types of demands that citizens can make (i.e. special representation, multicultural rights, self-government).[59] In discussing how citizenship can lead to better integration, liberal nationalists argue that only specific forms of political practice can lead to trust and loyalty from citizens such as a common identity.[60] On the other hand, postnationalists argue that a pluralistic society allows minorities to find their place within a state; instead, a pluralistic society centres around something other than nationalism like the constitution and a common political culture.[61] Still others may find the liberal nationalist approach too narrow,[62] focusing on different things such as whether a person is affected by a state decision[63] or has a connection to the territory or place.[64] In exploring the salience of the border and the right to free movement, some theorize citizenship through open borders or how members from poorer communities can and should access richer communities through a moral or human rights perspective.[65] Others theorize the protection of the integrity of existing communities and borders.[66] Membership somewhere is assumed. Indeed, Rainer Bauböck writes that the contemporary conundrum is that there are "citizens living outside the country whose government is supposed to be accountable to them and inside a country whose government is not accountable to them."[67] Irene Bloemraad goes so far as to assert that empirical evidence for the importance of citizenship is thin, finding that "most residents are citizens of their state."[68] Existing empirical research on statelessness however counters Bloemraad.[69] Studies of citizenship have not always acknowledged the existence of the stateless person, because their existence or presence is disruptive and disturbing when attempting to construct a theory of citizenship or statehood.[70] Theories of citizenship have privileged the voice of the insider and kept the stateless "at the margins of theory."[71] As Phillip Cole writes, rather than dismiss statelessness as "a leftover residue lying outside of the international system of sovereign states" or as "some minor inefficiency" that needs to be tweaked in the system, we should instead view this issue as "a structural failure, a product of that order" which may "involve rethinking everything."[72] Tendayi Bloom points to a special individual-state relationship of "noncitizenship,"[73] Lindsey Kingston maps out various kinds of hierarchies of personhood and the idea of "functional" citizenship,[74] and Kelly Staples discusses that the frame should be not one of member but of human and "bare life."[75]

This book presents an ontological position via ghost citizens to critically reflect on the assumptions some theories rest on: that the only salient relationship is the one acknowledged by the state and that the conditions with which recognition is conferred is sound. My research extends the work of Amar Bhatia who questions why the focus should be on "recognition by the state."[76]

Statelessness in Non-Western, Postcolonial Contexts

Tendayi Bloom describes liberalism as "a broad church" containing the core elements of individualism, equality, and liberty.[77] These Western values do not find prominence in non-Western states. For example, individualism contrasts sharply with Asian preferences for collectivism and its associated values. As Bloom notes, liberal thought claims, "universalism and a distanced rationality" giving "the appearance of being impartial" and "hiding its epistemic location" when scholars writing the "core texts of liberal theory" are "unfamiliar with the experience of activated noncitizenship."[78] Samantha Balaton-Chrimes concurs: "In keeping with this emphasis on autonomy in private life, the liberal political tradition turns a blind eye to difference associated with citizens' (or non-citizens') private lives, including identities such as ethnicity."[79] Kamal Sadiq writes, "While citizenship has a long lineage in developed Western states, we know very little about citizenship's advance in postcolonial developing states."[80] Sadiq further notes that "Missing from European accounts of citizenship are the rights and experiences of people in the colonies and their imperial centers"[81] and that "Europe's liberal claim becomes unstable once the conceptual lens is expanded to include a broader range of minorities and their various experiences of political, social, and economic discrimination."[82] Further, as Erin Aeran Chung states, "The study of citizenship in various non-Western contexts provides a distinctive lens through which we can analyze its contradictions and contingencies."[83] This book problematizes statelessness using narratives and storytelling in social and cultural contexts of postcolonial states.

Addressing the Rights Paradox: State Prerogative Versus the Right to Citizenship

Hannah Arendt is often invoked in relation to statelessness, given she was stateless for 13 years. She wrote that everyone has the "right to have rights."[84] The right, as explained by Seyla Benhabib is, "addressed to humanity as such and enjoins us to recognize membership in some human group."[85] Benhabib points out that "the use of the term 'right' evokes *a moral imperative*: 'Treat all human beings as persons belonging to some human group and entitled to the protection of the same.' What is invoked here is a *moral claim to membership* and *a certain form of treatment compatible with the claim to membership.*"[86] David Owen writes that while Arendt's appeal for a "right to have rights" has been "established as one of central importance to political reflection,"[87] the "problem of statelessness to which Arendt drew attention has not been resolved."[88] Michael Weinman agrees: "We have seen that the existing rights regime and the international institutions that support and give it codified expression are insufficient to the task of ensuring actual legal protections to non-citizens."[89] Further, Ayten Gundogdu, in reference to Arendt's paradox of statelessness points to "rightlessness of those who appear in their bare humanity."[90] In other words, statelessness necessitates a positionality of the absence of rights.

Since Arendt wrote about the right to have rights, the *Universal Declaration of Human Rights* has turned human rights discourse into, "a set of pleasant normative assertions."[91] Despite movements toward adopting a rights-based framework, much of the adoption of the rights-based approach has taken place among Western states.[92] The turn toward rights is not one that is as omnipresent in other parts of the world, including Asia, where a large proportion of the world's stateless rest. Even where some states take up human rights protections, however, these tools have not provided much comfort for stateless people in both Western and non-Western contexts.[93]

While many have benefited from the traction of and turn toward human rights, it is at the border, on the body of migrants and stateless persons, where human rights seem to either have a dampened effect or miss its mark. Sovereign privilege of the state almost always seems to trump any rights claims. Arendt's call for a right to have rights seems not to have been realized even in the West where it is most strongly embraced. Samuel Moyn writes that "to parade a list of rights before people who lack basic citizenship was 'something like offering a detailed inventory of the courses of a lengthy meal in the presence of the starving.'"[94]

There is an inherent belief that states will be assumed to act in bona fide ways to ensure its members will be conferred citizenship; the "human rights regime assumes one's relationship to a government."[95] Further, one can argue that rights associated with citizenship are still evolving and states are slowly coming around to recognizing certain obligations. The experience of stateless persons, however, shows a different story—that signing up to treaties does not mean they will automatically lead to resolution.[96]

The other consideration is the sovereign prerogative to say no. Scholars find a tension between borders and the egalitarian values pronounced by rights.[97] Other scholars go beyond identifying a tension and call sovereign prerogatives "punitive and disciplinary"[98] questioning the "weak presumption" states have to prohibit people from entering territories as well as the idea of property in service of this.[99] Duncan Ivison, Paul Patton, and Will Sanders, who write about Indigenous persons and political theory, state that "egalitarian political theory has often ended up justifying explicitly inegalitarian institutions and practices."[100] The presumption of borders leads to the legal rationale states turn to time and time again: the sovereign prerogative to govern within its jurisdiction and the right to decide who are its members.

Human rights protections are diluted by the state prerogative; rights are a paradox that mask and perpetuate structural conditions of harm and disparity, reinforcing rather than challenging established arrangements.[101] As Dean Spade has written in relation to trans rights in the United States, "law reform work that merely tinkers with systems to make them look more inclusive while leaving their most violent operations intact must be a concern of many social movements today."[102]

Acknowledging Stateless as Constructed Racial "Others" and "Foreigners"

My research builds on scholarly work on the construction of the Other[103] and how colonial rule relied on a graded, racialized and hierarchical conception of membership that informs the codification of citizenship.[104] The ontological turn to ghost citizens questions the label that states impose on persons without considering how stateless persons themselves understand their identity.[105] Scholars have discussed how migrants have been cast as illegal, deviant, strange, fraudsters, cheaters, and liars and so on.[106] The "phantasm" of "binary mode of self/other, clean/dirty, responsible/irresponsible, and independent/dependent" is "viewed as natural rather than political or economic" and that these attitudes, "take the individual as the unit of analysis and structural factors are ignored."[107]

In Malaysia, scholars have written about how British colonization created and reinforced segregated racialized communities[108] and "Indigenous" status among Malays.[109] Contemporary Malaysia is dominated, shaped and factualized by colonial knowledge[110] informed by colonial censuses,[111] and the bargains or compromises various racialized groups made to garner citizenship in nascent Malaysia.[112] This book builds on this literature to map out how the colonial vestiges of administrative and legal documentation, systems, and tools have persisted and evolved to shape a hierarchical and racialized national identity in

Malaysia. Further, this research explores how stateless persons perform citizenship and how they contest the label of foreignness.

Harsha Walia interrogates the formation and function of borders as a "spatial and material power structure"; that borders are an "ordering regime, both assembling and assembled through racial-capitalist accumulation and colonial relations."[113] This book furthers Walia's work in interrogating how colonialism and racial categories have created borders on the bodies of stateless persons, and expands existing interrogations into the state's obsession with purifying spaces from so-called contaminants — stateless persons — regularly identified as deviants, wayward, illegal, and foreign.[114]

Statelessness as a Development and Registration Issue

Statelessness has also been seen as a technical problem of documentation where one need only attend to the administrative task of registering with the government. Tied to this is the state's capacity to manage this technical or administrative work. Statelessness is thus seen as a consequence of developmental difficulties manifested through poverty and low levels of education.[115] Looking at statelessness through this lens, however, ignores the incredible capacity of the state to document and survey the population:[116] that states are using the technical under-registration of persons as an excuse for why there may be stateless persons within its borders, masking other structural reasons.[117] The turn toward sustainable development as a mechanism to solve statelessness has overlooked the work law has done to construct "citizens" especially in postcolonial states.[118] This book contributes to scholarship that reveals that states and their membership-making process is not one-dimensional but socially constructed and contested.[119]

The historical development of various forms of identity documentation demonstrates how the regulation of people's identities and movement are central to nation-state building.[120] The Holocaust and the Rwandan genocide show the extreme ways in which exclusion and even extermination was made possible with the use of bureaucratic records and documents to construct boundaries and notions of difference.[121] These practices have continued in the contexts of Myanmar with Rohingya and India with Muslim Assamese. Documents make "imagined communities" become realized on a practical level.[122]

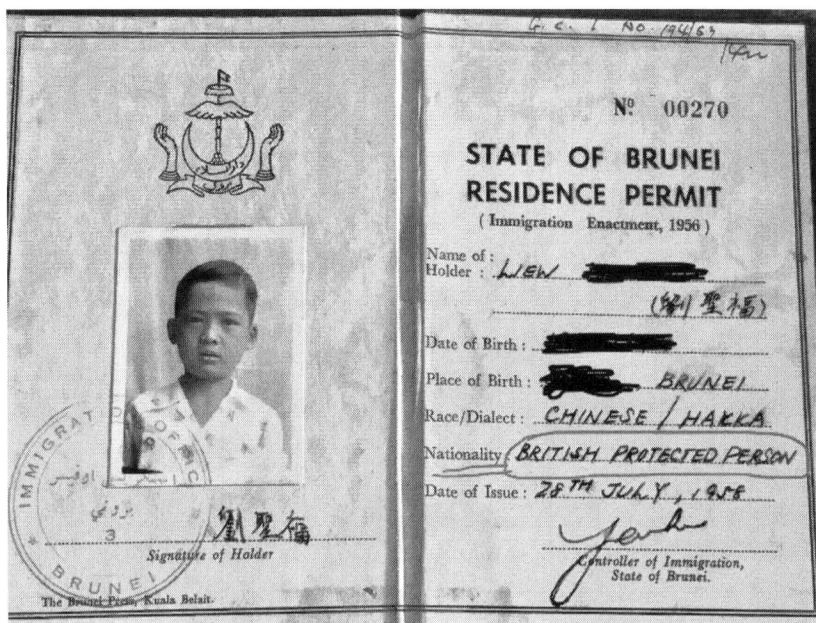

Photo Credit: Jamie Liew

The Case Study of Malaysia

Why Malaysia?

In the dark and murky waters of the Brunei River sits Kampong Ayer. Kampong, in Malay, means village. We could call it a suburb or neighbourhood, but those images are sure to conjure bungalows or two-storey houses flanked with manicured green lawns or condos and apartment buildings with sidewalks leading to open playgrounds and parks in Canada. Kampong Ayer is on water, framed by mangroves clutching edges of the river, sipping the salt water. Houses, schools, shops are perched on stilts over the restless river, connected by boardwalks, docks, and boats. Take away the water, the stilts, and the heat, and the images are no longer foreign. Clothes hang on lines adjacent to homes, children ride their bicycles, and potted vegetables and plants frame windows and porches.

My father grew up in a neighbouring water village that no longer exists, and Kampong Ayer is where my family takes me to bear witness to where we are from. My father has no love for his childhood home. This cannot be blamed on the lack of charm or community in the village that exists today. Born in Brunei, my father was stateless.[123] Brunei, a sultanate, did not confer citizenship to Chinese people. It was this lack of citizenship that led my father to migrate to Canada. His rootlessness in Brunei however, led me back to Asia to try to understand why. How could someone be born into a country and not have citizenship? How could the proboscis monkeys swinging from the trees above the water village feel more at home than he did?

My father's life story is for another time, but it is his lived experience that prompted me to try to understand the phenomenon of statelessness. When I am asked where my parents come from, I find it difficult to answer. How can I explain the purgatory my father was in as a place he came from? How can I attribute his existence to a place that wanted him invisible?

While I initially wanted to study the issue of statelessness in Brunei, this research is situated in Malaysia. The Sultanate of Brunei is not a democratic state and there are political barriers to interrogating why people are stateless there. Fear of the government, and a lack of openness and transparency made research impossible for a foreigner like me in Brunei. I turned to Malaysia, a country where my mother was born, and a country where I also have roots. There, statelessness was ubiquitous, not only on the bodies of thousands of people, but in political discourse. I chose Malaysia because it is a democratic state, a former British colony. It is a state that is not signatory to many human rights instruments, and there is a vibrant advocacy community for stateless persons.

I also felt that my face, shared culture, heritage, and language, combined with my father's own personal history of being stateless would allow me to connect with stateless persons there. My own personal connection to the place as both inspiration and instrument in this research is important to providing perspectives on statelessness. I try to point this out throughout the book. I follow the lead of other racialized scholars such as Heba Gowayed who found that her "insider/outsider status" as an Egyptian American and an Arab American woman enabled her to do her fieldwork on Syrian refugees resettled in Canada, the United States, and Germany;[124] and Kimberly Kay Hoang who recognized the "reflexive dialogue about the racialized, gendered, and classed relations that differentially reward and discipline white scholars, as opposed to scholars of color and male and female scholars from diverse class backgrounds" even as she was warned that studying sex workers in Vietnam would marginalize her as either an "area-studies scholar" or as someone who does "me-search."[125] This book provides reflexive dialogues that flow from research from racialized scholars like Gowayed, Hoang, and others.

Like Gowayed and Hoang, I do not appear much in this text, as a deliberate effort to place the stories of stateless persons at the heart of the analysis.[126] I hope their stories are represented in an honest and respectful way. Despite this, while I am hyper-aware of my place as a privileged, Western-born, educated lawyer and scholar, I do provide a few insights, given my personal positionality with statelessness, that I think are "worthy" of discussing.[127]

Statelessness in Malaysia

Some of the research in Malaysia details the challenges stateless persons face in accessing education,[128] while others provide accounts of statelessness in communities such as the Rohingya in Malaysia,[129] the Bajau Laut in Sabah,[130] the Tamils in Peninsular Malaysia,[131] and migrants.[132] Further, there is vital research on citizenship law in Malaysia.[133]

Catherine Allerton, in writing about child statelessness in Sabah, points out that "statelessness…is *always* embroiled in wider moral and political arguments" and "though laws exist to apparently prevent child statelessness, in practice, the path toward Malaysian citizenship … is unlikely to be straightforward."[134] Allerton argues that "statelessness is fundamentally an issue of (social, moral, and political) recognition and is not simply a question of the lack of citizenship."[135] Adding to Allerton's thinking, this book argues that the legal recognition is not simply one of neutral or benign operation of an administrative process. This book discusses how the state is actively reconstructing stateless persons as foreign or as ghost citizens.[136] My research compliments Allerton's writing to uncover the "work *against* recognition"[137] against stateless children.[138] This book documents how Malaysia, by rendering stateless persons as foreigners (ghost citizens) denies them citizenship of the state with which they have genuine and effective links.

Searching for Ghost Citizens in Malaysia — Methodology

Forty-five people, including nineteen stateless persons or their parents and/or siblings were interviewed in Malaysia over a period of approximately three months from January to April 2018. The interviews took place in Kuala Lumpur, Selangor; Georgetown, Penang;

Kota Kinabalu, Saba; and Miri, Sarawak. I also observed a registration rally in February 2018 where advocates gathered approximately sixty stateless persons and/or their parents to assist them in submitting their citizenship applications in a registration office. As well, I accompanied a stateless person on a day trip in March 2018 to meet with top officials in the Ministry of Home Affairs as part of her plea for citizenship. My observations and conversations as well as the papers gathered in these encounters document the lived experiences of ghost citizens.

Alongside this ethnographic data, I conducted a review of the *Federal Constitution of Malaysia* and related legislation, as well as all reported Malaysian case law involving stateless persons. Additionally, I acquired information for a few unreported cases via lawyers and the media up to April 2020. The discourse in the legal decisions enhances our understanding of how ghost citizens are created in law. Finally, reports, pamphlets, scholarly articles and other writings from advocates and scholars in the region provided context to the findings in this book.

The stories of the nineteen stateless persons and their families, as well as twenty-six advocates (lawyers, paralegals, NGO [nongovernmental organization] representatives, and a few academics) are heartbreaking. Their accounts were shared punctuated by tears, heavy sighs, anger, and frustration, but also hope that things will change for them individually and systemically. One of the most surprising aspects of this research project was how easy it was to find people to talk to and how forthcoming they were with me. They wanted to say something, to tell someone what they have been going through, and to appeal to anyone who could help them. Many were steadfast in asserting they were Malaysians, that they were not foreigners. Most of all, they wanted people to know they exist.

As a lawyer, it was painful for me to part after such personal encounters. I am used to hearing people's stories but then I take those stories, mash them up, rework them, and use them in legal documentation like affidavits, memoranda, and factums. I follow clients in their journey through a legal process. In those written actions, I feel I am taking a positive step for those who shared something intimate with me. In these encounters, I did not know if I would see or hear from these persons again; I did not have any concrete plans to help them on their journey except the promise that I would write about statelessness. This book, if nothing else, is a testament to the lives of stateless persons and a reminder of their brave act of speaking out.

I was jarred by the faces of children who accompanied their parents since they made me think of how I could have easily been one of them, that in my ancestral homeland, places could have been reversed, and I, or my parents, could have been telling someone about my struggles living as a stateless person.

I make several caveats. First, there is research on the experience of statelessness and the associated consequences.[139] This book supplements this research but does not provide a full picture of what stateless persons face in various aspects of social, political, and economic life.[140]

Second, in discussing each case, there is no nuanced legal opinion proffered as to the stateless person's eligibility or entitlement to citizenship. Nevertheless, on the face of the law in Malaysia, in my own legal assessment, many persons interviewed appear to meet the legal requirements for citizenship but face administrative and legal barriers from obtaining that citizenship.

Third, this book acknowledges that the labels of stateless and ghost citizens (foreign citizens) are being recreated here and that they invoke potential plural and diverse meanings.[141] While there is an exercise of categorization in identifying stateless persons in this book, this is not a finite list or a full picture of statelessness but a glimpse of what kinds of statelessness exist. The book hopes to illuminate the work of categorization. As Rita Kaur Dhamoon points out, the "re/making, re/organizing and managing" of "subjugating formations of difference" work to create relations of dominance.[142] This book describes how the colonial project of categorization and race-making manifests into the further classifications of statelessness allowing race to play the proxy for the foreign and wayward or disloyal Other.

Finally, a few terms are used to refer to persons stateless in situ (persons who are in their "home" country). I refer to a stateless person and de facto stateless synonymously as a person who is either stateless and is a migrant or a stateless person in situ because both include persons who have no legal recognition as a citizen in any state. I refer to three terms, de jure stateless, "administratively" stateless persons, and de facto citizens synonymously as persons who have no legal recognition as a citizen in any state but may have legal entitlement to citizenship, that is persons who are entitled to citizenship on the face of the law but due to various administrative or legal barriers, are unable to obtain the legal proof of citizenship. Some may question my use of the term stateless for persons who appear to meet the legal requirements for citizenship and prefer to use the term "undocumented citizen." My view is that the legal fact of being conferred citizenship is important. As such, persons should be considered stateless until they are legally recognized as a citizen.[143]

I refer to refugees as persons who self-identify or have been identified by NGOs/advocates (including the United Nations High Commissioner for Refugees [UNHCR]) as persons who are fleeing persecution, as outlined in the *Convention Relating to the Status of Refugees* ("*Refugee Convention*"),[144] and persons who are fleeing torture and unusual and undeserved treatment, as outlined in the *Convention against Torture and Other Cruel, Inhuman or Degrading Treatment or Punishment* ("*Convention against Torture*").[145] I refer to migrants as persons who have themselves moved to Malaysia. If the migrant person's child was born in Malaysia, I do not automatically consider the child a migrant.

Finally, Indigenous persons refers to any person in Malaysia that are Orang Asli, Orang Ulu or Anak Negeri. As I explain in Chapter 2, while people of Malay descent may be considered "Indigenous," this label is a social construction born of the postcolonial bargains made in the constitution. They form most of the population and are politically, economically, and socially dominant and therefore not ethnic minorities.[146] They are not included in the term "Indigenous" persons when I use it.

This book elevates voices of persons at the margins through narrative.[147] This project draws from research that interrogates the construction of the "imperial category of Native"[148] while recognizing the violence that the distinction between "natives," "Indigenous," and "Aboriginal" creates.[149] This book continues the work of Renisa Mawani on how the postcolonial state deploys indigeneity,[150] in this case, to advance or deny citizenship claims through jurisdictional terms of racial status and subjecthood, looking to the "histories of racial classification that animated the oscillating divides between 'aboriginal' and 'native' specific to the Malaysian and statelessness context."[151] The mobilization of indigeneity has been used to assert self-serving claims to citizenship and racial superiority. In this way, as Mawani asserts, Indigenous peoples were not vanishing or in the past, but indigeneity materializes in the present and future; indigeneity is "an effect of racial and colonial power, produced through protracted struggles and violent histories of British imperial rule."[152] This book uses this frame to complicate and bring to light the different "figures and forms of indigeneity"[153] in relation to statelessness in Malaysia. This research, however, also attends to the decolonizing practices interrogating indigeneity, being mindful of how such research may reproduce or amplify the ongoing colonization of Indigenous peoples. Where possible I point out gaps in the research and invite further research. This book uses ethnographic and sociolegal research to elevate the voices[154] and experiences of racialized stateless communities, to inform understandings of how "native," "Indigenous," "foreign," and "migrant" categories create statelessness.

Ghost Hunting: Outline of the Book

This book has eight chapters. This chapter introduces you to the concept of ghost citizens. Chapter 2 provides a brief overview of the historical context of the case study: Malaysia. The chapter discusses how British colonialization constructed segregated racial and ethnic identities and how these identities are reproduced in contemporary law, policy, and public discourse on who is a citizen.

Chapter 3 provides a brief overview of international law and how state practice and law-as-text (conventions and legal decisions) have held firm to the principle that the state has the prerogative to decide who are citizens. Flowing from this state prerogative is the emerging praxis where states deny citizenship to those with genuine and effective links with that state (ghosting citizens).

Chapter 4 presents an overview of Malaysian citizenship law but also reveals findings from a case law survey of Malaysian legal cases and ethnographic interviews on how stateless persons experience the legal system. In situ stateless persons with genuine and effective links are not only denied citizenship (where the state is ghosting their citizens) but are also prevented from utilizing the status of stateless, deeming them foreign citizens where there is no proof that citizenship by a foreign state has been conferred (conferring ghost citizenship).

Chapter 5 provides findings from the case law survey and ethnographic interviews to identify who are stateless in Malaysia. This chapter argues that many stateless persons are not necessarily "foreigners" and have genuine and effective links to states they reside in.

Chapter 6 presents findings that the government counter is not a neutral place but one where persons not only become stateless but are deemed foreigners, ghost citizens of other states. The chapter argues for a more focused gaze on administrative processes and the work of frontline government officials.

Chapter 7 follows Roisah, a young stateless person at the time of field research but has since successfully obtained citizenship in Malaysia. Roisah's case illustrates the strategic performance to *masuk Melayu,* become Malaysian, to become a citizen.

Chapter 8 summarizes the multiple state practices of ghosting in situ stateless persons who are de facto citizens by conferring ghost citizenship, invoking foreignness, otherness, wayward deviancy and illegality and invites further research on *ghost citizens* using voices and experiences of stateless persons elsewhere.

TWO

THE STATE
Colonial Vestiges of Racial Citizens

Malaysia, Truly Asia

I never get used to landing in Malaysia. The heat hits you immediately, like you are walking into an oven as you descend the stairs from your airplane. Flying in Malaysia has become easier and cheaper since Malaysia's low-cost airline came into the picture. Air Asia, Malaysia's largest airline, has a catchy advertising slogan: "Truly Asia." I have wondered how the airline could use such a slogan. This corporate mantra is not a benign catchphrase. Frederic Bouchon writes that the "brand relies on contrasted, if not blurred, images, echoing a society with contested identities" that "underlines the challenges in reconciling local values,"[1] revealing competing narratives of a unified but multicultural identity.

This chapter interrogates how Malaysia's colonial history has shaped citizenship laws. Scholars have pointed out that legal doctrines in the colony affected the development of legality in postcolonial spaces;[2] that legal discourse colonized individual subjects as subjects of law.[3] Following Edward Said's approach to identifying cultural artifacts,[4] this chapter presents the narratives and language used to possess colonial territory and articulate membership therein.

Although this chapter provides a brief historical background of Malaysia, it is important to acknowledge that the contextual orientation toward the past is not a fixed or ahistorical recollection. My summary is not exhaustive but serves as a reference point to discuss how Malaysia's common history as a former British colony provides social context for how race and statelessness is constructed.[5] It is beyond the scope of this book to critique the postcolonial journey Malaysia has taken in constructing a universal Malay identity and there is already a vibrant community of scholars undertaking this project.[6] Similarly, there is considerable research in different states about the way that ethnic or religious minorities may hold citizenship but have difficulties accessing rights and privileges.[7] Instead, this chapter provides the contours of the historical foundations behind the construction of statelessness through the lasting impact of the British colonial classification of race and ethnicity, thereby furthering the work of scholars on legacies of colonization.[8]

I use the term "race" throughout this book in a constructionist sense. Malaysians have adopted a British understanding of race that categorizes people using a mix of biological and cultural attributes. Such an understanding of race has allowed Malaysians to give new meaning to different categories of racialized people over time.[9] Similarly, I use the term "ethnic" and "ethnicity" to describe identities of social groups that are contextually constituted using several social and cultural attributes.[10]

I also use the terms nation and nationalism occasionally in this chapter and throughout the book. I borrow my definition of the term from Benedict Anderson, who treats it as belonging with "kinship" rather than an ideology such as "liberalism" or "fascism."[11] Anderson defines nation as "an imagined political community — and imagined as both inherently limited and sovereign."[12] In using this definition, I also want to emphasize that "nations" and in particular "nationalism" are used in this text as constructed concepts and therefore subject to explorations of who is defining or describing the "nation" or "national community." In this sense, I agree with Margaret Franz and Kumarini Silva that when we assume "nations" as "imagined," "we overlook the often-problematic ways that Anderson articulates how and why these communities are imagined." I agree that this "normative assumption sketches uniformity, legal and political inclusion, or a territory over which a sovereign power can declare and enforce law."[13] This book contributes to this scholarship to expose how particular "imagined" communities are propped up through the denial and stripping of citizenship and the creation of statelessness.

Finally, I also use the term "Indigenous" to refer to the peoples broadly identified as the Orang Asli, Orang Ulu, and Anak Negeri. Again, to some, the term "Indigenous" is a constructed identity which I briefly discuss next and throughout. I recognize that some communities find the term "Indigenous" to be too broad and prefer to be called by a particular name identified by their community rather than be included in a seemingly homogeneous group.[14] Where possible, I try to use the names used by the communities to refer to themselves.

All these terms (race, ethnicity, nationality, Indigenous) are terms that describe the constitutive making, doing, and evolving of identities; they are multiple rather than being universal and coherent. Further, they are produced, negotiated, and contested.

The Postcolonial Formation of the Malaysian State

Understanding the Malaysian context is informative for other postcolonial contexts where statelessness occurs. The Federation of Malaysia was formed in 1963 and united two geographically separate regions known as West Malaysia and East Malaysia. West Malaysia is situated on the Peninsula (sometimes called Peninsular Malaysia) and East Malaysia is situated on the Borneo Island. The Peninsula is a long land mass that extends southward from Thailand and is bordered on one side by the Straits of Melaka and the Indian Ocean and on the other side by the South China Sea. At its tip is the island city-state of Singapore. The Peninsula is where the political and administrative capitals sit (two federal territories of Kuala Lumpur and Putra Jaya). As a result, it often receives more attention than East Malaysia. East Malaysia, mostly accessible by plane, is comprised of two states on the Borneo Island, Sarawak and Sabah, and a federal territory, the island of Labuan. These two states encircle the state of Brunei and sit north of the Indonesian parts of the island.

Malaysia is a constitutional monarchy, and its political system is based on the Westminster parliamentary system. The Federation has traditional Malay rulers, Agongs or constitutional heads of the thirteen states. Every five years or when a vacancy occurs, these constitutional heads of state elect the federal head of state, the Yan di-Pertuan Agong.

The Birth of the Malaysian State

It is impossible to understand Malaysia without looking at its birth and its independence from colonial British rule. Alice Nah describes the early Malaysian nation as being comprised of "disparate groups of people" that were "hunters and gatherers, shifting cultivators of land, and harvesters of jungle and sea produce" who were "scattered across dense jungles, foothills of hilly terrains, riversides, and the mouths of seas."[15] Nah notes that "'jungle produce' — a resource closely linked with tribal communities — was transported between China and the Middle East" and that it was likely that "internal trade took place between interior groups of people and new, expanding coastal communities."[16] Nah writes that "Malacca flourished as an international port for commercial goods" and that historical accounts "identify Malacca with the beginnings of Malay civilisation, while others suggest that this growing centre had its origins as an aboriginal village."[17] In Nah's account, as Malacca grew, "various tribal groups were absorbed into the expanding community, becoming subjects of a Hindu-type ruling class" holding unchecked power over both "Malay" and "aboriginal" people who were "vulnerable to indebtedness" and "enslaved under a corvee system."[18] Nah suggests that Islam was introduced by Arab traders who then became the ruling and trading classes.[19] As other scholars note, there were Indian, Chinese, Arab, and others trading, travelling, settling and working in precolonial Malaysia with migration continuing in colonial times to meet labour demands in mines and plantations creating multiethnic communities.[20]

When Malacca fell to the Portuguese in 1511, the Dutch in 1641 and the British in 1824, "[l]arge groups of immigrants" flooded the Peninsula "to provide labour power for colonial administration and growing industries" forming enclaves of Chinese and Indian communities.[21] The British staked colonial claims in the region through the occupation of three port cities, Penang, Singapore and Malacca, known collectively as the Straits Settlements.[22] Though their initial imperial interest was in maintaining trading positions, the British began to see opportunities in expanding economic activity in the region, including in tin mining and agriculture.[23] The increase in economic activity led to waves of immigrations of Chinese, Indian, Indonesians and others to work in the tin mines, as well as rubber and other kinds of plantations, mainly between 1850 and 1930.[24] Scholars describe the British organization of migrants as a "segregated system"[25] or "pockets" of colonially produced spaces.[26]

Indigenous Identity During Colonial Times

While various forms of "aboriginal-Malay relations existed over the centuries,"[27] some interactions were violent and Indigenous persons were persecuted and exploited.[28] Indigenous persons saw themselves "as having distinct, separate identities from the 'Malays' — though this may not have been evident to others, such as colonial census takers."[29] During the British colonial period, "Malayness" became "Indigenous" in the sense that it referred to persons of the Islamic faith who practice and share a variety of regional cultures and customs.[30]

British Racial Categorization in Malaysia

British colonialists used three generalized categories of "'Malay,' 'Chinese,' and 'Indian,' along with a sense of 'whiteness,' that was to be held as the epitome of prestige and 'civilization,' to organize a plural society in service of the colonial economy."[31] Timothy Daniels finds that the British exploited "Indians" in various manual labour environments and "stereotyped them as loyal and trustworthy but docile and servile." The British exploited "Malays" in agriculture and food production industries and "stereotyped them as witty and lively but unreliable, uncivilized and unsophisticated." "Chinese" were exploited in trade and tax economies and "stereotyped as industrious and ingenious but also as cruel, immoral, and wicked."[32] The "Whites," Daniels describes, "were the chief administrators and traders who stereotyped themselves as civilized, industrious, and moral" casting themselves as "the principal model of prestige and status." Daniels concludes that "these essentialized categories" provided a "distinct mix of racial and cultural attributes" to define classes of persons used to govern British colonial society.[33] Charles Hirschman states, from the British perspective, that "the Malay is an idler, the Chinaman is a thief, and the Kling is a drunkard" all "cheap and efficient, when properly supervised."[34]

Colonial Categories Informing Identity and Citizenship

Historical accounts are incomplete because of who captured them.[35] Barbara Andaya and Leonard Andaya note that while "Indigenous" material from oral sources were committed to paper, the historical records are shaped by the recorder — often the colonizer's lens — leaving many questions unanswered.[36] Shamsul Amri Baharuddin writes that "the history of what is now Malaysia has been dominated, shaped and 'factualised' by colonial knowledge."[37]

Despite the scarcity of recorded historical accounts from the perspective of noncolonialist communities, there is research on the impact of colonization on concepts of nationhood and citizenship.[38] While "local individuals and groups have given new meanings and uses to social categories over time, the emphasis British colonial categories placed upon 'descent' and 'blood' and distinct cultural attributes has had a lasting impact on local constructions of social categories and identities."[39] Racial divisions are largely a product of colonial practices and European ideology.[40] Hirschman finds that while "Cultural barriers and hostility between Asian populations in the region predate European imperialism … these differences were bridged or accommodated in pursuit of other goals"[41] through geographical segregation.[42]

Sandra Manickam finds that censuses were part of the colonial imagining of the state to quantify and categorize people by race to "tame" areas and exert colonial power over colonized areas.[43] Manickam notes that "counting by race" resulted in "uneven conceptualisations and applications of ideas of race" that may or may not have encompassed "differences in bodies" as well as "language, religion, lifestyle and political status."[44] While presenting data in numbers and tables gave "the impression of clarity and ease in identification," meanings of race made their way into the census since various people were involved in counting and reporting.[45] Nah concurs, and finds that census "was not a straightforward matter" as there was perplexity in deciding between "Malays" and "Other Malaysians."[46] Scholars agree that the apparently "harmless" bureaucratic practices of census-taking served to invent, evolve, and consolidate racial categories whereby falling within a particular category came with material benefits.[47]

Shamsul A. B. finds that "the British interfered with the local thought system, and by doing this they increasingly disempowered the natives by limiting their ability to define their world; subsequently, the local order of things was replaced by a foreign one."[48] Shamsul A. B. posits that "the 'nation-state' has become dependent on colonial knowledge and its ways of determining, codifying, controlling, and representing the past as well as documenting and standardising the information that has formed the basis of government."[49] Shamsul A. B. writes, "The citizens of Malaysia rarely question these facts," which are "often invisible manifestations of the process of Westernisation."[50]

Defining Citizenship in a Newly Independent Malaysia

While the British originally proposed a framework that would confer the same citizenship rights to Malays and non-Malays, this provoked a reaction from Malays who did not want to give up their privileged position.[51] Shamsul A. B. finds that, when those involved in negotiations were formulating the constitution, negotiations ensued, and a bargain struck with the Chinese and the Indians. They could become citizens but had to accept *ketuanan Melayu* or Malay dominance, where they had to accept "'special Malay privileges' in education and government services, and 'Malay' royalty as their rulers, Islam as the official religion, and the 'Malay' language as the official language of the new nation-state."[52] Julie Pietsch and Marshall Clark show that "After much compromise between the Malays and non-Malays, the rights and privileges of Malays as the Indigenous people of Malaysia were to be written into the Constitution" and that "from the beginning, the Malays, somewhat undemocratically, were regarded as the legitimate owners of Malaya and the non-Malays who were viewed as immigrants."[53] Timothy Daniels concurs: "Non-Malays conceded a great deal of inequality to attain the best possible form of citizenship they could obtain."[54] Sharmani Patricia Gabriel shows that "This pre-independence formula of multicultural accommodation was predicated on a series of compromises — often invoked as the 'Social Contract' — that granted Chinese and Indians legal citizenship in return for the recognition of the Malays' 'special position' as the 'indigenous' people of the land." Gabriel explains that "The assumptions embedded in this formula of national identity were predicated on colonial constructions of 'Malay,' 'Chinese' and 'Indian' identities" that was "based on a division of labour and institutionally imposed domination-subordination relationships" where they lived "side by side, yet without mingling."[55]

Vestiges of colonialization were built into the constitution consecrating "differentiated citizenship."[56] Pietsch and Clark show that "the adoption of the Malaysian Constitution ... gave rise to a culture of ethnic nationalism, privileging the Malays"[57] by the guarantee of the special position of the Malay language, the adoption of Islam as the national religion, the adoption of a Council of Rulers composed of ethnic Malay Sultans, and the recognition of Islamic sharia courts and laws.[58] As Daniels writes, "the Constitution distinguishes Malays in cultural terms from other[s]."[59]

Yogeswaran Subramanium states, the word "Indigenous" is not contained in the constitution but instead refers to "natives" of particular states (Sabah and Sarawak) and confers associated rights and privileges.[60] Rusaslina Idrus asserts that "Ethnic Malays are the dominant majority in the government and claim special rights as indigenous peoples or 'sons of the soil' (*bumiputera*)." She points out that "While the government acknowledges the Orang Asli's [Indigenous] status as *bumiputera*, many do not enjoy the same special privileges that Malays do."[61]

In practice, Kamal Sadiq finds that while the constitution acknowledges "the natives of the states of Sabah and Sarawak," the constitution entrenches Malay dominance over other groups including the Indigenous[62] through a legal framework of "Malayised or ethnicized conception of citizenship."[63] Sadiq points to the "systemic attempt by the federal government to augment the three pillars of Malayness as national identity — bahasa (Malay languages), agama (Islam), and rajah (Sultan)."[64]

While this differentiated nature of citizenship has brought millions of Malays out of poverty, it has disadvantaged other groups.[65] Outwardly, Malaysia amplifies a message of one identity that is multicultural but "truly Asian." Sadiq shows that "Like other plural societies, Malaysia seeks to integrate diverse populations around the idea of a common citizenship."[66] Despite the desire to form this single, shared identity, there are fissures and fault lines as a result of "the hotly debated concepts" of "Malay identity" and "Malayness" which are "largely based on an Orientalist-colonial construction."[67] Racial and ethnic divisions from the colonial development economy continue to have influence on present-day Malaysia.[68]

Membership in the State: Bumiputera, Indigeneity and Citizenship

Bumiputera: Sons and Daughters of the Soil

The latest demographic information on the population of Malaysia comes from a 2016 census as follows:

> The largest group of Malaysians consist of three main races, namely the Malays, Chinese and Indians. Orang Asli are the natives in Peninsular Malaysia and is generally divided into three major groups, namely the Negrito, Senoi and Proto-Malay. Sabah's population consists of 32 ethnic groups and the major ethnic [group] is Kadazandusun while [the] Sarawak population consists of 27 ethnic groups and Iban is the major ethnic group. In 2015, the prefix data of Malaysian population is 30,995,700 and the divisions by ethnics are as follow: Bumiputera — 19,150,900 (61.8%); Chinese — 6,620,300 (21.4%); Indian — 1,988,600 (6.4%); Others — 270,700 (0.9%) and Non-Malaysian Resident — 2,965,300 (9.6%).[69]

I first heard the word Bumiputera when I first arrived in Kuala Lumpur. I was swimming in a pool with my kids when a Chinese man who professed to be a Malaysian citizen working in Singapore asked me where I was from and what I was doing in Malaysia on hearing my Western English accent. When I told him I was studying statelessness in Malaysia he told me simply that some people are just not Bumiputera. Since then, I have heard the word frequently, even among my own extended family. Bumiputera literally means "sons of the soil" and started appearing in official documentation around 1971 when Malaysia launched its New Economic Policy.

Sin Yee Koh writes, "Bumiputera is not an ethnic group per se, but refers to an 'indigenous' status with special rights protected in the constitution."[70] Shad Saleem Faruqi notes that the term is not legal and is of "political coinage" with no official definition anywhere.[71] Shamsul A. B. writes that "to most Malaysians, it is the *bumiputera* and non-*bumiputera* ethnic divide that is perceived as significant, used in official government documents as well as in the idiom of everyday interaction."[72] The Malaysian state has launched policies that specifically identify and privilege the Bumiputera although in different ways for its subcategories.[73] Bumiputera espouses a powerful "notion of indigeneity as a marker of cultural authenticity" that links ideas of race and ethnicity to literal imagery of soil and, therefore, territoriality.[74]

Who are the Bumiputera? In general, the category includes Malay and Indigenous peoples. They are often collectively described in three groups based on geography: the Orang Asli (literally means "original people") in Peninsular Malaysia; the Dayak or Orang Ulu (literally means "people of the interior") in Sarawak; and Anak Negeri ("citizen" or "child of the country") in Sabah. The International Work Group for Indigenous Affairs finds that

> In 2015, it was estimated that the indigenous peoples of Malaysia represented about 13.8% of the population of 31,660,700 million.
>
> The indigenous peoples of Peninsular Malaysia are collectively known as Orang Asli. The 18 Orang Asli subgroups within the Negrito (Semang), Senoi and Aborigen-Malay groups represent around 210,000 people or 0.7% of the population of Peninsular Malaysia.

In Sarawak, Indigenous peoples are collectively known as natives (Dayak and/or Orang Ulu). They include the Iban, Bidayuh, the Kenyah, the Kayan, the Kedayan, the Lunbawang, the Punan, the Bisayah, the Kelabit, the Berawan, the Kejaman, the Ukit, the Sekapan, the Melanau and the Penan, and the[y] account for 1,932,600 people, or 70.5% of the population of Sarawak.

In Sabah, the 39 different Indigenous ethnic groups are known as natives or Anak Negeri and constitute about 2,233,100 people or 58.6% of the population of Sabah. The main groups are the Dusun, Murut, Paitan and Bajau groups.[75]

While the Malaysian government has identified and acknowledged the different Indigenous communities, this tracking exercise is not benign. As Mahmoud Mamdani asserts, the state engages in creating a majority and minority permanent political identities. Mamdani explains that the constructed majority has sovereignty while the minority does not, reproducing colonial hierarchies, archetypes of colonial and imperial rule.[76] Yogeswaran Subramaniam explains that "A distinction should be drawn between ethnic Malays, the natives of Sabah, the natives of Sarawak and the Orang Asli because these four ethnic groups are ascribed different definitions and treatment under Malaysian law."[77]

The concept of Bumiputera has become a shorthand way to describe who belong, who are "legitimately" Malay, and who were the original habitants of Malaysia, but it is important to understand that Bumiputera does not describe a homogenous group with equal privilege or power. As Kamal Sadiq explains, "there are competing native claims on citizenship."[78]

Bumiputera versus Non-Bumiputera

When discussing the divide between Bumiputera and non-Bumiputera, much focus is placed on the difference between the Malay Bumiputera and other racialized persons who are characterized as migrants and foreigners. While there were significant historical communities of persons of Chinese[79] and Indian descent, they do not enjoy many of the citizenship rights and privileges that the Bumiputera do.

Sharmani Patricia Gabriel explains that Malaysia "was already highly diverse when it came into existence as an independent state in 1957"[80] and orientations of identity perpetuated views that some are "'immigrants' irrespective of the fact that they were born as citizens of the state."[81] Gabriel finds that

> Although the factors behind Chinese and Indian immigration to Malaya are both various and complex, the majority of the members of these minority ethnic groups are descendants of immigrants who arrived in Malaya in the late nineteenth and early twentieth centuries to serve British economic interests in its tin mines and rubber plantations [with a …] small percentage of these communities, known as the Peranakan, can trace their roots as far back as the fifteenth century.[82]

Nah describes this community, a sizable proportion of Chinese and Indian communities that were "locally born at the point of Independence" as "the racial groups rendered 'immigrants' [who] protested their socio-political positionality."[83] These communities had severed their ties to their ancestral homelands and "were keen to defend their rights to nationhood, but articulated their struggles without successfully dismantling the indigenous vs. immigrant distinction."[84] Gabriel posits that the state is clinging "to a model of national identity that was conceived in the colonial period."[85] Nah describes the emergence of the term Bumiputera as solidifying the "other" and "immigrant" labels attached to non-Malay communities. This term "simplified the way in which indigenous groups could be bifurcated into Bumiputera and non-Bumiputera or Malays versus non-Malays."[86]

Gabriel finds that the "category of *bumiputera* was a post-independence construction designed to protect Malay interests against claims for citizenship by Chinese and Indian" people and that the "exclusionary language" casts these minority ethnic groups as "the quintessential others — the *pendatang* and *penumpang*, 'newcomers' and 'squatters.'"[87] Ultimately, Bumiputera is a shorthand way to say, "They do not belong 'here' as they have come from 'elsewhere.'"[88] One reason that such groups are cast as "outsiders" is because of "the classic understanding of diaspora as groups with strong attachments to their ancestral homeland" and the way in which academic and public discourse define ethnic groups, "primarily, if not exclusively, in terms of their cultural and national past and of the existence of an ongoing relationship with that past."[89] This pervasive trope of "return and attachment" to the "true ideal homeland" fuels assumptions about identity and interests of minority ethnic groups.[90]

This has led to the hyphenated designations of "Malaysian-Chinese" and "Malaysian-Indian" where "the ethnic half serves as reminder of one's extra-national origins" which supports the "underlying proposition that Malays are *organically* Malaysian; they do not require a hyphen to mark their belonging or association 'here.'"[91] Gabriel argues that "The dichotomous tension between the 'immigrant' and the 'indigenous,' the 'ethnic' and the 'national' stabilizes these categories by keeping them apart."[92] Contemporary "hostilities toward Chinese minorities are a result of the lingering effects of a colonially-enforced plural society with a corresponding economic division of labour and institutionalized relations of dominance and subordination."[93]

"Becoming" Malay or assimilation is a strategy the state has used to maintain the dominance and privileging of Malay "authenticity."[94] A "'non-Malay' could only be a citizen by embracing Malay culture and history unequivocally, including the religion."[95] Non-Malays felt that "this belittled their contribution to the history and culture of Malaya."[96]

Malaysia, in 1971, after the racial riots of 1969,[97] launched the controversial New Economic Policy. The Sedition Act of 1948 was amended "to discourage discussions over 'sensitive issues'" including "questioning any matter, right, status, position, privilege, sovereignty or prerogative established or protected" by the Constitution including "those concerning Malay identity and special rights."[98] In the 1970s, the state's vision of national culture, as described by a minister, was as follows: "Culturally … the basis of integration is Malay — not because of racial arguments but because of the fact that … Malay culture is already the most Malaysian one that one can find in Malaysia."[99] Gabriel finds that "The state therefore becomes a bearer of a priori view of identity that assumes that Malay, and therefore also Malaysian, identity has fixed identifiers or markers" and that it is "this conception of identity as coherent and stable that underpins the 'plural society' framework."[100] Nah points out that once "Malay" identity was fixed, one way in which one could access privileges and rights was to *masuk Melayu* or "become Malay." Guidance on how to do this is in the Constitution, which states "'Malay' means, inter alia, a person who professes the religion of Islam, habitually speaks the Malay language, [and] conforms to Malay custom …."[101] Nah finds that, "[t]his definition, while historically located" also "serves as a timeless, ahistorical reference point upon which legal, political, economic and social arguments can be constructed and legitimised."[102] No other racial or ethnic group is defined in Malaysia's constitution. This is a deliberate strategy, Nah suggests, since some persons of minority groups can claim ethnic/racial similarities "to claim benefits assigned on the basis of indigenous identity" serving "to strengthen, rather than displace, the centrality of Malay ethnic identity as *the* 'sons of the soil' in the postcolonial nation-state."[103]

The effects of the differentiated citizenship for those who are not Malay are significant. For example, according to Koh, "the Malaysian-Chinese, in particular, have lamented their position as second-class citizens in Malaysia" and have sought migration as an exit strategy with media reports painting such persons as "disloyal."[104] Koh writes that "state-led constructions of the Malaysian citizenship has been one that is conflated with national identity and … loyalty," while at the same time prohibiting public debate on racial issues.[105] Koh finds that Malaysian-Chinese define their "Malaysian" identity alongside their "experiences of growing up" which includes childhood memories, geographical places and special events, and personal and familial social networks,[106] all enduring connections in legal constructions of citizenship as discussed in this book. Koh's interrogation of the meaning of citizenship among this group reveals distrust in whether the state will deal with Malaysian-Chinese fairly.[107] Koh concludes that "Bumiputera differentiation is a real and structuring factor."[108] Racial essentialism and the process of othering can explain state practices in the creation of statelessness.[109]

Among the Bumiputera in Peninsular (West) Malaysia — Orang Asli

The term *Orang Asli*, literally meaning "natural people," was a "term used to collectively describe the 18 official and distinct ethnic aboriginal subgroups in Peninsular Malaysia, classified into three broad categories of Negrito, Senoi and Aboriginal Malay."[110] The Orang Asli as a pan-tribal group have maintained "their respective languages, social organizations and spiritual values, culture and customs distinct from that of the Malays and mainstream society."[111] They face challenges in realizing their rights as "distinct Indigenous people despite being ascribed a measure of constitutional and statutory protection."[112] Many attribute this to

> a complex web of factors, including, historical prejudices and power imbalances, disparate affirmative action laws and policies,

> differentiated and contested constructions of … indigeneity vis-à-vis Malays, the extensive legal power possessed by the federal and State executives over [Indigenous people and their] lands, and the nation's priorities for the utilisation of lands and resources towards achieving economic progress.[113]

Many Orang Asli struggle to maintain their distinctive culture and identity that are inextricably linked with their close physical, economic, social, cultural, territorial and spiritual relationship with the environment.

> [The] Difficulties faced by the Orang Asli in their resistance to ethnic assimilation, fight for customary land rights, general lack of economic resources and minimal political clout have necessitated Orang Asli leaders having to speak about themselves through singular voices while being aware of their own plurality, internal fractures and unresolved differences.[114]

Subramanium finds that British colonization positioned the Orang Asli "as a marginalised community with limited rights while the Malays [were] constructed as indigenous peoples with special privileges"[115] and that British intervention exacerbated Malay preconceptions of Orang Asli as primitive and culturally inferior, fuelling practices of integration or assimilation.[116] Nah asserts that the Orang Asli are "menacing" to the Malay Self in three ways: (a) one cannot become Orang Asli as they can slip into Malay by adopting the language, religion and culture and Orang Asli are not historical migrants as the Malay are; (b) Orang Asli identity was constructed by the British and did not specify a religious prescription, which allows them greater flexibility in negotiating personal decisions; (c) the presence of Orang Asli as a marginalized group disturbs the narrative that Malays necessarily need affirmative privileges and benefits.[117]

One such strategy to deal with the disruptive presence of Orang Asli is the *dakwah* or Islamic missionary that was aimed at Islamising Orang Asli.[118] Subramanium argues that "becoming Malay" was the way through which Orang Asli could enjoy their citizenship rights fully.[119] Nah describes the *dakwah* as including the "implementation of a 'positive discrimination' policy for the converted, with some distribution of material benefits individually and through development projects."[120]

Some Orang Asli leaders maintain that the "becoming Malay" strategy is a means to erase their community.[121]

Regional Citizenship in Malaysia: Bumiputera in East Malaysia — Dayak and/or Orang Ulu

Indigenous communities in the states of Sabah and Sarawak are many and distinct and yet they are often discussed collectively as the Dayak or Orang Asli in West Malaysia.[122]

One stateless person told me about difficulties he had in travelling within Malaysia and that he had to seek authorization to travel from East Malaysia to West Malaysia.[123] At the time, I thought the restriction in his movements were linked to his statelessness, but I discovered that there were immigration controls regardless of citizenship. Kamal Sadiq confirms this in his own observations[124] and finds these East Malaysian border controls reveal "fissures" in the country's conceptions of citizenship and discontent with the federal government's failure to meet historical concerns about the protection of language, religion, and culture as well as their claims on local natural resources, rights that are grounded in the Constitution.[125]

Fuelling the concerns of the Bumiputera in Sabah is the "demographic concerns" related to "the influx of Muslim immigration from the southern Philippines and Indonesia."[126] Sadiq explains that "migrants can claim native Malay status due to ethnic/religious overlap" because they can speak Malay or related dialects, are Muslims and "find extended kinship communities among the local Bugis, Javanese, Sulus, Bajaus, and others."[127] Non-Malay and non-Muslim Indigenous Bumiputera are threatened by the migration of populations "condoned by federal authorities since it demographically overwhelms non-Muslim native communities."[128]

Thus, the permissible movements granted by the federal government are perceived to create a common citizenship centred on the Malay language, Islamic religion, and Malay culture. Sadiq explains that "the effort to integrate, to create a common will, a common labor and resource market, and a common 'social demand' is in direct conflict with the desire to protect the culture, land and resource rights of a major regional ethnic [Indigenous] group."[129]

James Chin agrees and finds that Muslim powerbrokers have been invested in making a Malay Muslim state rather than promote a multiethnic and multireligious Malaysian Federation.[130] Chin cites the celebration of "new Malays" and the campaign, "It's easy to become Malay."[131] The idea of *masuk Melayu* or becoming Malay has promoted a particular racial and religious identity as paramount in Malaysia.[132]

A Contemporary Unitary Malay Identity

Recently the Malaysian government, while acknowledging it is a modern democratic state with a growing economy, has identified "ethnic disunity" as a concern and called for efforts to "reconstitute" its "imagined community" based on "a shared culture" that is "embedded in the state."[133] Malaysia appears committed to a "modernization" project based on a strategy to homogenize its members in a sociocultural sense.[134] This nation-building project, as this book discusses throughout, includes a strategy to exclude, deny, and strip citizenship from certain racialized persons who have genuine and effective links to the state of Malaysia but who do not fit the mould of a unitary national identity.

Statelessness: Constructing Ghost Citizens and Non-Malaysians

Understanding Malaysia's historical colonial past is important to comprehend how statelessness is created and maintained in Malaysia. Scholars posit there is a "range of gradations in the qualities of citizenship."[135] In Malaysia, however, these gradations and differences mask the systemic and outright exclusion of some people. As Linda Bosniak points out, "While the second-class citizenship critique is an indispensable form of political and legal criticism … the focus on the denial of rights to status citizens often renders the critique insensitive to the history of systemic denial of citizenship status itself to members of subordinated groups."[136] The linking of conceptions of nationality, ethnicity, and race with statelessness is not new. This book further discusses what it means to be loyal to a nation and how this perpetuates and creates statelessness.[137]

As Chapter 5 demonstrates, many of the categories of stateless persons in Malaysia are long-standing residents who have genuine and effective links with the state. An understanding of the national conflict related to identities around citizenship helps inform why, despite such links, certain groups of people are not only deemed stateless but cast as "Others" or "foreigners" and therefore as not kin or community members. In this book, I call stateless persons ghost citizens because of their de facto perspective that they are citizens due to the enduring, long-lasting links to the state they claim to be citizens of but who have been ghosted by the state and denied that status. They are also ghost citizens because the state renders them as the responsibility of another state, making them a ghost citizen of a foreign state, even though they have no legal connection or actual conferral of citizenship from any other state.

The project of nation-building and the creation and maintenance of national identity is fraught with historical traumas, choices, and oppression especially in postcolonial states.[138] Malaysian "nation-building … reinforces a sense of competition between and within racial categories"[139] and is one that aims for a singular identity that is dominated by the Malay language, religion, and culture. The construction of statelessness is more than a symptom, remnant, or legacy of colonialism. It is a persistent, relentless, and enduring rot decaying a community. As scholars like Nandita Sharma and David Pearson theorize, there are "linked processes" of aboriginalization (of aboriginal minorities), the ethnification (of immigrant minorities) and the indigenization (of settler majorities).[140] These processes were sown and pollinated during colonization.

The project of *masuk Melayu*, to me, seems disingenuous to the fabric of Malay society. Part of the pride I have in having roots in that region is exemplified by my desire to share the cuisine unique to that region. For example, curry laksa personifies the best of Malaysian fusion cuisine incorporating Chinese, Indian, Indigenous, and Malay features. I lament the fact that the happy coexistence of these multiplicities assembled in the cuisine is not mirrored elsewhere in Malaysia.

How one is conferred citizenship in Malaysia is coloured by the identity a person is perceived to carry. Are they Bumiputera? If they are Bumiputera, what kind are they? If they are not Bumiputera, have they *masuk Melayu*, become Malay? These are the questions behind the proxies embedded in the legal and administrative requirements and processes discussed in Chapters 3, 4 and 6.

THREE

THE LAW
The International Legal Construction of Ghost Citizens

Law-as-Text Shrouding States

We cannot discuss how one is stateless without examining the law. Alice Edwards and Laura Van Waas call international statelessness law "the clear runt of the international legal regime."[1] Mark Manly writes that statelessness is a "highly specialized but obscure area of international law" and this is in part explained "by the complexities of wide divergences in approach between nationality laws of different states" and the "sheer range of issues and standards involved" pertaining to not only the prevention and reduction of statelessness but also protection of stateless persons.[2]

Although statelessness is ultimately a legal status, there is a tendency to essentialize statelessness as a legal problem. For example, in 1950, the US representative in the Ad Hoc Committee on Statelessness and Related Problems stated that the refugee problem was a humanitarian one whereas the problem of statelessness was primarily legal and one that "should be dealt with by a body of legal experts."[3] Manly points out that while the UNHCR has engaged in a number of activities (awareness raising; building partnerships with NGOs to train and conduct mapping and consultative exercises; the identification of stateless persons; and improving civil registration), much of its work in relation to statelessness promotes the accession to the *Statelessness Conventions* and the reform of nationality laws.[4] The work of legal reform is laudable but as Manly acknowledges, "Even where nationality laws appear on their face to be consistent with international standards, there may continue to be problems with implementation."[5]

This chapter builds on the work of legal scholars[6] but also explores the limitations of law reform. Sustained focus on law-as-text distracts from problems individuals encounter when engaging with state institutions and processes as they attempt to obtain citizenship. This chapter challenges the normative position of two assumptions: first, that where law-as-text meets international standards, states are doing all they can; and second, that the law is neutral and objective.

The chapter critically examines the law-as-text in conventions and jurisprudence and confronts two concepts. The first is the adherence to the state's prerogative or right to decide who are its citizens and the inexorable turn to a human rights framework despite its lacklustre performance in the contexts of migration and statelessness. The second is the deference shown to the law-as-text, which distracts from the experiences of stateless persons when they interact with the law.

This chapter outlines how the legal framework is deployed by states to simultaneously deem persons ghost citizens of other states while also allowing states to ghost their own citizens and treat them like foreigners. Law and its processes are used to justify the stripping of the status of stateless and the deeming of persons as foreigners. The legal development of ghost citizens is alarming because it thins the definition of statelessness. This identification of a person as a ghost citizen also distracts and diverts attention from valid claims made by stateless persons who have genuine and effective links to a country they consider their home.

International Law: The Definition of Stateless and the Right to Nationality

The following discussion does not provide a comprehensive overview or a complete depiction of the issues, critiques, or potential sites for opportunity for reform; it presents how the law is implicated in creating not only statelessness but ghost citizens.

The International Legal Definition of Statelessness in Conventions

The Statelessness Conventions

There are two international conventions that directly address statelessness: the *1954 Convention Relating to the Status of Stateless Persons,*[7] which has eighty-three state parties; and the *1961 Convention on the Reduction of Statelessness,*[8] which has sixty-one state parties. The number of parties to each convention indicate less state interest relative to other human rights conventions. Despite this, these conventions provide a foundational understanding of the aspirations of the international community, a guide to measure state behaviour, and a rubric from which states can borrow. Importantly, they are a legal pronouncement of the existence of stateless persons and that stateless is a legal category of persons.

The *1954 Statelessness Convention* provides that a stateless person is one who is not considered a national of a state by operation of law. Although the definition of statelessness in the text of the *1954 Statelessness Convention* seems clear that a person is stateless when they do not have citizenship conferred to them by law, state practice seems to indicate otherwise. States deem persons citizens (notably of other states) even where there is no legal conferral of such citizenship, thereby creating ghost citizens. It is one of the wildly diverging ways in which states thin the definition of statelessness.

The 1954 Statelessness Convention
The *1954 Statelessness Convention* establishes the legal definition of stateless and associated civil, social, and economic rights such as the right to education, employment, housing, identity and travel documents, and administrative assistance. The convention is silent on how to implement it.

The 1954 Convention is home to the widely accepted definition of stateless: "a person who is not considered as a national by any State under the operation of its law."[9] Laura Van Waas states that "What underlies the stateless person's 'unprotected' status and what renders him or her in need of international protection, is simply the absence of a nationality. It is neither relevant how the individual came to be without nationality nor where the person subsequently finds him or herself."[10]

While several other international instruments refer to statelessness, the *1954 Statelessness Convention* is the *only* place where international law defines the term.[11] The International Law Commission recognizes this definition as customary international law.[12] There is strong recognition for "statelessness"; however, the *1954 Statelessness Convention* does not confer a right to nationality, but instead calls on states to facilitate the naturalization of stateless persons, encouraging states to resolve statelessness quickly and as easily as possible.

This convention provides a strong normative view on two concepts. The first, that while states may encounter stateless persons, they are not necessarily obligated to confer citizenship on them. Second, in using the term "naturalization," stateless persons are presumed to be foreigners or strangers of the state and need to apply for citizenship.

The 1961 Statelessness Convention
The *1961 Statelessness Convention* focuses on the right to nationality with the aim of preventing and reducing statelessness. It provides positive rights for persons to acquire nationality in certain situations. Van Waas explains: "it sets out safeguards for the avoidance of statelessness in three broad contexts: acquisition of an original nationality at birth, including by foundlings (Articles 1 to 4); loss, deprivation or renunciation of nationality in later life (Articles 5 to 9); and in respect of succession of states (Article 10)."[13] While there are guarantees provided, the early decision to proceed with a text that prescribes only the *reduction* and not the *elimination* of statelessness means that some cases may still slip through, "displaying the unfortunate hallmarks of an international compromise shaped by ... tension between states' sovereign interests ... and the shared interest of avoiding statelessness."[14] Van Waas acknowledges that the convention "respects the overall freedom of states to legislate as they see fit in the area of nationality and does not attempt to create an international law on nationality."[15] William Conklin concurs, finding that the convention was "predisposed to retain and protect bounded reserved domain of states over nationality issues."[16]

Thus, there are three main normative concepts that emerge from the 1961 convention. The first is that this convention creates a thick conception of birthright citizenship, encouraging state parties to grant nationality to a person born in its territory. The second is that the convention encourages states to confer citizenship on persons who are habitually resident in the territory, also giving weight to the concept that territorial link is an important factor in indicating an entitlement to citizenship. Finally, despite the calls to grant citizenship owing to territorial link, the state ultimately has the discretion to determine the terms under which citizenship should be conferred, if at all. That a state holds the ultimate power, a veto, to decide who are its citizens is the arch holding up our current understanding of citizenship law around the world. As discussed in the following section, this state prerogative power is the basis upon which states justify their power by not only ghosting stateless persons or denying them citizenship, but by stripping stateless persons of their status as stateless and deeming them ghost citizens of other states.

The Scope of de Jure Statelessness and the State Prerogative

The legal definition of statelessness is generally understood in a singular manner as encompassing a homogenous group of people who share one characteristic: they do not have any citizenship whatsoever. Despite confusion about whether de facto statelessness (ineffective nationality[17] or someone understood to have nationality but has problems substantiating it[18]) figures in the definition, it is de jure that drives the interpretive engine of the definition. Carol Batchelor opines that the definition refers to de jure statelessness, "because it delineates a specific, quantifiable fact: either one is, or one is not a national by operation of a State's law."[19] She explains that "the definition itself precludes full realization of an effective nationality because it is a technical, legal definition which can address only technical, legal problems."[20]

The UNHCR Handbook on the Protection of Stateless Persons provides that:

> Where the competent authorities treat an individual as a non-national even though he or she would appear to meet the criteria for automatic acquisition of nationality under the operation of a country's laws, it is their position rather than the letter of the law that is determinative in concluding that a State does not consider such an individual as a national.[21]

Van Waas explains that "even if an objective third party would determine that a certain person enjoys nationality on the basis of their reasoned reading of the legislation in force, if the state reaches the opposite conclusion, this latter viewpoint is decisive."[22]

The de jure interpretation of the definition is important. The Statelessness Conventions rely on the preliminary finding of statelessness before calling on states to grant citizenship. As Conklin affirms, "each state has retained the freedom to decide whether a person is really stateless" since the de jure definition of a stateless person, "is phrased as 'under the operation of *its* laws'" — the state's "reserved domain."[23]

The state's final say, prerogative, or right to decide provides states with immense power. Under international law, given that there is no right to nationality or mechanisms to monitor state processes in citizenship conferrals, the Statelessness Conventions place much faith in states to confer citizenship where merited. The normative assumption is that states act permissively, in the best interests of the persons claiming citizenship, and that the main barriers are the creation of legal pathways to citizenship.

Other International Human Rights Conventions

The Refugee Convention
The *Refugee Convention* is the formative legal source for refugee protection. It has garnered more state uptake than the Statelessness Conventions with 145 signatories, and it has been implemented domestically with more vigour. There is a plethora of literature on refugee protection, and a robust community of advocates and scholars working in this area of law. However, the *Refugee Convention* provides limited protection to stateless persons.

The convention provides a tightly circumscribed definition of refugee that does not include all situations of statelessness. The very fact of being stateless does not trigger protection in this regime. Under the convention's definition, statelessness needs to have a nexus with a well-founded fear of persecution on an enumerated ground of race, religion, nationality, political opinion, or membership in a particular social group.

During the early drafting of the *Refugee Convention*, suggestions were made to include stateless persons within the protective framework.[24] State negotiation however, took "persons who are not nationals of any state" off the table as a ground for protection.[25] As a result, nothing in the convention is specific to the plight of stateless persons, unless they are also within the definition of refugee.[26] In September 1954, the decision was made to create a separate convention relating to statelessness.[27] Some claim that the plight of refugees was perceived as more urgent than stateless persons.[28] Others saw it as an issue of "remedy vs cure"; that the elimination of statelessness was different from that of the protection of refugees and that solving statelessness was a more elusive endeavour.[29] Michelle Foster and Hélène Lambert argue that "the decision to excise statelessness [from the *Refugee Convention*] was not as clear-cut as may sometimes be assumed or implied," and that "the arguments against inclusion were largely practical rather than principled."[30]

Admittedly, the *Refugee Convention* has provided opportunities for protection where stateless persons are able to fit in the refugee definition. Normatively, however, the definition necessarily treats stateless persons as foreigners and therefore only provides protection to the extent that stateless persons want status in another country rather than "their own"

— a legal distinction discussed by litigants in the cases cited in this chapter shortly. This convention therefore does nothing for in situ stateless persons — those within their "own" countries who have significant ties with that country. Finally, as with the Statelessness Conventions, states have ultimate discretion in conferring any status on persons requesting protection under this regime reinforcing the system of state recognition.

Other Conventions

Several international legal instruments set out rights to nationality. The *United Nations Declaration of Human Rights* provides in Article 15: "Everyone has the right to a nationality."[31] The language in Article 2 provides that everyone is entitled to the right "without distinction of any kind, such as race, colour, sex, language, religion, political or other opinion, national or social origin, property, birth or other status."[32] Similarly, the *International Covenant on Civil and Political Rights (ICCPR)*[33] provides, in Article 12, the right to lawfully enter or leave any country, "including his own"[34] and Article 16 states, "Everyone shall have the right to recognition everywhere as a person before the law."[35] Beyond this, there is also language about non-discrimination when it comes to status[36] and also the right to recognition as a person before the law.[37] Further, there are explicit references for the right to nationality, for example, in Article 24, which provides: "Every child shall be registered immediately after birth and shall have a name," and that "Every child has the right to acquire nationality."[38] The *International Covenant on Economic, Social and Cultural Rights (ICESCR)* does not expressly deal with nationality but does support the access to economic, social, and cultural rights provided in the *1954 Statelessness Convention*.[39] The *Convention on the Rights of the Child* (CRC) asserts as a primary consideration the best interests of the child in state interactions with children (including in adoption proceedings)[40] and recognizes the right to birth registration and the right to nationality, particularly "where the child would otherwise be stateless."[41] Related to this, the CRC also calls states to "respect the right of a child to preserve his or her identity, including nationality" and that states have an obligation to "provide appropriate assistance and protection, with a view to re-establishing speedily his or her identity."[42] This is significant, because the CRC acknowledges a heightened obligation where a child is at risk of statelessness. The CRC also provides that states do not discriminate against a child or the child's parent/ legal guardian's "race, colour, sex, language, religion, political or other opinion, national, ethnic or social origin, property, disability, birth or other status."[43] Finally, the CRC also supports the access to economic, social, and cultural rights provided in the *1954 Statelessness Convention*.

The *International Convention on the Elimination of All Forms of Racial Discrimination* (ICERD) provides measures for states to undertake to condemn, eliminate and prevent racial discrimination.[44] Article 5(d)(iii) provides that states must undertake to prohibit and eliminate racial discrimination in relation to the right to nationality.[45] This convention, however, has a caveat in Article 1: "Nothing in this Convention may be interpreted as affecting in any way the legal provisions of States Parties concerning nationality, citizenship or naturalization, provided that such provisions do not discriminate against any particular nationality."[46] This instrument also supports the access to economic, social, and cultural rights in the *1954 Statelessness Convention*.

While many international legal instruments seem to go further than the Statelessness Conventions in providing rights to nationality, they do not identify specifically in what circumstances the obligation is triggered and provide no mechanism by which the determination of nationality can be resolved or monitored. They simply pronounce a broad notion of the right to nationality. The idea that an individual is then to be attributed nationality and that no one should be without citizenship gives weight to the state practice of identifying for themselves the citizenship that stateless persons have in theory. As the case law discussed in this chapter and in Chapter 4 demonstrates, instead of conferring citizenship themselves, states are pointing to the hypothetical, the imagined, and the presumed citizenship stateless persons must have from another wayward country (ghost citizenships) because one must be a citizen somewhere (but not here). The international legal framework permits states to engage in the practice of ghosting their de facto citizens and conferring ghost citizenship on persons to justify their own ghosting. The legal framework reinforces the default arrangement of state recognition.

Regional Adoption of the Definition of Stateless

There is a significant stateless population in Asia.[47] Malaysia is one of ten members of ASEAN, the Association of Southeast Asian Nations, an organization aimed at cooperation in the region.[48] The Philippines and Cambodia are the only ASEAN countries to have ratified the *1954 Statelessness Convention* and the Philippines is the only state to sign the

1961 Statelessness Convention. While the right to nationality is in the ICCPR, Brunei, Malaysia, Myanmar, and Singapore are not state parties. All ASEAN members are parties to the *Convention on the Elimination of all Forms of Discrimination against Women (CEDAW)* and the CRC albeit with reservations. A majority of Asian countries have not signed on to one or both Statelessness Conventions.[49]

While ASEAN has a mandate that is committed to human rights, it is at the whim of the political will of state members, and there is no enforcement mechanism to ensure that ASEAN members are adhering to any human rights instruments.[50]

As early as 2016, Malaysia was making calls to act on the Rohingya crisis in Myanmar. Reuters reported in December 2016 that "Malaysia … called for … ASEAN to coordinate humanitarian aid and investigate alleged atrocities committed against [the Rohingya]" marking "a break with ASEAN members' tradition of non-intervention in each other's internal affairs."[51] In November 2018, it was reported that "ASEAN is pushing the Independent Commission of Enquiry, established by the Myanmar government, to 'carry out an independent and impartial investigation of the allegations of human rights violations and related issues and hold those responsible fully accountable,'" and that this "firm tone is a departure from ASEAN's usual mild attitude toward Myanmar, based on the group's principle of non-interference in each other's internal affairs."[52] This has been attributed to "Muslim-majority nations in the region such as Indonesia and Malaysia … driving the criticism against Myanmar."[53]

Despite these small movements to call for adherence to human rights, the tepid regional response is not surprising given that the wider international legal infrastructure prioritizes state prerogative in matters of citizenship. Rodziana Mohamed Razali writes that "the legal frameworks for nationality in the ASEAN region are essentially shaped by the restrictive doctrine of *jus sanguinis* and single nationality, causing statelessness to be highly transmissible across many generations."[54] This, coupled with ASEAN members' reluctance to sign on to key human rights conventions, shows a strong resistance to any legal interference with the state's prerogative to decide who are its citizens.

Limitations Within Human Rights Conventions

Scholars claim there are emerging norms of a state's obligation to confer nationality.[55] State practice with regards to statelessness cases show otherwise. The refusal to sign onto a convention, the use of reservations or limitation clauses in treaty ascension, the reserved domain for treaty right to nationality, and the ascension but weak interpretation of a right are but a few tactics states use.[56] Conklin finds states "continued to reserve their freedom to confer, withdraw or withhold nationality from natural persons" and that "[s]uch an approach to treaty reservations is usually accompanied by a list of peremptory norms that by their very nature exclude the right to nationality and the right to legal personhood."[57] Conklin also finds that "despite the Vienna Treaty's object and purpose test for reservations, state parties ... continuously fall back upon their own internal jurisdiction as the source of legality."[58] International legal instruments are not only "hortatory"[59] but are limited by language with phrases like "provide appropriate assistance";[60] "undertakes to take the necessary steps";[61] "pursue by all appropriate means";[62] and "use their best endeavours."[63] Further, while "The non-discrimination clauses of the human rights treaties are invariably phrased in strong terms ... nationality as such is invariably excluded from the list of proscribed categories"[64] as it is, for example, for example, Article 1(2) of the ICERD states the non-discrimination norm "shall not apply to distinctions, exclusions, restriction or references made by a state party to this Convention between citizens and non-citizens."[65] Article 1(3) also provides that "Nothing in this Convention may be interpreted as affecting in any way the legal provisions of state parties concerning nationality, citizenship or naturalization ...."[66] Overall, the limitation clauses are active barriers to realizing a true right to citizenship for stateless persons.[67]

International Jurisprudence: Interpreting Genuine Links and One's Own Country

Genuine and Effective Links: The Nottebohm Case

International jurisprudence appears to increase a state's obligation to confer nationality.[68] Peter Spiro finds that "state discretion is no longer unfettered" and that there are emerging norms toward naturalization of long-term or habitual residents and a *jus soli* basis for birthright citizenship giving heft to territorial link as a basis for citizenship."[69] Spiro notes that the Liechtenstein v Guatemala case (the Nottebohm case) "may supply a sort of inverse conceptual guide to the future international law of citizenship."[70]

The Nottebohm case involved a claim by Liechtenstein against Guatemala for the wrongful seizure, without compensation, of the property of a Liechtenstein national.[71] Friedrich Nottebohm (born 1881) was a German national by birth but became a citizen of Liechtenstein in 1939.[72] Nottebohm was, however, a long-term resident of Guatemala and had few ties to Liechtenstein.[73] Guatemala challenged the admissibility of Liechtenstein's claim on the grounds that Nottebohm's naturalization to Liechtenstein was defective.[74] ICJ agreed, peering behind the veil of naturalization to find that his citizenship with Liechtenstein was not "real and effective."[75] ICJ noted that "nationality is a legal bond having as its basis a social fact of attachment, a genuine connection of existence, interests and sentiments, together with the existence of reciprocal rights and duties."[76]

Since the Nottebohm case, there have been a series of international law cases dealing with dual nationals that have adopted this "dominant and effective" test espousing the examination of relevant factors such as "habitual residence, center of interests, family ties, participation in public life and other evidence of attachment."[77] As Charles Brower and Jason Brueschke suggest, the increasing number of cases in which, for example, the Iran-US Claims Tribunal have turned to the dominant and effective nationality test (albeit in the context of dual nationals) "certainly represent a large source of precedent on the subject, which should serve as useful examples in other contexts."[78] They comment that the Nottebohm case "is seen as authority for the position that there should be an 'effective' or 'genuine' link between the individual and the State of nationality, not only in the case of dual or plural nationality (where such a requirement is generally accepted), but also where the national possesses only one nationality."[79] While some question the importance of the Nottebohm case on legal concepts of citizenship given that this was a case about diplomatic protection,[80] the case, nevertheless, provides a useful framework.

The Nottebohm case not only provides support for in situ stateless persons to claim a legal entitlement to citizenship but provides legal sustenance to the conditions under which a right to nationality may be invoked or triggered. The words "genuine" and "effective" qualify the links that one may have to a country to allow a person to make claims on citizenship. The Nottebohm case, however, is a double-edged sword, on the one hand providing opportunities for stateless persons who have long-standing residence and connection to a country to make a legal claim for citizenship, and on the other hand providing fodder for states to engage in practices of conferring ghost citizenships by pointing to connections elsewhere like a parental link. Indeed, the Iran-US Claims Tribunal provided that a person could have more than one effective nationality, notwithstanding the need to identify one as "dominant."[81] Kim Rubenstein and Niamh Lenagh-Macquire point out that the Nottebohm case, which is "the basis of 'effective nationality,' recognized under international law, is not simply social connectedness with a state but allegiance to the state, and that such allegiance is exclusive."[82]

Colouring the quality of "genuine and effective link" with the veneer of allegiance allows states to question whether persons do have genuine and effective links despite possible factual findings of long-term residence (and even birth within the territory), familial connections, and economic or employment integration. Other than the practical links, ultimately, it is the question of allegiance that may arise in cases where claims to citizenship are made. What kinds of proxies can be used to confirm allegiance? As discussed elsewhere in the book, even where long-term residence and family links can be shown, race and historical categorizations of race may colour the question of allegiance to some extent.

"One's Own Country"

While the Nottebohm case and cases from the Iran-US Claims Tribunal provide some traction for the right to nationality where one has significant ties to a specific state, legal pronouncements elsewhere have watered down this approach, particularly in the human rights context.

Article 12(4) of the ICCPR provides that "No one shall be arbitrarily deprived of the right to enter his own country."[83] The phrase "his own country" has received some interpretive attention at the United Nations Human Rights Committee. The *travaux préparatoires* of the ICCPR, in relation to Article 12(4), provide that the provision was meant to prohibit exile as much as possible.[84] Beyond this, Article 12(4) also created a "right to enter one's country."[85] The *travaux préparatoires,* however, reveal that "The general consensus was ... the right was not absolute" and that "'his own country' should be taken to mean the country of which the individual concerned was a national or citizen, the necessity of being able to submit ample proof of the fact was also emphasized."[86] As illustrated in case law discussed next in this chapter and in Chapter 4, the standard of "ample proof" required on the part of stateless people is high, while proof on the part of a state to find that a person is a citizen of a foreign state is correspondingly low.

The Human Rights Committee has provided a frequently cited approach to interpreting "own country" in Stewart v Canada.[87] Stewart was born in Scotland but at the age of seven moved to Canada.[88] Stewart considered himself Canadian despite his parents never having applied for citizenship on his behalf.[89] He discovered he was only a permanent resident when immigration officials found him inadmissible to Canada due to a series of criminal convictions.[90] Stewart, facing deportation, made a claim to the Human Rights Committee asserting that "article 12, paragraph 4, is applicable to his situation since, for all practical purposes, Canada is his 'own country'" and "[h]is deportation from Canada would result in an absolute statutory bar from reentering Canada."[91] Stewart seemed to concede that Article 12(4) did not apply to everyone but only to those who can claim "his own country" and that the UK was no longer his "own country" since he left it at the age of seven and since his entire life centred on his family in Canada; he considered himself a de facto Canadian citizen.[92] Canada, for its part, argued that "the right to remain in a country and not to be expelled from it is confined to nationals of that state"[93] and that "the most fundamental principle of immigration law is that non-citizens do not have an unqualified right to enter or remain in the country."[94] Canada also argued that the procedures undertaken to evaluate the decision to remove Stewart were within the bounds of domestic law and there was no evidence of bad faith or abuse of power.[95]

The committee, in considering whether Canada was "one's own country" in relation to Stewart stated "the concept 'his own country' is not limited to nationality in a formal sense," and "it embraces, at the very least, an individual who, because of his special ties to or claims in relation to a given country cannot there be considered to be a mere alien."[96] Further, the committee held that "The language of article 12, paragraph 4, permits a broader interpretation, moreover, that might embrace other categories of long-term residents, particularly stateless persons arbitrarily deprived of the right to acquire the nationality of the country of such residence."[97]

The committee then asked whether a person who has not acquired citizenship but has citizenship of another state, can regard the state he does not have citizenship in as "his own country" and does contemplate it being possible but only in circumstances where the state can be regarded as placing unreasonable impediments.[98] In this case, the committee cast Stewart as failing in his obligation to acquire his citizenship given that Canada provided mechanisms to acquire citizenship after a period of residence.[99] The committee held that "Individuals who do not take advantage of this opportunity and thus escape the obligations nationality imposes can be deemed to have opted to remain aliens in Canada."[100] Thus, the committee concluded that none of Stewart's rights were violated.

Nine committee members in the Stewart case provided their own individual opinions, many on the scope of interpreting "own country." Member Laurel Francis disagrees "with the Committee's restricted application of his 'own country' concept" characterizing Canada's actions vis-à-vis Stewart as terminating his "own country" status.[101] Members Elizabeth Evatt, Cecilia Medina Quiroga, and Francisco José Aguilar Urbina write that the committee's view was too narrow, and contemplated the case of stateless persons.[102] They find that individuals should not be deprived the right to enter "their own country" where it would be unacceptable to deprive a person of "close contact with his family, or his friends or, put in general terms, with the web of relationships that form his or her social environment." They point to factors that illustrate "strong personal and emotional links" a person may have "with the territory where he lives and with the social circumstances obtaining in it."[103] These members go further and find that "there are factors other than nationality which may establish close and enduring connections between a person and a country, connections which may be stronger than those of nationality" and they point to long-standing residence; close personal family ties; and intentions to remain.[104] The three members questioned Canada's reasoning that "criminal offences alone could justify the expulsion of a person from his own country, unless the State could show that there are compelling reasons of national security or public order which require such a course."[105] The committee members took issue with the framing of the issue—that the focus was on whether proceedings to decide whether to deport Stewart were arbitrary versus what grounds existed for taking away Stewart's right to enter "his own country."[106]

Committee member Prafullachandra Bhagwati provides an opinion that gives some thought to the precedential effect of the decision: "people who have forged close links with a country not only through long residence but having regard to various other factors, who have adopted a country as their own, who have come to regard a country as their home country, would be left without any protection."[107] Bhagwati argues the test should be stated as a person "who, because of his special ties to or claims in relation to a given country cannot there be considered to be an alien."[108] Despite advocating for this wider test, Bhagwati acknowledges that "it is the sovereign right of a State to determine under what conditions it will grant nationality to a non-national" and "[i]t is not for the Committee to pass judgement whether the conditions are reasonable or not."[109]

The Stewart case highlights the core problem with any claim to a right to citizenship: the "sovereign right" or prerogative of states to confer citizenship. Even while international law is increasingly recognizing that individuals may have deep relationships with a state, ultimately, the exclusive power rests with a state to grant or deny citizenship.

Several cases before the Human Rights Committee have since relied on or clarified the Stewart case. In Canepa v Canada, the committee remarked, in relation to Article 12(4) and the Stewart case, that "a person who enters a State under the State's immigration laws, and subject to the conditions of those laws, cannot regard that State as his own country when he has not acquired its nationality and continues to retain the nationality of his country of origin."[110] The committee found the efforts of the claimant to obtain citizenship a significant factor in deciding whether a state is "one's own country."

In a 2001 decision of Madafferi v Australia, the committee relied on the same rationale: that persons cannot claim as "their own country" a state they have not acquired citizenship from and where there were no unreasonable impediments in the process to acquire said citizenship.[111]

In the 2010 decision of Ilyasov v Kazakhstan, the committee declined to provide views on Article 12, but a few committee members provided their own opinions. Members Gerald Neuman, Yuji Iwasawa, and Walter Kälin write that "Overextending article 12, paragraph 4, would also risk undermining the essential protection that this provision was designed to afford. The primary function of the right to enter one's own country is to impose an extremely high barrier against a State's exile of its own citizens, or blocking of their return."[112] Specifically they state, "Extending the coverage of article 12, paragraph 4, to all foreign residents with permanent resident permits, or to foreign residents with families that include nationals, would inevitably lead to dilution of the protective standard."[113] Member Anja Seibert-Fohr also writes that "Though article 12 does not refer to nationality, the reference to everyone's right to enter 'his own country' protects first and foremost a State's own nationals."[114] Member Yuval Shany writes, "there are strong indications in the *travaux préperatoires* that the original version of the text of the paragraph, which covered only nationals, was changed specifically with a view to accommodating the interests of certain permanent residents."[115]

A 2020 decision of Warsame v Canada explores the tensions in Article 12(4).[116] The committee found that Warsame "has established that Canada was his own country within the meaning of article 12, paragraph 4, of the Covenant, in the light of the strong ties connecting him to Canada, the presence of his family in Canada, the language he speaks, the duration of his stay in the country and the lack of any other ties than at best formal nationality with Somalia."[117] Six members of the committee provided their own opinions, two of which dissented while four concurred. Interestingly, all six opinions disagreed with the committee's interpretation of Article 12(4) in finding that Canada was Warsame's "own country" with one member pointing to the lack of effort on Warsame's part to secure citizenship.[118]

The 2011 decision of Nystrom v Australia also acknowledges that "close and enduring connections" inform as to whether a state is "one's own country" specifying that "The words 'his own country' invite consideration of such matters as long-standing residence, close personal and family ties and intentions to remain, as well as to the absence of such ties elsewhere."[119] In the Nystrom case members Gerald Neuman and Yuji Iwasawa again advocated for a less expansive interpretation of Article 12(4) stating that an expansive approach "vastly increases the number of non-nationals whom a state cannot send back to their country of nationality, despite strong reasons of public interest and protection of the rights of others for terminating their residence."[120] They call for a more narrow approach arguing that the broad interpretation would lead to the "dilution" of the protection in Article 12(4).[121]

Budlakoti v Canada provides positive traction for the identification of certain links as indicating "one's own country."[122] In this case, Budlakoti claimed he was a Canadian citizen by birth but Canada contested this citizenship, claiming his parents were employed by Indian consular officials at his birth. The fact of employment by a foreign consular office was the basis for finding Budlakoti exempt from birthright citizenship in Canada[123] Budlakoti was rendered criminally inadmissible and Canada has, ever since, sought to deport him to India (they do not claim him as their own).[124] The committee noted that Budlakoti was born in Canada and lived in Canada his entire life, never having resided in India or possessing any connection or relationship to anyone in India.[125] The committee also acknowledged that Budlakoti was issued a Canadian passport and has strong ties to Canada given the presence of his family, the language he speaks, and the duration of his presence in Canada. Budlakoti argued that Canada was "his own country."[126] The Human Rights Committee found that Canada's actions in deporting Budlakoti would violate his rights under the ICCPR providing strong reasoning that Budlakoti's "own country" was Canada. Despite this positive determination, because the Human Rights Committee's recommendation was limited to the prevention of deportation, Canada's actions remained narrow. Budlakoti remains stateless and in limbo but within Canada.[127] As Daiva Stasiulis points out, Canada is normalizing citizenship deprivation resulting in cases of statelessness.[128] We see in this case a state engaging in the practice of rendering a person a citizen of another country. In this case, Budlakoti was cast as a citizen of India to justify the deprivation of citizenship. Canada denied Budlakoti was stateless and instead referred to him as a national of India given the speculative potential to acquire such citizenship and despite the absence of evidence that he was a citizen of India.[129] This practice of conferring ghost citizenships acts as a premise to ghost a citizen from their access to citizenship is becoming a common state practice.

Aside from the Budlakoti case, the jurisprudence of the Human Rights Committee is moving away from its own general approach in interpreting Article 12(4) in General Comment No 27 which provided that Article 12(4) "recognizes the special relationship of a person to that country."[130] More importantly, it stated that Article 12(4) "does not distinguish between nationals and aliens" given the use of the words "no one."[131] In relation to the phrase "his own country," the committee provided that it "is broader than the concept 'country of his nationality'" and that "[i]t is not limited to nationality in a formal sense" but rather that "because of his or her special ties to or claims in relation to a given country, cannot be considered to be a mere alien."[132] The committee acknowledges the three categories of examples in the Stewart case (nationals stripped of citizenship in violation of international law, persons whose country was incorporated or transferred to another national entity where citizenship has been denied to them, and stateless persons arbitrarily deprived of the right to acquire citizenship) but also states that "other factors may in certain circumstances result in the establishment of close and enduring connections between a person and a country" permitting a "broader interpretation that might embrace other categories of long-term residents."[133]

The interpretation of "one's own country" in Article 12(4) of the ICCPR have highlighted two things. First, in law, there is a normative understanding that a person's relationship with the state is not simply that of a citizen or foreigner; there is a spectrum and the links, connections, and ties one has with a state can inform where one belongs. This in-between place confers a ghostlike veneer of citizenship on persons who can point to the links or ties. It points to a space that is akin to purgatory or an otherworldly place, sometimes unrecognizable to those with status.

Second, the cases show an imbalance of power in the relationship between states and individuals; states invoke "one's own country" to evoke the idea that persons are foreign citizens and not citizens of the claimed state with greater success than claims made by individuals in their stated home country. In the cases discussed, individuals claimed "one's own country" and were ghosted by the states they claimed as their own. In domestic state practice, however, as will be seen in the case study of Malaysia, such links, even if tenuous, speculative, and even non-existent, are enough for states to prop up the ghost citizenship of a stateless person — citizenship in an alternative state. For states, the legal concept of "one's own country" is being invoked in ways that fosters state practice of creating ghost citizens allowing states to avoid examining claims of citizenship made within their borders. For individuals, this ability to turn to factors of an enduring or long-standing connection can only take one so far — it can trigger an examination of what is one's state but it reaches a ceiling whereby states are pushing back with questions about their efforts to obtain citizenship or nefarious activities they have engaged in whether it be due to neglect (in obtaining citizenship) or criminal intent (as reasons to banish a person).

The State Prerogative and the False Promise of International Law

International law has acknowledged the plight of statelessness and has proposed an approach to create obligations among states to address statelessness. There are several reasons, however, for why international law has not provided relief for stateless persons. One limitation is that many states simply are not party to or adhere to the Statelessness Conventions or the provisions in various international legal instruments to call for robust and fair treatment of stateless persons within their borders. Practically speaking, the strongest legal tools are not usable in the many contexts in which stateless persons are found.

A second limitation is that the state's prerogative to decide who its citizens are is embedded in international law. On its face, in various international legal texts, there are pronouncements to rights to nationality, but when it comes down to it, international law cannot take a person to the finish line. The current legal framework may appear to be inching toward a right to citizenship but in practical terms, there are limitation clauses, exclusions, reservations, and interpretations in domestic settings, as well as the lack of an enforcement or incentive mechanism for states to recognize a right to nationality. As such, the law-as-text has not lived up to its promise of eliminating or even diminishing statelessness but has been carefully crafted to allow states to do two things. First, such legal constructions have allowed states to circumvent their obligation to grant nationality to those with genuine and effective links to their states when they make claims for citizenship. Secondly, and perhaps most disturbingly, states are gaslighting stateless persons by referring to tenuous or non-existent connections elsewhere so they can deem that person a citizen of an alternative state (and hence the responsibility of a different state) even though there is no legal confirmation of citizenship, effectively withholding the status of statelessness from them.

A third limitation is that states invoke international law to engage in questionable practices to deny the identification of a person as *their* citizens by creating ghost citizens — citizens of states elsewhere.

International law seemingly gives a stateless person leverage in claiming that even in situations where citizenship has not been conferred, certain factors, such as one's ties and bonds to a state, may raise questions as to why a state is not doing so. While international legal pronouncements regarding factors such as enduring connections to a country colour the quality of the relationship between an individual and a state, as explored in Chapter 3, this is often ignored when claims of citizenship or claims of associated rights are made. Claimants are ghosted, rendered invisible and unable to grasp the status or rights as a result of evidentiary requirements under international jurisprudence that demand evidence of sustained attempts and efforts to acquire citizenship to bolster a claim that the state is their "own."

Further, on the flip side, states use international law to argue that while the person is not their citizen, they point to factual findings of links, ties, and connections, no matter how tenuous, to confer ghost citizenship of alternative states on people. This arises in cases where states deny the person has a claim for citizenship in their state because they see them as having an existing connection or link to a different state, denying them the status of stateless person. This construction of the ghost citizen allows states to not only deny their responsibility to that individual but also allows states to deem such persons as foreigners, wayward figures, or deviants that are not worthy of the state's attention. Given this state practice, we cannot take for granted the fact that states are acting in bona fide, good faith ways with stateless persons.

This double-edged sword of ghosting citizens (despite ties and because they did not do enough to obtain status) and conferring ghost citizenship (despite no proof of conferral, of a foreign state where they might have tenuous links) raises questions about whether we should rely on state recognition as a defining feature in our communities.

FOUR

THE CITIZEN
Domestic Legal Construction of Ghost Citizens

Malaysia: A Universal Case Study

The case study of Malaysia provides important insights for understanding the creation and maintenance of statelessness in general. Malaysia is a democratic state that is multijuridical with a common law and an Islamic legal system. It is also a former British colony and has a multicultural population, but does not adhere to many international human rights instruments. Given that many postcolonial countries have similar features of a democratic governance structure with an extensive administrative system, the insights gained from this case study are apt for places where statelessness is surging.

This chapter will provide a brief overview of the law on citizenship in Malaysia while highlighting legal trends and ethnographic experiences of stateless persons. This chapter does not provide a comprehensive tour of citizenship law; I leave that to my learned colleagues in Malaysia.[1] The analysis considers Malaysia's constitution, legislation, public policy, reports, and documents. I also consider ninety-seven cases pulled from interviews with forty-five people and thirty-seven reported cases, as well as thirteen unreported cases since January 1975 to April 2020, with one exception of Malaysia's Apex Court decision delivered in 2022.[2]

A Thin Conception of Human Rights in Malaysia

Malaysia is a signatory to the *Universal Declaration of Human Rights*[3] and the CRC with reservations, both of which provide rights to citizenship.[4] However, Malaysia is not a party to the 1954 *Statelessness Convention* or the 1961 *Statelessness Convention*,⁵ the *Refugee Convention*,⁶ the ICERD,⁷ the ICCPR,⁸ or the *Convention against Torture*,⁹ among others. In response to calls to sign and ratify some of these conventions, Malaysia has stated it is not ready and that it is in consultation to ensure its preparedness to sign.¹⁰ As a result, there has been very little use of human rights language in domestic legal cases. Some advocates mentioned the turn to human rights sometimes harmed a legal case involving a stateless person.¹¹ During an interview with one lawyer, they stated:

> Unfortunately some lawyers pushed arguments from a human rights perspective rather than a legalistic black letter law approach. There is a difference. We need to recognize that we are a legislative system. If there is a conflict in the law, no matter how a judge feels for a child, they cannot help. This is more so when it touches a political issue. To make it easy for the judge to decide, you need to focus on legal arguments.¹²

A different lawyer argued that human rights was important but commented on its muted efficacy: "When we argue that Malaysia is a party to the Convention on the Rights of the Child … the court does not think it is obliged to follow such conventions. For me, this is utterly wrong that this is happening."¹³ Another lawyer commented: "I did refer to the Convention on the Rights of the Child to which Malaysia is a signatory, but Malaysia has reservations, so it is limited."¹⁴

A review of case law confirms that human rights law has little to no impact on a stateless person's case. For example, in Than Siew Beng, the Court of Appeal states that "International conventions, such as the CRC have no force of law as it has not been incorporated into municipal legislation."¹⁵ Aside from three cases, none of the other thirty-three reported decisions considered human rights at all.¹⁶

Citizenship Law in Malaysia

The Constitution

To understand how statelessness is created in Malaysia, one must briefly examine Malaysia's citizenship law. While citizenship law finds its home within the Federal Constitution of Malaysia ('Federal Constitution'), other pieces of legislation inform access to citizenship, including the 1952 Adoption Act¹⁷ and the 1961 Legitimacy Act.¹⁸

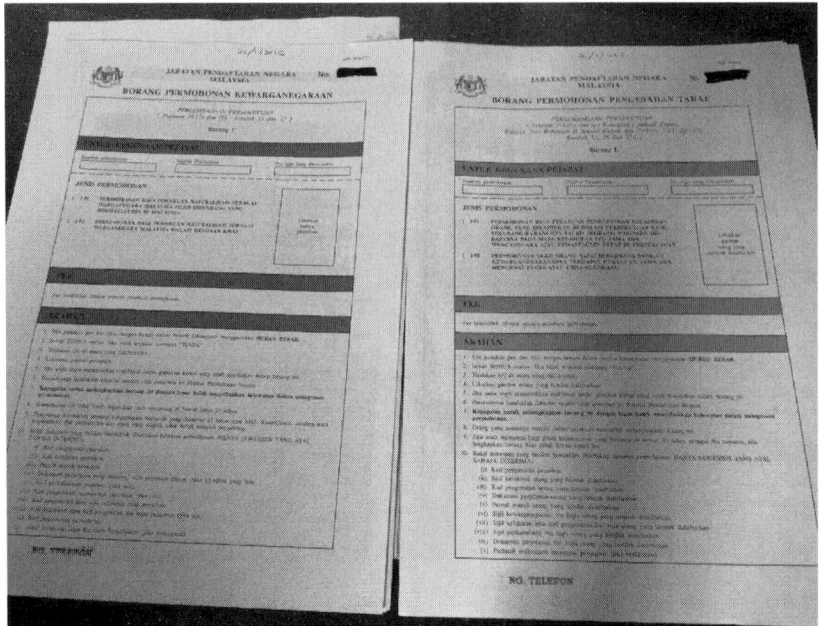

Examples of blank citizenship application forms. The serial numbers have been redacted. Photo Credit: Jamie Liew.

There are four different ways a person can acquire citizenship in Malaysia: by operation of law or automatically;[19] by registration;[20] by naturalization;[21] or by incorporation of territory.[22] When applying for citizenship, different forms (*borang* in Malay) with individualized serial numbers are submitted. The forms are colour-coded, for example in blue, yellow, green, and purple signifying which one of the four ways one is applying for (i.e. by operation of law etc.). As discussed in Chapter 6, some forms are more accessible than others.[23]

All the cases of statelessness discussed in the case law and with those interviewed dealt with citizenship applications under Articles 14 (operation of law or automatic) and 15 (registration) of the Federal Constitution. This chapter focuses on these two modes only.

Operation of Law (Automatic; Article 14 — Purple Borang)

Citizenship by operation of law (automatic) is enunciated in Article 14 of the Federal Constitution, which provides that person/s born before Malaysia Day who were citizens of Malaysia prior to independence are automatically Malaysian citizens. It also provides that persons born after Malaysia Day, if they meet certain requirements, are also automatic citizens. Those born after Malaysian independence have to meet requirements set out in part II of schedule II, section 1 including, in general, (a) those born in Malaysia of a parent who was a citizen or permanent resident of Malaysia; (b) those born outside of Malaysia whose father is a Malaysian citizen; (c) those born outside Malaysia whose father is a Malaysian citizen and whose birth is registered with the Malaysian consulate within one year of the birth; (d) those born in Singapore to a parent who is a Malaysian citizen; (e) "every person born within the Federation who is not born a citizen of any country otherwise than by virtue of this paragraph."[24]

A superficial reading of the constitution makes it seem that the simple fact of being born within Malaysia by a parent who is a Malaysian citizen or permanent resident entitles one to citizenship automatically.[25] Relying on a parental link, however, is complicated, as Article 14 has been read with part II, schedule II, section 17 which has been interpreted to mean that where a person's parents are not legally married, a child is considered "illegitimate" and that child's citizenship follows the mother's citizenship and not the father's,[26] even if the father is her only Malaysian parent.

Arguably, this provision is irrelevant if a child was born in Malaysia; it is not necessary to have a Malaysian parent. The constitution under Article 14(1)(b), part II, schedule II, section 1(e) provides a safety net for statelessness by providing that every person born within Malaysia, "who is not born a citizen of any country otherwise," is also a citizen.[27] This provision should be read with sch II pt II s 2(3), "For the purposes of paragraph (e) of section 1 a person is to be treated as having at birth any citizenship which he acquires within one year afterwards by virtue of any provision corresponding to paragraph (c) of that section or otherwise."[28] Subsection 2(3) then provides an interpretive guide for s 1(e) in that a person "who is not born a citizen of any country otherwise" includes persons born in Malaysia who have not acquired citizenship within one year after their birth.

The fail-safe provision, however, has not been interpreted this way. The Malaysian government has interpreted the words, "who is not born a citizen of any country otherwise" as a requirement to assess whether a stateless person has explored obtaining alternative citizenship, especially where one parent is suspected or known to be a citizen of a country other than Malaysia.[29] This has been the vehicle by which ghost citizenship is found in jurisprudence. Some, however, interpret the provision as not including this requirement to look for a parental or blood link in another country.[30]

Registration (Discretionary; Article 15A — Green Borang)

Article 15A of the constitution states: "Subject to Article 18, the Federal Government may, in such special circumstances as it thinks fit, cause any person under the age of twenty-one years to be registered a citizen."[31] Article 15A provides wide discretionary powers to the Minister of Home Affairs to grant citizenship.

Automatic Versus Discretionary Conferral

Articles 14 and 15 may lead to the same result, namely, the conferral of citizenship, but the process by which one acquires citizenship differs under these two articles. Article 14 confers citizenship by operation of law or automatically and is the preferred application by stateless persons and their advocates because once a person meets the criteria listed in Article 14, citizenship is as of course. Article 15 is a different legal path as it relies heavily on the discretion of the Minister of Home Affairs; aside from the criteria that one must be less than 21 years of age, there is nothing guiding the Minister or their delegate as to when citizenship should be granted.

One of the lawyers I interviewed stated that "Lawyers have interpreted Article 14 as one that you cannot reject; if it is operation of law, then you must grant [citizenship]."[32] The High Court in the Haja Mohideen MK Abdul Rahman case has aptly described the different modes:

> An application under art. 14 is quite unlike an application under art. 15 where a person has to apply to be a citizen in which case the Federal Government has the right to consider his application on a substantive basis which may include matters of policy in arriving at its decision whether or not to grant him citizenship ....[33]

Stateless persons are often directed or encouraged to apply under Article 15 rather than Article 14 by state agents. The fact that stateless persons, when aware of the difference, have chosen the automatic conferral over registration demonstrates their perceptions that they are de facto citizens seeking documentation to prove their citizenship. Stateless persons are loath to apply for citizenship via registration or naturalization processes given that these processes raise questions as to the genuineness of their claims and may imply they are necessarily foreigners who must earn or prove they are worthy of the conferral.

It is the existence of these different citizenship application processes that have fuelled the practice of ghost citizenship. The state practice of asking stateless persons to apply under Article 15 reinforces narratives that persons need to earn or demonstrate their ties, bonds, and allegiances to the state, rather than treat them as kin that need to be furnished with proper identification documentation. The differential modes of citizenship are used to not only taint applicants with a varnish of foreignness but also shields and protects the state from having to confront claims of citizenship from kin. Advocates, since research was conducted in 2018, are still struggling with this distinction. In a 2023 news report an advocate was quoted as saying: "There is no need to apply, no need for approval from the Home Minister. They are entitled to citizenship by the Federal Constitution."[34]

Ghost Citizens as Judicial Facts

As discussed, rights to nationality are tempered with the state prerogative to decide who is a citizen. When confronted with claims for citizenship, states raise questions as to which state does owe the obligation. This legal approach — pointing to foreign citizenship — is not only being adopted at the international level but also in domestic legal venues. In Malaysia, the jurisprudence reveals this practice justifies the denial of citizenship, the ghosting of citizens.

Admittedly, law could be tweaked to address gaps and shortcomings. However, many people I interviewed saw legal interpretation as a significant barrier to citizenship.[35] One lawyer commented that "Laws are not being applied fairly and as per the constitution. A lot of interpretation is arcane. [Judges ask for] a lot of extra-legal requirements. These requirements are not those that flow from the spirit of the constitution."[36] One NGO representative stated that "The government is not following the constitution ... Citizenship by descent should also be given automatically to adopted children."[37] One lawyer said that "The same arguments in front of different judges yields different results. Successful cases show how it should be done; a fair interpretation is possible but there is a string of cases that show an adverse position."[38]

Factual Findings: Not Meeting the Requirements

A common argument put forward by government lawyers is that applicants did not satisfy the requirements for citizenship.[39] The question of whether one meets the legal requirements is a question of fact. In making factual findings however, we see stateless persons confronted with a reinvention of their lives and identities without any evidence. Legal fictions cast persons as citizens of foreign countries, as ghost citizens. The next subsection discusses how people are made to be ghost citizens through a variety of legal devices all enacted through issuance, reissuance, or denial of birth certificates.

Ghost Citizens via Birth Certificates

In Malaysia, birth certificates identify persons as either citizens, or not a citizen, or as an unknown. Stateless persons talked about how birth certificates were taken away, reissued, or denied and how these actions led to the conferral or confiscation of citizenship. Indeed, in at least five of the reported cases, Identification Cards and birth certificates were confiscated and reissued with the information around citizenship altered to say they are not citizens of Malaysia.[40] For example, in the Lim Kai Lin case, parents of a stateless child challenged the decision to issue a new birth certificate and identity card marking their child as not a citizen.[41]

In this section, I look at how the issuance, reissuance, confiscation, and denial of a birth certificate is a central and critical interaction in the construction of statelessness and ghost citizens.

The Birth Certificate: The Pronouncement of Citizenship

The birth certificate is valuable and important because of its function of pronouncing citizenship and is a contested site. While, in the Haja Mohideen MK Abdul Rahman case, the High Court commented that "A birth certificate in any case is a certification of birth and not of citizenship" and found that the fact the plaintiffs had birth certificates stating they were citizens "did not necessarily indicate that they were citizens," in other cases where birth certificates list a person as not a citizen, birth certificates are seen as establishing the legal fact of (non)/citizenship.[42] For example, in the Madhuvita case, the claimant sought an order from the High Court to have her birth certificate reissued with "citizen" listed on it as per Article 14(1)(b) of the Federal Constitution.[43] In this case, the stateless person's parents (Malaysian father and Papua New Guinean mother) were married after the birth of the stateless child. Despite having a Malaysian father and being born in Malaysia, the applicant's birth certificate listed her as not a citizen. While the government pointed to the citizenship of the mother, the court, in finding for the stateless person, leaned on the social facts establishing her links to Malaysia: "The applicant had lived all her life in the Federation, and had no intention of applying for citizenship of Papua New Guinea. The appellant's birth was not registered in Papua New Guinea and was registered here instead."[44]

Similarly, in Tan Lee the applicant argued that the government officer's decision to take away a birth certificate that listed a person as citizen amounted to citizenship revocation.[45] In this case, a child, who was born before the child's parents were married (Malaysian father and Indonesian mother), was rendered stateless when the initial birth certificate listing the child as a citizen was taken away and a new one reissued listing the child as not a citizen.[46] The court noted that the amendments made to the birth certificate were significant; that it changed her status from citizen to non-citizen and her race from "Cina" to "Indonesia."[47]

These cases reveal normative understandings of the function of birth certificates. First, the birth certificate is a significant document, not just mere proof, marking a legal fact related to citizenship that amounts to a decision that can be challenged and judicially reviewed.[48]

Second, the Court of Appeal in the Mandhivita case considered the markers that form the genuine connection between the applicant and the state (the fact of birth on a territory, the fact of a citizen parent, and the fact that the applicant lived her entire life in Malaysia and had no intention of applying for citizenship elsewhere). This kind of legal approach allows context to inform a decision, is supported by international law (as discussed in Chapter 3) and provides an important precedential value to future legal strategies.

Third, the practice of taking judicial notice of the unsubstantiated fact that there is a mere possibility for a person to obtain citizenship elsewhere (due to the mother's citizenship) is displacing evidentiary requirement of actual conferral of citizenship elsewhere. This troubling practice of deeming a person a ghost citizen simply because of a mother's citizenship in a foreign country thins the definition of statelessness and distracts from the merits of whether a person is in fact a citizen of the claimed country. Relying on the marker of "not a citizen" on a birth certificate is a concerning practice given findings presented in Chapter

6 where stateless people were treated with lack of respect and hostility by officials at government counters when their birth certificates were confiscated, issued, or reissued.

The Birth Certificate: Proof of Citizenship

In a few cases, the courts have emphasized the requirement to prove one's citizenship through only the birth certificate. One example is the Ong Boon Hua case, which involved an 80-year-old individual who was born in pre-independent Malaysia in 1923.[49] The applicant was outside of Malaysia and wanted to enter but could not prove he was a Malaysian citizen. He provided documents that proved his parents, his siblings, and children were all Malaysian citizens, but he no longer had his birth certificate. The National Registration Department (NRD) indicated that there was no record of the applicant's birth. He then provided affidavits from his family members. In denying Ong Boon Hua the remedy to be declared a citizen, the Court of Appeal concluded that the applicant must provide a birth certificate and discounted other means, such as affidavits or other documentary proof, to show proof of citizenship.[50]

Similarly, in the Nalaln Kunji Kanan case,[51] a stateless person provided the death certificate of a parent which also listed the parent's citizenship. This document was deemed insufficient. It was not clear why a birth certificate could not be proffered, but the court held that the burden is on the stateless person to produce evidence they meet the requirements under Article 14(1)(b), in this case, the preferred document being the birth certificate.[52]

The case of Yong Lee Hua involved an 80-year-old person born in pre-independent Malaysia. Yong was issued an identity card that listed her as a citizen in 1963, 1973, and 1966.[53] In 2007, Yong lost her identity card and she applied for a replacement. She was issued an identity card that listed Yong as a permanent resident.[54] The government relied on the Ong Boon Hua precedent to argue that Yong needed to produce her birth certificate to prove she was a citizen.[55] The High Court distinguished Ong Boon Hua from this case however, stating that the birth certificate was not essential given the requirement was not listed in the constitution. The court recognized that "It is common knowledge that there are citizens, particularly those in the rural and deep interiors of Sabah and Sarawak who do not possess any birth certificate. Documentation is a concept that is alien to them. To demand that they produce their birth certificates before they can be considered as citizens would be to perpetrate a grave injustice." Further, the court held that citizenship is "purely a question of fact," that "production of a birth certificate is but one of the ways to prove this fact" but that "It is not the only way."[56]

These cases raise three important considerations for stateless persons. First, the burden of proof is on the stateless person to offer documentary evidence that they are eligible for and meet the requirements for citizenship.

Second, the birth certificate may be considered proof of citizenship, and in some cases may be considered not only essential but the sole proof of citizenship. The absence of a birth certificate could be fatal to the chances of obtaining citizenship. While the High Court distinguishes the Yong Lee Hua case from Ong Boon Hua, the decision in Ong Boon Hua is from the Court of Appeal, a higher, appellate court and its opinion may be seen as more determinative.

Third, the courts' treatment of birth certificates has meant that the markers of "citizen" or "not a citizen" are default indicators of whether a person is a citizen or not. To change or resolve this, stateless persons must judicially challenge or review the markers placed on these certificates. This is concerning given that in Chapter 6, research findings reveal racist and hostile approaches on the part of government officials in confiscating, reissuing, or issuing birth certificates.

Further, even where the judiciary finds that an error has been made, the hardships of statelessness are downplayed. For example, Yong sought damages for what she faced while she was not recognized as a citizen. The High Court acknowledged that she felt she "became an alien in her own country of birth"[57] but they did not award her damages.[58]

Children as Ghost Citizens

Adopted Children as Ghost Citizens

Eight of the thirty-two reported cases[59] and five unreported cases[60] involved adopted children. Fifteen of the sixty cases that interviewees discussed involved adopted children. Three of the five amalgamated cases that reached the apex court in Malaysia, the Federal Court, involved adopted children.[61]

Why is it that adopted children are stateless in Malaysia? In four of the eight reported cases, when the children were adopted, the adoptive parents were listed on the birth certificate as biological parents and the children as Malaysian citizens.⁶² In all cases, when the child, at the age of twelve, became eligible to obtain an Identification Card (IC), the registrar notified the families that the birth was not registered or registered improperly, confiscated the birth certificate, and reissued a new birth certificate listing the child as a non-citizen. In three of the eight remaining cases, after an adoption had been processed, the children were issued a birth certificate listing the adoptive parents' names and identifying the child as a non-citizen.⁶³ In the eighth remaining reported case, a father (a Malaysian citizen) adopted his biological child in the hopes of being able to assist his child's application for citizenship.⁶⁴

In the reported cases, the ultimate issue was whether an adopted child can enjoy the same rights as a biological child to automatically acquire citizenship by operation of law under Article 14(1)(b) of the constitution if their adoptive parent is a Malaysian citizen. In the eight reported cases involving adopted children, the court denied them their requested relief of recognition as a citizen by operation of law. This body of jurisprudence cements the idea that adopted children do not enjoy the same access to citizenship as biological children. As the Court of Appeal stated in the Than Siew Beng case, "An adoption order does not confer a right of citizenship by operation of law consequent upon the making of an adoption order."⁶⁵

My interviews with advocates confirmed that there was a systemic practice of excluding adopted children from the automatic conferral of citizenship. One lawyer commented that "the law is interpreted where if you adopt a stateless child, it doesn't automatically obtain citizenship by descent of the adoptive parent. The birth certificates of adopted children list their adoptive parents and under adoption laws, adoptive parents are considered true parents, but they are not for citizenship purposes."⁶⁶ This approach was applied in cases where parents sought legitimacy orders as well; where a child is deemed the child of a parent, they do not automatically acquire the citizenship of that parent.⁶⁷

It is interesting that all five unreported cases were resolved out of court during litigation leading to the successful acquisition of citizenship. Without a reported decision however, there is no legal precedent to point to. In three of the cases, the government awarded citizenship literally at the doorstep of the highest court in Malaysia prior to a scheduled hearing.⁶⁸ These cases are celebrated in the media and the outcome of the cases would not otherwise be known.⁶⁹

How the courts reached the conclusion that adopted children do not automatically acquire the citizenship of their adoptive Malaysian parent is crucial to understanding the persistence of statelessness and the creation of ghost citizens. Judicial decisions consider a few aspects of Article 14(1)(b) and section 1(b) of Part II of the Second Schedule, specifically, the legal meaning of (a) "parent"; and (b) "at the time of the birth." Further, the courts also contemplate how the constitution interacts with the Adoption Act 1952.

The Case of Foo Toon Aik

The case of Foo Toon Aik[70] is illustrative not only because it is an example of the strange practice of parents adopting their biological children to try to create a legal link for citizenship, but it is also the most cited precedent of the judicial view that adopted children do not automatically acquire the citizenship of their adoptive Malaysian parent.[71]

Foo Shi Wen was born in Malaysia in 2006 to his father, Foo Toon Aik, a Malaysian citizen and his mother, a Thai citizen.[72] Foo's parents were married but their marriage was not registered in either Thailand or Malaysia at the time of Foo's birth.[73] His birth certificate stated his citizenship status as, "Bukan Warganegara" or non-citizen.[74] Subsequent to Foo's birth, his parents' marriage broke down and his mother returned to Thailand, relinquishing her parental rights over Foo Shi Wen.[75] Foo Toon Aik adopted his biological son and after receiving an Adoption Order pursuant to the Adoption Act 1952, he applied for a new birth certificate for Foo Shi Wen.[76] The second birth certificate also stated Foo Shi Wen's citizenship status as "Bukan Warganegara."[77] Foo Toon Aik applied to the Federal Court for writ of certiorari to have the decision to list his son's citizenship status as non-citizen quashed on the grounds that this was an error in law, followed by a mandamus to register the child as a citizen.[78]

Counsel for Foo used the case of Lee Chin Pon to argue that as consequence of the Adoption Order, it is an automatic operation of the law that the adopted child takes on the citizenship of his adoptive father.[79] Foo's lawyer also relied on section 9 of the Adoption Act 1952 which discusses the effect of an adoption order: "all such rights, duties, obligations and liabilities shall vest in and be exercisable by and enforceable against the adopter as though the adopted child was a child born to the adopter in lawful wedlock" and the adopted child is "included within the meaning of the expressions 'parent' and 'child' and adopted child shall be treated as being the child of the adopter born in lawful wedlock and not the child of any other person."[80]

Frozen in Time: Assessing "Parent" + "At the Time of the Child's Birth"

Justice Rohana Yosof of the High Court made two findings when rejecting Foo's judicial review. First, she found that for a person to qualify for citizenship by operation of law, he must be born to a "lawful" parent as understood in Article 14(1)(b) of the Federal Constitution.[81] Justice Yosof found that, at the time of the child's birth, he was not born to a lawful parent and hence she deemed the child "illegitimate."[82] In other words, even though Foo's parents were married, their marriage was not registered and therefore not valid, rendering the child "illegitimate" in law. This is where it gets complicated. The argument that Foo is "illegitimate" is relevant if one considers how the constitution confers citizenship in a discriminatory manner. Where a child is "illegitimate" the child cannot acquire citizenship from his father; he can only acquire citizenship from his mother. In this case, Foo's mother was a Thai citizen and not a Malaysian citizen. This led to the strange practice that some parents of biological children are adopting their own kin to try to pass on citizenship by jus sanguinis via the adoption. However, in this case, the judge notes that the Adoption Act 1952 is silent on matters of citizenship of an adopted child and that without an express provision to indicate that an adoption order has any effect on citizenship of an adopted child, such an implication cannot be read into law.[83] The High Court focused on the specific noninclusion of citizenship in the Adoption Act rather than interpret what section 9 in the Act includes under the terms, "all rights, duties, obligations and liabilities of the parent." While acknowledging the objective of section 9 was to deem an adopted child as a "natural child" in all kinds of legal settings, it restricted its interpretation to exclude citizenship.[84] The court also interpreted Article 14 of the constitution to exclude adopted children from its purview since it "also does not make specific reference as to whether an adopted child can be treated as being born to a lawful parent for the purpose of art. 14" finding it "inappropriate to infer or imply that an Adoption Order also deems an adopted child to be a natural child for purpose of citizenship when both the Adoption Act and the constitutional provisions are silent on the same."[85]

This reported decision sets in place a disturbing precedent that has been followed in subsequent cases.[86] The legal interpretation imposes a temporal limit — that children can only acquire citizenship by descent at the time of birth and no action taken after the time of birth can change that situation.

This case perfectly demonstrates the discriminatory way the constitution excludes children whose non-Malaysian mother is not married to a Malaysian father. The examination of one point in time — the birth of the child — excludes the examination of other relevant social facts: the father is the only active parent in the child's life; the father is a Malaysian citizen; the biological father is adopting the child; the parents were married but had not yet registered their marriage; and the child's birth in Malaysia. Instead, the High Court chose to take a narrow interpretation of the law, ignoring the complex matrix of factors that inform genuine and effective links to one's own country. This legal approach forever freezes in time a person's chance for conferral at the time of their birth. It promotes a noncontextual approach to interpreting law and an insistence to prove who the biological parents are in cases where there may be no relationship with or knowledge of the persons.

Subsequent cases have tried other ways to convince the courts that the adoption of a child should matter when deciding citizenship. For example, in the case of Samuel Duraisingh, it was argued that if the identity of the biological parents at the time of an adopted child's birth must be examined, there should be a rebuttable presumption favourable to that child — that for any child born within Malaysia, there should be a presumption that the child's biological mother was a permanent resident, and that until the contrary is shown, a child should be presumed to have met the second criteria under Article 14(1)(b) of the constitution.[87] Courts have not adopted this approach.[88]

These cases signal an enormous evidentiary burden for adopted children and their families — they must identify the biological parents and investigate whether they were Malaysian citizens and married at the time of the child's birth. For children abandoned at birth, this is a herculean and sometimes impossible task. As the applicant argued in the Chin Kooi Nah case, "The applicant submit[s] that it is not the child's fault that the child was abandoned … Thus, it would be a grave injustice and ridiculous if the child is punished."[89] Counsel in the Than Siew Beng case argued that providing proof of citizenship of biological parents is "placing an excessive and unrealistic burden."⁹⁰ Courts have ignored efforts to locate biological parents.⁹¹ It appears that courts are not moved by facts that show genuine and deep links to Malaysia.⁹²

In effect, courts are looking beyond the veil of the adoption order and misinterpreting the spirit of not only the adoption law but the constitution.⁹³ As one lawyer explained, "Even where two parents adopt a child, the courts still look at the biological parents and where they are from. We should reconsider how the Adoption Act is interpreted. Why follow the biological parents when it is the adopted parents we should be looking at?"⁹⁴ Another lawyer concurred:

> Under the Adoption Act, once you are adopted, the prior birth certificate is surrendered, cancelled and a new birth certificate is issued. Section 25(a)(4) and (5) of the Adoption Act states that whatever is on the birth certificate shall be received without further proof. Once a birth certificate is issued, you don't look behind it. The NRD [registrar] increasingly demands to see who are the [biological] parents or whether there are other opportunities for citizenship. They are going behind the birth certificate. Citizenship should not be determined by these factors or by looking for other proof.⁹⁵

In summary, the legal test for citizenship by operation of law calls for a person to be (a) born within Malaysia (jus soli); and (b) born to at least one parent, who, at the time of the child's birth, was a citizen or permanent resident (jus sanguinis) and qualifies for citizenship by descent.⁹⁶ The burden is on the applicant or the adopted child to identify their biological parents and their citizenship.⁹⁷ In situations where an adopted child's parents are unknown, any bid for citizenship is bound to be complicated if not impossible.⁹⁸ In situations where an adopted child is a product of a mixed relationship in which the biological parents were not married and the mother is not a Malaysian citizen, the child's bid for citizenship will fail.⁹⁹ Where an adopted child is a product of a marriage in which one of the parents is Malaysian, if there is no proof substantiating both the validity of the marriage and the citizenship of the parent, the child's bid for citizenship may be at risk.

In all eight reported cases dealing with adopted children, the adopted children did not meet the criteria set out in Article 14(1)(b). This neutral depiction that some people did not meet the mandated criteria or simply did not furnish the proof of having met the requirements allows the courts to hide their role in creating ghost citizens. These judicial precedents have deemed adopted children automatically as foreigners and ghost citizens of other states by virtue of their link to a biological mother that is either unknown or a non-citizen of Malaysia, sometimes where they play no role in a child's life.

Since research was conducted in 2018, the apex court in Malaysia awarded citizenship to a 17-year-old adopted child in 2021, but this decision has not been followed by lower courts.[100]

"Illegitimate" Children as Ghost Citizens

The prevailing interpretation of the law in Malaysia is that the Federal Constitution treats children born of married parents differently than children born of parents who were not married at the time of their birth, or "illegitimate" children. Ten of the thirty-two reported cases dealt with stateless persons whose mother was not a Malaysian citizen and could not obtain citizenship because of late registration of births or marriages, or because their biological parents were not married. In three cases, there was an intersection of factors: children born outside of Malaysia to married parents (Malaysian father and non-Malaysian mother) whose births were registered late.[101] In a fourth case, the intersection of factors was that a child was born outside of Malaysia to parents who were not married at the time of birth (Malaysian father and a non-Malaysian mother) who registered the birth late, and married and registered their marriage after the birth of the child.[102] Yet another case involved a child born of unmarried parents (Malaysian father and non-Malaysian mother) who was adopted by a Malaysian citizen.[103] The five remaining cases involved persons born in Malaysia to parents who either were not married at the time of their birth or they registered marriages after the birth of the child.[104] In all of these cases, the mothers were not Malaysian citizens but were Thai,[105] Papua New Guinean,[106] Filipino[107] or Indonesian[108] citizens. In one of these five cases, the parents of the stateless child could not marry before the birth of the child because the mother's divorce from her former husband was not finalized.[109] Two of these six cases were appealed to the apex court in Malaysia and were resolved before a hearing was held.[110]

In seven of the ten cases, the courts held that the children were citizens by operation of law as they met the criteria in Article 14(1)(b) of the Federal Constitution.[111] One case involved a person in detention.[112] Two cases led to a denial of citizenship, finding that the child did not meet the requirements in Article 14(1)(b) of the Federal Constitution.[113]

Different Temporal Limits "At the Time of Birth"

Unlike adopted children, biological children and their parents have had better success in the courts. The main reason is that the factual matrix for biological children will likely not have changed from "at the time of birth" to any time following that, and biological children have greater access to their parents and their documents.

In several cases, the courts have looked at social facts and taken a contextual approach to legal interpretation. For example, in the Mohamed Sadik Mohamed Ali case, the court looked at the facts that the applicants' father was a Malaysian at the time of the births; that the applicants' mother is a permanent resident of Malaysia; and that the applicants had taken all steps and measures to register the births in Malaysia.[114] Similarly, in the case of Haja Mohideen MK Abdul Rahman, the court referred to the wider purpose of citizenship law, which is to allow fathers to pass on their citizenship to their children, finding the temporal requirement as facilitating or encouraging birth registration rather than adding a limit to accessing citizenship.[115] Further, in the Ramanoojum case, the court held that despite the late registration of births, they "considered the factual matrix" that militated the conferral of citizenship.[116] The court emphasized that the timing of registration was not fatal since the rule was meant to facilitate registration.[117] These cases demonstrate a willingness to look at the genuine and effective links stateless persons have.

Ghost Citizens and Their Mothers

Not Every Parent is Equal
— Foreign Mothers and Malaysian Fathers

In cases involving automatic conferral of citizenship (Article 14(1)(b)), it has been widely interpreted that this mode is "anchored" with "both concepts of jus soli and jus sanguinis."[118] As discussed earlier, the constitution provides, on its face, a legal presumption that an "illegitimate" child shares the same citizenship as their mother.[119] In most cases, it is not disputed that a child is born within Malaysia. A major question in every case involving an "illegitimate" child is whether the requirement of jus sanguinis was met (the requirement of having one parent as a Malaysian citizen). The problem is not every parent is equal. In cases of "illegitimate" children, the child is presumed to follow her mother's citizenship even if the father is a Malaysian citizen and citizenship poses a significant challenge where the mother is not a citizen of Malaysia.

While many decision makers have acted on this presumption, the Court of Appeal in the Madhuvita case provides a diverging and contrasting interpretation of "parent" and "at the time of birth"[120] as compared to the adoption cases.[121] The court interprets the constitution as a "living piece of legislation" and provides a flexible approach. Specifically, the fact that the parents were not married at the time of the birth, "does not alter or diminish their capacities as parents" given "she is no longer illegitimate by reason of legitimation by the subsequent marriage of her parents."[122] The Court of Appeal reasoned that as long as the child *becomes* legitimate, they can benefit from the conferral of citizenship from a Malaysian father.[123]

Contrast the Madhuvita case with that of Lim Jen Hsian.[124] In Lim's case, the child was born of a Malaysian father and a Thai mother when the parents were not married. The difference is that the parents in Lim's case never married so the social fact of subsequent marriage and registration could not be deployed as it was in Madhuvita's case. The child in this case was forever cast as "illegitimate" but also deemed a foreign citizen by virtue of the mother's Thai citizenship. Subsequent marriage seems to erase the negligence or error on the part of the parents, allowing the court to justify a flexible interpretation of the constitution as it has for other cases.[125]

Thus, this case also makes some normative statements about citizenship in Malaysia. First, the decision adds value to ideas of legitimization, illegitimacy, and the importance of marriage in citizenship applications. Second, the decision normalizes the inequity in citizenship law, disadvantaging children who have mothers that are not Malaysian and are not married to their Malaysian fathers whether at the time of their birth or subsequently. Third, the decision entrenches the dual requirements; that birth in Malaysia is not sufficient but that jus sanguinis must also be met. Finally, despite the erasure of "illegitimacy" in some cases, there is another line of cases that show some courts are simply not willing to see the social fact of subsequent marriage as having a corrective effect.[126]

While the Malaysian government has proposed legal reform in 2023 to allow citizenship for children born overseas to women with Malaysian citizenship, it reinforces the normative understanding that non-Malaysian mothers are still strange or Other.[127] The overall judicial trend is that wherever there is doubt of the purity of one's links to Malaysia via one's parents, one can be rendered a ghost citizen of another state and therefore a foreigner.[128] This judicial practice allows any tangential or thin link to another nation to be proof that the child is not a citizen of Malaysia.

At the time of writing, the Malaysian government was not only proposing legal reform to allow Malaysian mothers to confer citizenship to children born outside of Malaysia, but the government quietly proposed a constitutional amendment to remove section 1(e) of part II of the section schedule. This amendment would remove citizenship by jus soli — or birthright citizenship by being born in Malaysia. Lawyers and advocates have voiced concerns that this could create "countless stateless persons in Malaysia."[129] Further, the government proposed removing Section 19B in Part II of the Second Schedule. This would remove the presumption that any child born in Malaysia was born to a mother who was a permanent resident until the contrary is shown. Again, advocates have argued that this would leave many children stateless.

Interpreting "Who Is Not Born a Citizen of Any Country"

It is not an accident that many of the statelessness cases before the courts involve persons whose mothers have foreign citizenship. Courts refer to this foreign figure through the interpretation of the following language in the constitution: "who is not born a citizen of any country."[130] The Malaysian government has taken the position that these words "must relate to the citizenship of the biological parents of the said child"[131] and that evidence must be proffered to show they are not a citizen of other countries.[132] Stateless persons and their advocates, however, are claiming that the phrase "not born a citizen of any country" does not require proof of the identity of biological parents.[133] The courts see this phrase as inviting them to speculate as to the potential citizenship a stateless person *may* be able to obtain or acquire. They have created a burden for stateless persons to prove that they are indeed stateless.[134] This approach focuses on the wayward foreign mother who has come within the borders of Malaysia to give birth, signifying a foreign link or tie as a proxy for citizenship elsewhere.[135] For example, the Court of Appeal in the

Than Siew Beng case stated that "A plain reading of s. 1(e) 'was not born a citizen of any country' refers to the relationship of the [child] to his biological and lawful parents at the time of his birth."[136]

An overview of these cases reveals some troubling trends. First, there is a tendency by the courts to have hyperfocus on the link a stateless child has with their foreign or non-Malaysian mother. Courts have placed a spotlight on this foreign woman to cast the stateless child as a citizen of another state. Using the citizenship of a foreign mother to act as a neutral device for fact finding ensconces the practice of looking at the child's circumstances in a static form — at the time of birth. The foreign mother in this case has become a figure in the courtroom smothering the child with the veneer of otherworldliness and therefore lacks allegiance.

Aside from the temporal limitation of looking at the citizenship status of a mother at the time of birth, courts have also placed importance on the marital link; a child born of a wayward foreign mother has no genuine or effective link to Malaysia unless their mother is married to a Malaysian citizen.

In many cases, the government argues that such persons cannot be Malaysian citizens because Malaysia does not recognize dual citizenship,[137] and therefore there is no need to attend to merits of the citizenship application.[138] In sixteen reported cases, the fact that a stateless person had a foreign mother played a significant role.[139]

In Lim Jen Hsian's case, the High Court held that "the citizenship of the Applicant is determinable" identifying the stateless person as Thai.[140] Substantiating that factual finding, the court pointed to the Nationality Act of Thailand and the fact that the stateless person's mother was Thai.[141] The Court of Appeal agreed, finding that the stateless person in this case, "cannot be said to be one, 'who is not born a citizen of any country'" as stipulated in the constitution.[142] The court found that "it is not disputed" the stateless person's biological mother "is a Thai national."[143] In the case of Chan Tai Ern, for example, the court found, "P1's biological mother's non-citizenship is an impediment to any application for citizenship."[144] In all these cases, there was no proof that citizenship had been conferred by the foreign state.

Children are deemed ghost citizens of the countries their mothers harken from, even if they have never been there, have no citizenship from that country, and have no relationship with their mother. This status of ghost citizen has allowed courts in Malaysia to disown these children; they are treated as illegal aliens in a country where they have long-standing, genuine links.

Finding Ghost Citizenship: A Thin Evidentiary Foundation

The factual finding of a stateless person as a foreign citizen is more concerning if we consider the evidence relied upon to render the person a ghost citizen. In a generous light, it is the testimony of a stateless person or their family member or the documentary evidence of the citizenship of the stateless person's mother where courts then infer citizenship of the stateless person. This is disturbing considering, as documented in this book, how difficult it is to obtain citizenship and how courts take no notice of the procedural and legal barriers that may be in place in other jurisdictions.

In some cases, there is no evidence of citizenship of a parent, whether biological or adopted. Here, the courts are purely speculating.

Some may argue that courts are taking judicial notice of the fact that some stateless persons can apply for some far away citizenship and may obtain citizenship in the future. This is problematic given what we know about judicial notice. Judicial notice is "the acceptance by a court, without the requirement of proof, of any fact or matter that is so generally known and accepted by the community that it cannot be reasonably questioned, or any fact or matter that can readily be determined or verified by resort to sources whose accuracy cannot reasonably be questioned."[145] Judicial notice is a mechanism that constitutes an exception to the general rule that matters of fact are established by the introduction of evidence. For example, "We know that children can drown in lakes; we need no proof of that. We also know that alcohol can impair a person's faculties; we need no proof of that."[146] Essentially, judicial notice dispenses with the need for proof of facts that are clearly not controversial. Facts that are judicially noticed are notorious, generally accepted, and are not proven by evidence or tested, and therefore the threshold for judicial notice is strict.

Finding a person to be a citizen via speculation with no certainty as to the outcome of a citizenship application in a foreign jurisdiction does not fit within the category of judicial notice. Citizenship is an adjudicative fact requiring verification from a state.

Despite the lack of evidence that a stateless person is a citizen elsewhere, courts have avoided scrutiny of this specious practice by claiming that the evidentiary burden is on the stateless person to prove they are not a citizen *anywhere*. Confirming citizenship or lack thereof is part of their due diligence to meeting preliminary requirements under law to establish they are stateless. It is extremely difficult to obtain such proof if a person has never set foot in the state or has no actual link to that state, not to mention the administrative labour required to do this. This judicial practice is concerning as it thins the international legal definition of stateless via the use of legal tools of presumptions and burdens of proof to create a fiction that persons are foreigners.

Ghost Citizens Via Discretion: The Alternative Remedy

So far, the Malaysian cases we have examined have largely dealt with claims to citizenship made under Article 14(1)(b) of the constitution, which provides automatic entitlement to citizenship "by operation of law." Article 14 claims are preferable to stateless persons as they explained they feel they are citizens and should be granted citizenship automatically. As discussed in Chapter 6, however, some applicants are not aware of this avenue or are denied the application forms to apply under this provision, leaving them to apply through Article 15A if they meet the age requirement of being under 21 years of age.

In many cases, even where applicants claim they have an automatic entitlement to citizenship (Article 14(1)(b)), courts are denying such claims and pushing applicants to seek, what the courts consider to be the appropriate alternative remedy which is the discretionary application under Article 15A.[147] This is significant for two reasons. First, by denying claims under Article 14(1)(b) and pushing applicants to apply under Article 15A, decision makers (whether administrative or judicial) are downplaying, thinning, or even gaslighting stateless persons' claims that they are truly citizens of Malaysia. Instead, directing applicants to apply under Article 15A reinforces the narrative that such stateless applicants are necessarily foreigners or ghost citizens of other states and need to apply or ask for the state's exercise of prerogative power, the permission for citizenship.

Article 15A provides a less stable approach to acquiring citizenship: (1) the provision provides a temporal limitation where only children under the age of 21 years can apply for citizenship; (2) the primary mechanism for granting citizenship is via discretion, leaving applicants at the whim of the decision maker; it is not an automatic conferral.[148]

Another problem is that the courts have ruled that they do not have jurisdiction to judicially review Article 15A decisions characterizing them as policy decisions beyond the court's purview.[149] Closing the ambit of review of these discretionary decisions is a strong normative statement that it is solely the state's prerogative to grant citizenship in cases where there is no automatic entitlement.

Finally, courts have engaged in a troubling practice in identifying an "alternative remedy" in Article 15 when denying citizenship via Article 14(1)(b).[150] Simply pointing to another remedy is not in and of itself problematic, but what is troubling is using the existence of an Article 15A application to find that the applicant did not exhaust all of her remedies. It also forecloses a full analysis of the merits of an application under Article 14(1)(b). For example, in the Chin Kooi Nah case, the court stated that "the applicant has failed to exhaust the alternative remedy open to her of applying for citizenship of the child by way of registration pursuant to art. 15A of the Constitution."[151] The court characterized the lack of attempt at an Article 15A application as a failure to take a preliminary step and "Not having exhausted this window of avenue, it is premature for the applicant to contend that the Child is rendered 'stateless.'"[152]

This approach has subsequently been adopted, for example in the Pang Wee See case, citing Article 15A as a path "still available for him to explore" and that "he had not exhausted his available avenue for redress."[153] In the Lim Kai Lin case, the court was not convinced that Articles 14(1)(b) and 15A applications were "separate and distinct" and stated, "the Applicants ought to have exhausted the avenues available before they can come to this court."[154]

This preliminary requirement thins the commitment articulated in Article 14(1)(b). It seems absurd that true citizens, entitled to automatic conferral of citizenship, must attempt to get citizenship through the discretionary mode first. The judicial approach requiring one to access a discretionary Article 15A application before challenging an erroneous Article 14 decision is a curious procedural requirement not found explicitly in the constitution.

Outside the courtroom, lawyers had much to say about Article 15A. One lawyer commented that Article 15A applications should be permissive and that the only requirement is whether the child is under 21 years of age.[155] This view was not shared by other lawyers. Another lawyer said that "The problem is that the issue rests with the Minister of Home Affairs."[156] A different lawyer provided that

> I don't think this is an issue for the courts. Citizenship is in the minister's hands; it is up to the minister. One more citizen is a vote. The discretionary aspect in Article 15A can remain. Every government has similar policies. But, when you are entitled to citizenship, they should not deprive you. It is irritating that the Attorney General's arguments keep raising argument that if you think you have been deprived go to 15A. The courts buy it. This is rather than going through the operation of law [Article 14].[157]

The majority of lawyers interviewed advised clients to seek applications where the operation of law could be applied under Article 14.

Advocates who were not lawyers also saw discretion as a problem. One NGO representative commented that "the Minister makes decisions, and it is completely out of our control."[158] Interestingly, one NGO representative felt that they had some success in obtaining citizenship for persons through discretionary avenues.[159] It was unclear how or why the NGO was able to persuade decision makers to exercise their discretion favourably except that this NGO had ties with the political party that formed the elected government at the time.[160] This NGO representative's experience and views were an anomaly in the discussions I had with many people. Most advocates I interviewed felt that there was less chance of garnering citizenship under Article 15A than Article 14(1)(b). One NGO representative explained: "I believe there should be certain parameters for this. You can't wake up one day and feel good and sign but tomorrow tear up the application. It seems arbitrary. No one knows when things will be approved and why."[161] One person stated, "The JPN [Jabatan Pendaftaran Negara] and the Home Minister is a black box. It is hard to get insight into the decision-making process and why some are successful and others not. Maybe it is not a logical or rational process."[162] The discretion afforded in Article 15A makes this alternative remedy exceptional and mysterious.

Ghost Citizens in Prison

Three of the thirty-two reported cases dealt with stateless persons in immigration detention because they did not have documentation.[163] Interviews with stateless persons and their advocates identified detention as a real risk for stateless persons. One advocate stated she came to know about this problem indirectly when she was working on issues related to children in detention:

> It is hard to know how many people in detention are stateless as this information is not collected. There is no transparency in how the government characterizes people. There is no screening process and no individual assessments …. There is no statelessness resolution procedure here. It means people just stay in detention. No one is addressing the issue of long-stayers.[164]

She commented that their advocacy has been perceived as "seditious" and lamented: "I want to have a relationship with the government where immigration will call and say we have a case and help us figure out what to do."[165] News in 2023 showed positive steps of removing children from detention.[166]

Ghost Citizens Outside the Courtroom

Challenging State Narratives with Legal Remedies

Stateless persons frequently told me they did not want to compromise their position that they were entitled to citizenship. Perhaps the best way to explain this is how one lawyer told me that there are two choices when a citizenship application has been denied: (a) judicially review the decision to deny citizenship; or (b) ask for a declaration or originating summons that the applicant is a citizen.[167] In seeking a declaration, this lawyer explained that clients felt they were asking what they are entitled to, and not simply contesting a bad decision made by an administrative decision maker.[168] In an overwhelming number of cases dealing with stateless persons' citizenship applications — eighteen of the reported cases — declarations were sought as the preferred remedy for stateless persons involved.

One lawyer did state that judicial review of decisions to list a person as non-citizen on a birth certificate is his preferred route.[169] His rationale was that such a person should not have to *apply* for citizenship because they should already be recognized as such on their birth certificate based on the ground that the child was born in Malaysia.[170] The lawyer noted that most successful decisions were not reported and therefore no precedent is available.[171]

The choice of application, remedy and legal strategies point to an active challenge on the part of stateless persons to narratives that stateless persons are foreigners and subject to the state's discretion.

Abandoning the Remedy of Declaration of Citizenship

One lawyer described a case where she requested both a declaration of legitimacy (to establish a parental link with her client and the child) and a declaration of citizenship and how the court, while granting legitimacy, refused to grant citizenship. She explained:

> The judge told me I had to withdraw the prayer for citizenship, or he was not going to proceed. I did not. The judge granted all remedies except citizenship …. I am not sure why the judge wanted to separate out proceedings and lengthen the process. Why would he deny this even after he granted the declaration for legitimacy? In a different case, I did withdraw the prayer for citizenship because I was not confident I would get the declaration for legitimacy if I did not.[172]

Another lawyer confirmed the difficulty of asking for citizenship as a remedy: "I ask for a prayer to include not only adoption or legitimization but also recognition of citizenship. Often, courts strike this out and just award adoption or legitimization forcing people to go through another legal process [to acquire citizenship]."[173]

One NGO that has recommended at least 130 cases to lawyers to litigate also faced pushback for asking for citizenship as a remedy in cases that were formalizing adoption or legitimacy, explaining that remedies for citizenship were dropped during litigation unless the case was strong.[174]

Unfeasible Remedy of Mandamus to End Waiting

One lawyer explained, "Where there are older kids, the strategy has to include thinking about what time they have to wait and whether it is worth doing an Article 15A application [because of the age limitation of 21 years old]. Can they afford to wait?"[175] In the administrative law context, the common law remedy of mandamus requires the decision maker to decide without delay. When I asked whether mandamus is a viable remedy, advocates said that this kind of remedy would be viewed by the court hostilely and may jeopardize any favourable ruling on the underlying judicial review.[176] An advocate said that "A mandamus would not be seen by judges well."[177]

Adopting One's Own Children

Stateless children were adopted by their biological parents as a desperate strategy to acquire citizenship for their children.[178] One lawyer said:

> It is difficult to explain to parents that yes, in reality, the child is theirs, but that the law doesn't recognize it and they need to go through multiple processes which is no guarantee. Sometimes ridiculous things happen like a biological father adopting his own child so that the child can inherit benefits from him. The courts never question it or say it is absurd. They just rubber stamp if the welfare report is okay.[179]

When I asked this lawyer whether clients are ever advised by them to adopt biological children, the lawyer replied: "My practice is to go the legitimization route and not adoption. You don't want to encourage a bad practice."[180] However, one lawyer did talk about doing adoption processes for parents who were adopting their biological child.[181] When I asked why the lawyer embarked on this process, the lawyer stated that the court directed that an adoption must be done.[182] The lawyer then spoke of an example where she was assisting a grandmother in adopting her grandchild. The adoption was denied as the court said it would be strange for the father then to become the child's brother.[183] The court then recommended that the father adopt the child despite the presence of a DNA test showing the child was his biological child.[184] Another lawyer told me: "I am concerned about the move that people are adopting their own [biological] children. This is a perverse application of the law. This makes children more vulnerable and normalizes a bad practice."[185] NGOs also confirmed seeing such strategies undertaken even though it did not guarantee citizenship.[186]

Settling Cases

Some cases are settled before a decision is rendered by a judge. As one lawyer stated, "Sometimes they settle out of court to avoid precedents. Many cases are unreported as a result."[187] While the settlement may be positive for the individual in the case, the piecemeal resolution of statelessness cases means there is no systemic solution for such cases after a settlement, and there is no precedent shaping future decisions that do seek judicial guidance.

Lack of Legal Fees Driving Strategy

As one lawyer explained, "I try to resolve cases out of court to save money, but I will go to court if it is the only recourse."[188] Another lawyer said her advice and her client's decision about how to proceed are affected by the lack of funds. She added that "To save legal costs for the client, I try to avoid appealing decisions. The NGO that refers me clients prefers that we work with the bureaucracy to try to get citizenship rather than appeal decisions because it is cheaper."[189] The absence of legal aid or funds to pay for legal services has meant that fewer cases are brought into judicial venues. This may explain why some advocates turn to the media or advocate directly with the Home Ministry.

Ghosting the Legal Process

Many expressed frustration with the legal process. They thought that it was slow, that it did not appear fair or did not operate logically, and that it did not lead to the desired result. In many cases, stateless persons gave up altogether and stopped pursuing any legal avenues.[190]

It became clear in my discussions with NGOs that they played a gatekeeping role to legal venues. In some cases, NGOs referred stateless persons to competent or trusted legal counsel and provided financial assistance alongside moral and psychological support.[191] In other cases, they discouraged going to lawyers or the courts[192] and instead adopted other strategies such as direct advocacy with politicians or submitting multiple administrative applications.[193] The NGO representatives I interviewed revealed an active role in assisting stateless persons with deciding what legal strategy to employ.[194]

Interventions and Watching Briefs

Lawyers and NGOs have intervened in cases by submitting "watching briefs." One advocate stated that "We always file written submissions, but the courts are reluctant to accept the submissions of watching brief counsel."[195] When asked why watching briefs are still submitted despite the lack of reception, the advocate noted, "It's about planting seeds. If someone searches a file, documents are there on the record. Someone can use it, expand on it …. Watching briefs include an affidavit with letters, and legal arguments with case law."[196] In some cases, watching briefs may play a positive role. For example, in the case of Navin Moorthy, where citizenship was ultimately granted, the court drew from the watching briefs filed by the Human Rights Commission (SUHAKAM), the Association of Women Lawyers, and the Bar Council.[197]

State Practice Thinning of the Definition of Statelessness with Ghost Citizenships

State practice shows there is a thinning of the definition of statelessness through the manifestation of ghost citizens. The creation of the ghost citizen is done by simultaneously casting stateless persons as foreign citizens, denying they are stateless, and rejecting accounts of their genuine and effective links.

In addressing this trend, one proposed solution is to provide a statelessness determination procedure.[198] Gàbor Gyulai, however, points out that while it may be ideal to provide an identification mechanism, this is an impossible, lengthy, and cumbersome task, akin to proving the existence of particles in physics, and may undermine the protection objective of the 1954 Statelessness Convention.[199]

While the Geneva Conclusions state that "determination procedures should adopt an approach to evidence which takes into account the challenges inherent in establishing whether a person is stateless,"[200] as discussed earlier in this chapter, evidentiary burdens are often placed on stateless persons without regard to the hardships it creates. The growing state practice is that individuals must show not only proof they are not a citizen *anywhere*, but now, also proof that they are not merely *entitled to* or have *opportunity* or *access* to citizenship elsewhere.

Both the Geneva Conventions and the UNHCR Guidelines state that the burden of proof is a shared onus between states and stateless persons with the burden on stateless persons being that they cooperate with the determining authority.[201] As the jurisprudence and state practice discussed earlier reveals however, the burden has been placed solely on the stateless person themselves to not only confirm their statelessness, but to also exhaust any opportunity to obtain citizenship. This is despite the practical difficulties stateless persons have in confirming their status. Aside from the costs and administrative labour of obtaining confirmation, Gyulai states, "stateless persons often face insurmountable difficulties in demonstrating their lack of nationality, and if they were left alone in this task, most of them would never have access to protection" as "foreign authorities have diverging attitudes towards claims for the confirmation of citizenship coming from individuals and state offices."[202]

Attention should be paid to the conferral of ghost citizenship. States should be scrutinized on the ways in which they construct the foreigner especially among in situ stateless persons who are claiming kinship and genuine and effective links. Moreover, in thinking about structural ways to end and resolve statelessness, questions should be raised as to the salience of state recognition.

FIVE

OUR KIN
Homegrown Stateless Persons

Experiencing Statelessness

There are conflicting reports about the number of stateless persons in Malaysia. One report states that an NGO had helped reduced the estimated number of stateless persons in Malaysia from 40,000 persons in 2009 to 12,368 in September 2017.[1] Lawyers for Liberty states, "While the actual number of stateless persons is subject to 'guesstimate' — a not uncommon challenge having regard to the nature of the problem, whether the number is 30,000 or 300,000 should not be the issue."[2]

This chapter does not speculate as to the number of stateless persons. Even one stateless person is too many. There may be interest in quantifying statelessness to measure the extent of the problem (to downplay or play up the fact that statelessness exists); to identify a benchmark to measure whether the state is adequately addressing the problem (that it is not a large problem or the state is reducing it); or to use it to frame particular discourse about who actually is stateless (that the numbers reflect foreigners or those not eligible for citizenship). The problem is that there will never be certainty in any number that arises due to the nature of statelessness and because the measurement of stateless persons is fraught with problems associated with measuring including the stripping of social life of context and meaning, or the hiding or distorting of the experience of stateless persons.[3] This chapter moves away from the computation of statelessness because numbers, while they convey an aura of objective truth and scientific validity, cannot provide a full picture of why we should care about statelessness. Numbers, while seductive in their promise of providing concrete knowledge, are hard to come by and are not always grounded in qualitative accounts or local knowledge.[4]

In the statelessness context, there are obvious reasons why an accurate number cannot be garnered: persons may not be known to the state or may not want to be identified[5] (for fear of deportation, detention and other consequences). One lawyer commented, "Stateless people fear repercussions if they become known by registration offices, but now they have no choice because their kids can't go to school, or they can't get certain benefits. This is a social problem."[6] The purpose of this chapter, therefore is to give a qualitative description of the characteristics of stateless persons, not to provide specificity as to the scope.

This chapter provides context as to who stateless persons are and what circumstances may give rise to statelessness. The appendix provides more detail on the cases of stateless persons documented in this study. Six categories are identified in the Malaysian context. Five of the six categories of stateless persons in Malaysia are in situ or persons who have genuine, enduring, and deep links to Malaysia. While these categories may or may not exist in other states around the world, this discussion provides a frame or typology by which to interrogate the characteristics of stateless persons in postcolonial, multicultural states that hold constitutional and rule of law principles as well as an administrative state as part of its legal infrastructure. As Gàbor Gyulai writes, "Many people who are currently living without a nationality have strong ties to a certain country, many in fact having lived there since birth, the nationality of which they have reasonable and well-founded grounds to claim."[7]

Identifying who is stateless is important because the findings in this chapter show that many stateless persons are not necessarily foreign or migrants even though they may be forced to be due to their status as stateless.[8] This is important given the discourse that stateless persons are, in Malaysia, mostly foreigners[9] and because it upsets the narrative the state evokes that stateless persons are citizens of states elsewhere: ghost citizens.

After identifying six categories of stateless persons in Malaysia, the chapter discusses how the perceived identities, categories, and characteristics of stateless persons both reinforce and unsettle the state's suggestion that such persons are necessarily foreigners, strangers, and non-citizens.[10] This research continues the work of scholars looking at in situ statelessness[11] and argues that legal ideas of kinship, genuine and effective links and *jus nexi*[12] should play a role in creating a stronger relationship between states and stateless persons.

The Identification of Six Categories of Statelessness

The identification of six categories of stateless persons arose from forty-five interviews with persons in Malaysia, and the scan of reported legal cases up to April 2020. The forty-five interviews revealed sixty cases of statelessness and the case law provided thirty-six accounts. In all, ninety-six instances of statelessness were examined to identify common experiences.

In some cases, a story of statelessness fits into more than one category. Where such a case was spotted, an evaluation of the dominant reason why the person could not obtain citizenship was identified. For example, while many cases were affected by the lack of documentation, if the reason for statelessness was also that the child was born prior to their parents getting married, the lack of marriage was seen as the dominant reason. Only those cases that were solely premised on lost or missing documentation and no other reason were counted in the documentation category. As well, many lawyers, stateless persons and NGO persons discussed the same case with me. I counted the case once, even though many persons may have brought it to my attention.

I want to note that in sorting stories into categories to discuss the instances of statelessness, I am reproducing the very actions that colonizers took to organize people. This ordering exercise, however, has the aim of upsetting or overturning assumptions made by colonial and racial labels discussed in Chapter 2 and the labels that persons are not bona fide citizens given by legal venues as described in Chapters 3, 4 and 6. In organizing the cases of statelessness in this way, the aim is to point out the deep genuine and effective links stateless people have with a country they consider their own. Further, this classifying system is borne out by the descriptions stateless persons, their families, and advocates provided and is grounded in their own perceptions and aspirations to be acknowledged as citizens. The accounts and resulting categories challenge state-described labels and explain why this mode of state recognition of people is problematic.

Category 1: Persons with Long-Standing Residence Since Pre-Independence and Their Descendants

This category involves persons who have been living in Malaysia prior to independence on August 31, 1957 (Merdeka Day) and forming a federation on September 16, 1963 (Malaysia Day). Subsection 14(1) of the Federal Constitution provides that every person born before Malaysia Day who was a citizen of the Federation are automatically citizens of Malaysia.[13] As well, sections 16 and 16A of the Federal Constitution provides, in general, citizenship by registration to persons who were born in Malaysia before Merdeka Day where they can show they have resided in Malaysia seven years preceding the date of application, that they intend to reside permanently in Malaysia, are "of good character," and have elementary knowledge of Malay.[14] Despite this pathway to citizenship, a large number of persons with lengthy connection to Malaysia are deemed stateless. This category of stateless persons includes persons — and their descendants — who were in Malaysia during British colonial times. There are two subcategories: those who worked in plantations and those who did not.

Category 1a: Persons Working in Plantations During Colonial Times and Their Descendants

Mapping done by UNHCR and an NGO identified a population of 12,400 Indian Tamil people that has no citizenship in Malaysia.[15] Statelessness in this group is attributed to several generations of Indian Tamils living in Malaysia at remote, rural plantations prior to Malaysia's independence.[16] Work in plantations did not require identification, or marriage or birth registration.[17] Plantations were self-contained communities that had employment, schools, health centres, and other amenities.[18] When plantations were shut down, people were confronted with issues when trying to access education and health services because they did not have any documentation.[19]

At the time of writing, 12,000 people applied for citizenship resulting in 2,300 persons acquiring citizenship. Only 12 per cent of cases have been resolved leaving 9,700 persons still awaiting a decision. The Malaysian government has acknowledged the existence of this stateless population in the Malaysian Indian Blueprint.[20]

While many of the documented cases are of Indian Tamils in Malaysia, there is a population of Filipinos and Indonesians in Sabah who work in the forestry and palm oil plantations that arrived during pre-independence who may be eligible for citizenship.[21] There has been little effort to identify the extent of the problem of statelessness in this population.[22] Interviews with stateless families, however, revealed that there may be more persons than known in this category. For example, 2S is a 33-year-old who is a stateless descendant of plantation workers. 2S is stateless because her mother is also stateless, despite the fact that 2S's mother was a citizen during colonial times.[23]

While currently there are plantations in other parts of Malaysia (for example in Sabah) that employ migrant workers, these contemporary plantation workers and their descendants (who may be stateless) do not fall within this category.

Category 1b: Persons Not Living in Plantations During Colonial Times and Their Descendants

Interviews conducted revealed stories of persons and families rendered stateless because they did not register or apply for the appropriate documentation after Merdeka Day or Malaysia Day. These persons did not live or work on plantations. For example, one NGO identified a 70-year-old stateless Chinese man in immigration detention.[24] Another case involved three generations of persons within one family who were stateless despite the eldest family member having been born in Malaysia in pre-independence times.[25] One stateless person explained she was stateless because, as a child, her birth was not registered.[26] She has not been able to get citizenship even though her parents have Malaysian citizenship due to their birth in Malaysia in pre-independent times.

Category 2: People Who Lack Documentation

As researchers have noted, "long-term exclusion and problems in acquiring birth certificates and other documents mean that many children are 'at risk' of statelessness."[27] In Malaysia, persons are stateless simply because they do not have the appropriate documentation to apply for citizenship. Eleven of sixty cases examined — identified through interviews with persons — fit this category. In many cases, the missing document was either a birth certificate or a marriage certificate or both. However, even where a person had a birth certificate, sometimes the information on the birth certificate was lacking, such as who the parents of a child were, prompting a search for other supporting documentation such as a DNA test or other proof. While lack of documentation may intersect with other causes of statelessness, documentation alone can be a substantive barrier to acquiring citizenship. For example, 6S is an 18-year-old girl. She and her 12-year-old brother are stateless. 6S told me that when her father died, her mother lost all her documents and was unable to obtain new copies.[28] 14S is a 32-year-old stateless woman whose birth certificate indicates that her citizenship is *belum ditentukan* or not specified. 14S did not know her father and did not have any documentation related to her mother. She and two of her children are stateless as a result.[29] 15S is a 63-year-old woman of Indian Tamil descent who holds a permanent residence card even though her mother (age 86) is a Malaysian citizen, and her three siblings have Malaysian citizenship. 15S's mother lost her birth certificate and attended three separate registration offices to get a new one but has been unsuccessful.[30]

The question is not one of entitlement — persons in this category have a legal entitlement to citizenship but lack the documentation to substantiate genuine and effective links.

Category 3: Abandoned Children or "Foundlings" and Adopted Children

Fifteen of the sixty cases — identified through interviews with persons — dealt with abandoned and/or adopted children. Eight of the thirty-six reported case law involve abandoned and/or adopted children.[31] One NGO representative noted that 90 percent of the hundreds of cases of abandoned children that came to her in the last decade are statelessness cases.[32] Statelessness is persistent among abandoned children or "foundlings" in Malaysia because they often come to NGOs without any documentation or information about their background.[33] While some stateless children are adopted by Malaysian parents, children do not always obtain citizenship automatically.[34]

Several stateless adopted children shared their stories with me. For example, 3S,[35] 5S,[36] and 17S[37] were all born in Malaysia and were adopted by Malaysian citizens with little to no information about their birth parents. All learned they were stateless when they were 12 years old and applied for their identity cards.

Category 4: Children of "Mixed" Marriages or Alternative Families

This category brings together cases involving stateless children whose entitlement to Malaysian citizenship arises from the fact that they were:

(a) Born of parents where the father is a Malaysian citizen, and the mother is not; and

(b) Born of parents who were not legally married at the time of their birth.

These legal qualifications entrench gender discrimination in Malaysian citizenship law, providing preferential treatment to married couples and, where couples are not married, denying children the opportunity to acquire citizenship by descent from their father. Twenty of the sixty cases reported by interviewees involved children who are stateless because of the marital or lack of marital status of their parents or the timing of the legal recognition of the marriage. Eleven of thirty-six reported case law involve mixed (mixed referring to nationality) marriages and alternative families. These circumstances arise due to various reasons including the following: the divorce of the first marriage was not finalized; there was a delay in getting married; parents did not know the importance of legitimizing/registering the marriage (even though a customary or religious marriage, or a marriage in a foreign place had taken place) before a child was born; and/or the parents were not married. These two subcategories (children of mixed marriages or alternative families and children born out of wedlock or before a marriage was registered) are discussed in the next few paragraphs.

One NGO representative described cases arising from children born in alternative family situations involving non-Muslim persons in Malaysia (i.e. Chinese men having multiple families with women without Malaysian citizenship).[38] While Muslims are legally permitted to have multiple marriages, non-Muslims are not. Children born of women who are not Malaysian citizens, and who were not legally married to the father (who is a Malaysian citizen) may not be recognized as citizens.

Further, children born of a Malaysian father and a foreign mother, who were not married, or their marriages were not registered, were rendered stateless. For example, 13S was born to a Malaysian father and a

Thai mother.[39] One lawyer I interviewed told me that in her legal practice, she had several clients who were Malaysian men of Chinese descent who married or were in relationships with women who had citizenship in Indonesia, Thailand, Cambodia, or the Philippines and had children who were stateless.[40] Thus, children who have two parents who were not married at the time of their birth may find themselves stateless despite the fact one parent may be a Malaysian citizen.[41] This is especially true of children born to unwed parents where the mother does not have Malaysian citizenship.[42]

Reported case law also shows stateless cases dealing with children born before a marriage takes place or is registered.[43] 4S and 13S were fathers of stateless children. They attribute the statelessness to the fact that they were pursuing divorces in their first marriage when their children were born in Malaysia because of a second relationship with women who did not have Malaysian citizenship. 4S explained that his daughter has never been to Indonesia, where the mother is from, and has lived her entire life in Malaysia.[44] 13S explained that the mother of the child has since returned to China, where she is from, and has no contact with the child.[45]

Several stateless persons and advocates spoke of cases involving women with foreign citizenship that gave birth to children after they married their Malaysian citizen spouses.[46] 11S (Malaysian citizen of Chinese ethnicity)[47] had marriage registration issues. 11S is a father of a child who is stateless because his marriage to an Indonesian woman was not registered before the birth of his child. He stated that he was in fact married before the child was born but that the marriage was not registered because he received erroneous advice to the effect that he could register the marriage after the child was born. Finally, there are those that never married the parent of their child.[48]

Category 5: Indigenous Persons

This study did identify two instances of statelessness that affected Indigenous people. One paralegal detailed how he travelled to Sarawak for six months to provide paralegal assistance for 150 people in an Iban community to obtain identity cards.[49] He described having to take a bus and then boat to reach this population and that the reason why such a large group of people was stateless was because of their remote rural location. Moreover, some village chiefs refused to sign documentation to attest that the individuals were living in the village as a protest or refusal to become part of the state system.

The study recognizes a gap in knowledge when it comes to stateless Indigenous persons in Malaysia. This category, like the earlier named categories, also has genuine and effective links to Malaysia by virtue of a generational and long-standing existence within the country. The Federal Constitution acknowledges the special rights attached to Indigenous persons in Malaysia. The identification of this category does not necessarily support notions that Indigenous people should obtain Malaysian citizenship but highlights that more should be gleaned from the communities themselves about their occurrence of statelessness and their own ideas and aspirations with regards to citizenship or community recognition.

Category 6: Refugees and Children of Migrant Workers

Interviewees identified eight cases dealing with stateless migrants who came to Malaysia either as foreign workers or as refugees. One notable group of persons are Filipino and Indonesian migrants in the state of Sabah.[50] The proximity of the Philippines and Indonesia to Sabah, civil conflicts in the Philippines in the 1970s and 1980s, and the demand for cheap labour in forestry and palm oil industries attracted migration from neighbouring countries.[51] Some Muslim Filipinos who fled to Sabah were recognized as refugees by the UNHCR and initially received special permission to stay and work from Sabah's Chief Minister.[52]

I interviewed persons who had migrated to Malaysia and had children who were born in Malaysia since they had been residing in Malaysia for a significant period.[53] For example, 8S was born in Indonesia but claims not to have any Indonesian citizenship. He is a permanent resident who has lived in Malaysia for 39 years and is married to an Indonesian citizen. 8S is the father of five children, all of whom are stateless.[54]

A notable group of stateless refugees is the Rohingya from Myanmar and interviewees discussed them.[55] Approximately 150,000 Rohingya refugees are registered by UNHCR in Malaysia as of 2017, and many are stateless.[56] 9NGO works primarily with refugees in Malaysia and identified that, other than Rohingya, the main groups of stateless refugees include children identified as Palestinian, Syrian, and Thai.[57] 9NGO revealed that many refugees are not preoccupied with obtaining citizenship in Malaysia but are more concerned about obtaining refugee status (which is not always given by UNHCR), and access to basic services such as health care and education. 11NGO substantiated this by saying that some refugees see Malaysia as a pit stop to other locations and don't understand the concept of statelessness nor do they realize they are stateless.[58]

In some of these cases, long-standing residency in Malaysia may allow migrants and refugees to eventually qualify for citizenship but it is not an automatic conferral. Migrants and refugees must apply through the naturalization process or apply through registration (if they meet those requirements).[59]

Malaysia is not a signatory to the Refugee Convention and the decision as to whether to recognize a group of persons as refugees is highly politicized. It is widely understood that the reason why the Filipinos in Sabah in the 1980s and now the Rohingya are allowed to be recognized as refugees is because they are Muslim.[60] Malaysia has made some positive statements with its ASEAN counterparts supporting Rohingya refugees and allowed the UNHCR to register them as refugees. However, other refugee groups are not eligible for registration with the UNHCR.[61] Further, there is no pathway for permanent residence or citizenship for refugees. One Rohingya woman I listened to at a public lecture described how she had lived in Malaysia for over twenty years and still has no hope of obtaining citizenship.[62]

Intersection of Factors

Some stateless persons may encounter their status as stateless in a multitude of ways or via an intersection of factors. For example, 16S is stateless on a few different axes: she is an "illegitimate" child born out of wedlock to a non-citizen; her birth was registered late; and her adoptive mother did not have the appropriate documentation because 16S was abandoned at birth and adopted without any knowledge of who her birth parents were.[63] Another example involved persons who were eligible for citizenship by virtue of their long-standing residence since pre-independence. These persons were children in plantations who were adopted by persons who were not their biological parents.[64] A person's ability to obtain citizenship is complicated by this duality of being a descendant of a plantation worker and of being adopted.

Disturbing the Ghost Citizen Concept: Genuine and Effective Links and Legal Ideas of Kinship

This chapter has described six categories of stateless persons in Malaysia. Five of the categories can be characterized as encompassing persons who have long-standing residence and other ties in Malaysia, an indicator suggesting a genuine and effective link with the country. Further, persons within five of the six categories may also have at least one lawful parent that is a Malaysian citizen, another factor suggesting deep connection to Malaysia.

These attributes of place of birth, residence (sometimes generational), parental relationship, and others suggest thick bonds with a state. The self-identification of stateless persons in five of the six categories as being within their "own country" suggest the need to attend to the perception, discourse, and rationales for why these persons have not been able to acquire citizenship.

International law recognizes a variety of connections or elements when identifying "one's own country" as discussed in Chapter 3. There is much fodder here to prop up claims of citizenship for in situ stateless persons and to upset state accounts or findings in legal settings that such persons are foreign and therefore ghost citizens by turning to international law's understanding of in situ statelessness, the definition of genuine and effective links and legal concepts of kinship.

International Legal Concepts of In Situ, Genuine and Effective Links, and *Jus Nexi*

The legal ontological tools of "own country," in situ, "genuine and effective links," and kinship as explained in Chapter 3 are useful in establishing a claim for citizenship and contesting findings that persons are necessarily foreign or citizens elsewhere. Basing one's positionality in these terms can steep one's claim within recognizable legal principles that activate adherence to the rule of law. Specifically, turning to these known legal concepts can help first identify how stateless persons are made to be ghost citizens by first showing how states are ghosting people that have deep roots in the state. Second, the legal principles can be used to contest claims that stateless people are necessarily foreign or citizens of states elsewhere by pointing to the factors demonstrating a bond with the state.

In Situ Statelessness

Scholars have described statelessness as occurring in two different contexts: in the migratory context and in situ or persons who are within their "own country."[65] This chapter is not preoccupied with creating an exhaustive list of factors that would be used to determine what constitutes stable ties or genuine and effective links. However, factors such as place of birth, long-term residence, and birth to a parent with citizenship are the most obvious factors.

The majority of the stateless persons I talked to emphasize their connections and bonds to the state. Understanding that some stateless persons are in situ by virtue of their entrenched and profound links disrupts notions that stateless persons are necessarily foreign or strangers.

Genuine and Effective Links

As discussed in Chapter 3, the terms, "genuine and effective link,"[66] "dominant and effective,"[67] "special ties" or "close and enduring connections,"[68] and "one's own country"[69] provide legal sustenance to claims made by stateless people that they are citizens being ghosted by their home country. While these legal tools were developed to identify a primary citizenship in dual or multiple citizenship contexts to identify a responsible state, these legal factors can animate what a person's "own country" is in the context of statelessness. These legal principles provide a framework by which stateless persons can ask states to contest claims that they are foreigners or non-citizens. As discussed in Chapters 3 and 4 however, these same legal tools are being deployed by states to claim that stateless persons have links and therefore citizenship elsewhere, conferring a ghost citizenship, one tied to a foreign state not the state that the individual considers as theirs. This practice raises questions about whether state recognition should be the default governance structure in citizenship and statelessness matters.

An Inclusive Version of *Jus Nexi*

There is much scholarship critiquing the turn to attachments to land or territory as a marker of belonging and citizenship. Some have discussed how citizenship should be "deterritorialized."[70] While there are valid challenges to the normative claim that borders are needed and boundaries are determinative communities of self-governance, the case study of Malaysia shows there is still a stickiness to not only territorial attachment but to genuine and effective links in the way that stateless persons identify themselves. Even though stateless persons do discuss how they and others, "develop and sustain multiple allegiances and networks across nation-state boundaries," they attest that disproportionate weight is given to any tangential or possible link or bond outside of a home state. States use speculative findings of a tie elsewhere to deem them foreign; stateless persons are conferred ghost citizenship. One lawyer stated that "In many of these cases, these are not foreigners masquerading as citizens."[71] Another lawyer stated that "They treat them like foreigners."[72]

Ayelet Schachar's turn to genuine and effective links through her term *jus nexi* supports the theoretical foundation that states owe allegiance to their own members.[73] However, I would like to expand Schachar's concept of *jus nexi* and question Schachar's exclusion of birthright citizenship as a method of acquiring citizenship. Schachar readily abandons the mechanism of birthright citizenship with theoretical rationales as it being arbitrary and akin to a lottery.[74] The experience of stateless persons calls for a move away from the hypothetical toward a thicker and more inclusive form of *jus nexi*: that we should not get rid of *any* tools that could confer citizenship on any person, including birthright citizenship. In other words, in my opinion, we should not give states another reason to deny citizenship to those who consider themselves part of the fabric of that state. Eliminating birthright citizenship reinforces notions of the state prerogative that they ultimately get to choose and leaves some persons without the ability to point to a connection through birth to contest a state's characterization of their identity.

There are two reasons why there should be a heftier concept of *jus nexi*. The first is that the experiences of stateless persons tell us that even in situations where a person is born within a state the fact of birth in a territory does not always lead to or guarantee the conferral of citizenship. This book provides accounts of how those with birthright entitlements do not always get it. In this sense, Schachar's theory relies on the proper operation of law-as-text and has faith in states properly conferring citizenship where other markers of genuine and effective links are present.

Second, practically speaking, stateless persons' accounts raise questions of the need to confine or limit the ways in which connection to a state is established. Schachar does mention theoretical reasons for why birth is not necessarily an accurate measure of the kind of relationship a person may have with the state.[75] The incidents of statelessness, as explored in this chapter and in Chapter 6, however, tell us that many who are born in a state do feel a connection and make efforts to continue to build links with that state. Further, living through statelessness is a horrific existence and why would we want to circumscribe ways in which a person can acquire citizenship, even if they are imperfect in indicating the kind of tie that a person has? For stateless persons, a viable tie, however imperfect, should trigger state response. The foregoing research in this chapter brings to the forefront how an absence of birthright citizenship (or the effect of it) raises issues of inequality that are missing from Schachar's theoretical analysis. This is particularly stark when you consider that the denial of citizenship is informed by the question of which racialized persons are deserving of citizenship. An inclusive version of *jus nexi* should be used when identified as a factor for establishing ties or bonds with a state.

Kinship in Law

An alluring principle is one of kinship that can be found in many Indigenous legal traditions.[76] In turning to this concept here, I recognize that I cannot provide a fulsome understanding or depiction of this concept as I consider myself still a student of Indigenous legal traditions. However, concepts of kinship in, for example, Cree law in Canada, can help inform the aspirational quality of state–stateless relations. In fact, legal ideas of kinship can disrupt our reliance on the state and postcolonial recognition model and move us into a discussion about who should be recognizing membership and how communities can be formed without the harmful vectors of borders.

As this chapter has outlined, many of the categories of stateless persons feel a kinship to Malaysia—they considered the state their home. Cree law places importance on the concept of kinship. Their law includes terms such as *miyo-wîcêhtowin* which refers to having or possessing good relations with one another individually or collectively; *wîtisânîhitowin* which refers to kinship and establishing relationships governed by kinship; *wâhkôhtowin* which refers to good relationship; and, *kisêwâtisiwn* which refers to kindness.[77]

Kinship has also been invoked as an important consideration in law in other contexts, for example, in discussing ideas of social policy;[78] in reunifying families in immigration law;[79] and in family law.[80] Relations between persons we consider family or those in familial type relations give rationale to policy. In this sense, the kinship concept is pervasive in our understanding of important legal considerations. Indeed, citizenship policy invokes jus sanguinis, the concept of blood link, to justify the conferral of citizenship.

Questions and critiques around how kin are treated emerged in my discussions with stateless persons and their advocates. Many people were perplexed by the move to cast out of the community persons they have relations and bonds with. Kinship provides a universal legal approach to pay attention to and also attend to our relations. Legal factors informing "genuine and effective links" and "one's own country," among others that flow from other areas of law (Indigenous, family, and immigration law) can also animate who is kin. Using the parlance of kin can help a stateless person mount questions about state claims that they are strangers or foreigners. Ideas of kin can also interrogate why the state is the default mechanism that confers citizenship. Further, the concept of kin allows us to question the quality of state–person relationships and whether they are reciprocal, attentive to respectful obligations, and make space to contest or reappropriate narratives of kin.

SIX

THE GOVERNMENT COUNTER
The Discretionary Creation of the Stateless Person

At the Government Counter

How many of us remember our last visit to a government counter to apply for or to renew our driver's licence? Do you remember what the government official said to you? Do you remember what the forms looked like? Do you remember the questions that were asked of you?

Some of us can treat the acquisition of a driver's licence as, at best, an exciting moment of privilege to join others on the road, and, at worst, an administrative hassle or one of the many errands you have to run in a day. Many of us take for granted the fact that we are bound to receive the identification documents we ask for. When applying for such documents, we expect to receive the appropriate forms, to talk to a person at a counter to answer questions about how to fill out the forms, submit the forms and fees, and have it processed in a timely manner. This kind of encounter is seemingly innocuous, even forgettable. My own recent renewal of my driver's licence, during the COVID-19 pandemic, took less than 15 minutes including the wait time and the obligatory new photo. My son's passport application during the pandemic, however, was a harrowing 19-hour wait at an office over the span of three days.

What if your attempt to renew your driver's licence was met with a hostile government employee who insisted that you did not pass your driving test and that you had to retake it? What if that employee refused to book the test or give you the forms for you to fill out? What if you passed the test and the officer then told you there were other requirements you did not know about that you now had to meet before you could receive your licence? What if the registrar reissued your licence but a learner's licence instead—meaning that you could not drive without a licensed driver in the car—with no explanation as to why this was being done?

For stateless persons applying for citizenship, standing at the government counter may lead to denials, refusals, obstructions, misunderstandings, judgement, and deceptions preceding life-altering outcomes. The counter is where stateless persons experience an "administrative death" where life as they knew it is over.[1]

Interactions at the counter are "not a discrete spatio-temporal event" but "carries with it traces of broader power relations."[2] This chapter looks at what occurs at the counter from the perspective of the stateless person and explores why and how stateless persons are being administratively denied citizenship even though, ostensibly, they meet the criteria under the law. The conversations I had with stateless persons revealed that it was in the everyday interactions stateless persons had at government counters where they felt their chances of obtaining citizenship withered away. Public servants "have substantial discretion in the execution of their work"[3] and the counter is an "unchecked space susceptible to political interference."[4]

Rather than presume that the administrative state functions as it should or as one may expect, this chapter suggests that the government counter is a frontier that should receive greater attention. The findings here pertain to any jurisdiction that relies on a regulatory state. Given much scholarship that focuses on "administrative justice," "street-level bureaucracies" and discretionary decision-making through the perspectives of the decision makers themselves,[5] this research focuses on those on the other side of the counter. Insights on the stateless person's experience add to wider scholarly discussion on how marginalized persons experience the administrative state.

This chapter does not provide commentary on the part of the government or the frontline bureaucrats. First, civil servants were not willing to be interviewed. Second, there is much research that discusses how persons working in the administrative state may perceive their roles of policy making, legal interpretation, and implementation.[6] While research has examined viewpoints including those of "clientele-agents," "citizen-agents," or "state-agents" as well as high-level managers,[7] this position does not capture the experiences and interests of those directly affected by decisions made at the government counter. This chapter focuses on the voices of stateless persons.

The chapter provides a brief overview of the administrative state, the concept of administrative justice, "street-level bureaucrats"[8] and discretionary decision-making and then distinguishes between the terms "administrative work" and "administrative barriers" and then explores the administrative work stateless people are burdened with and how stateless persons are cast as ghost citizens by the administrative state.

The Administrative State and Administrative Justice

The rise of the regulatory state has affected the way people interact with government. Policies and programs are implemented and delivered by agencies, tribunals, and registrars. These offices employ government officers who have been delegated decision-making power by a democratically elected government. Their power includes the ability to create procedures and make substantive decisions about whether to confer benefits.

Administrative law scholarship has focused on "boundaries designed to distinguish the legal from the administrative aspects of decision-making."[9] Where deemed administrative, deference is given to administrative decision makers. There are, however, calls for a "re-examination of whether these boundaries are tenable or desirable" given that decisions they make, "often affect vulnerable people with few alternative recourses."[10]

Administrative law encompasses both procedural fairness (the process by which a decision is undertaken) and substantive justice (the outcome).[11] This chapter challenges the bifurcated notion that some decisions are purely procedural and interrogates what legal decisions deserve scrutiny, specifically discretion.[12] Experiences of stateless persons reveal that some procedural decisions amount to substantive decisions.

"Street-level bureaucrats" have a certain measure of autonomy or discretion in conducting their work.[13] Most scholars writing about administrative justice and how law is experienced at the street-level do so from the perspective of government officials and how they interpret and understand the law.[14] Frontline officials have a "legal consciousness" and "professional norms,"[15] that inform their understanding of law[16] and of "formal law [that] is not determinative."[17] Discretion is a "central and inevitable part" of decision-making.[18]

There is debate about where discretion sits in law, with some arguing that it is political, an exercise of power, a one-way projection of authority, arbitrary, outside of or antithetical to the realm of law, and others arguing that it is decision-making that occurs within a "space controlled by law"[19] and takes meaning from the context of rules and standards surrounding it.[20]

Sociolegal scholars find that it cannot be assumed that decision-making is guided by formal policy or law-as-text, that other factors are at play.[21] Decision makers can be guided by different conceptions of what the decision makers' legal mandate or goals are,[22] hidden aspects such as shared meanings and personal feelings,[23] and the social context they find themselves in.[24] For example, some social factors that inform decision-making include social status (of both the person served and the official), including race.[25] While some scholars find some "frontline workers use their discretion in more or less beneficial ways,"[26] such findings make assumptions about who decides what is the best interests of persons before them and that decision makers always act in the interests of that person. Research already acknowledges differential treatment of people based on race, class, and socioeconomic status.[27] This chapter builds on this work in questioning the assumptions behind the view that "law is the primary instrument of social regulation" and that "discretion is a residual category of law."[28] Thinking about administrative decision-making and statelessness is important as Jennifer Elrick posits—policy making, and indeed nation-building, is generative and influenced by the bureaucracy's implementation of law.[29]

This chapter draws attention to the relevant yet "low visibility" discretionary decisions made by government officials.[30] Focusing on law-as-text, be it as legislation or jurisprudence, ignores the context for which decisions are made and that discretionary power involves political and social factors.[31] As Anna Pratt and Lorne Sossin point out, "many settings of discretion are not subject to meaningful oversight."[32]

As discussed in Chapters 3 and 4, legal reform has done little to change occurrences of statelessness. Legal scholars in statelessness have tended to overplay the influence of legal reform and underplayed other potential sources of influence. Casting discretion as a residual category of law has meant less attention on such decisions.[33] This chapter will problematize this.

Administrative Work Versus Administrative Barriers

Elizabeth Emens defines administrative (or admin) work as, "the organizing and coordinating and managing and faxing and emailing and calling and texting of information and our lives."[34] As Emens writes, "Admin seems trivial. This is part of its dangerous logic. By appearing to be small and unimportant, admin rarely commands our full attention or inspires sustained protest." She affirms that "Admin shapes life outcomes"[35] and so, "we need to see admin as labor."[36] Emens provides the following examples of admin work: completing institutional paperwork; managing and coordinating schedules; managing inflow and outflow of mail, messages and other communications; handling finances; managing health, medical, and insurance matters; researching and applying for activities, schools, financial aids, and public benefits; keeping track of important documents; and, planning and arranging transportation and travel, among others.[37] Emens finds "awful admin work" can include redoing something you have already done, renewing an identity document, paying a parking ticket.[38] The task just gets you where you started. Awful admin work, "involves painful human interactions … where you are basically powerless and the result depends on other people who are indifferent to your suffering" citing "government desk clerks" who "seemed to make the rules up as they went along."[39]

Challenges Stateless Persons Face Before Getting to the Counter

There is an abundance of administrative work imposed on a person before they can apply for citizenship.

Understanding the Status of Statelessness

Resolving statelessness means that one needs to be aware they are stateless. Of the nineteen stateless people interviewed, fourteen did not know that either they themselves or their children were stateless until they talked to someone at a government office.[40] Three of the nineteen persons did not understand the full implications of statelessness until they tried to register their children for school.[41] In one case, a parent who was interviewed admitted that their child did not know that he was stateless and that they wanted to shelter him from this reality.[42] One lawyer stated that "In some cases, the child does not know," explaining that parents do not want the child to feel they have limited opportunities or were prevented from doing anything when, in fact, the child's statelessness was a hardship on the family as they could not travel together for example.[43] Another lawyer stated she represented parents who have children who do not know they are stateless because the parents have not told them they are adopted.[44]

One stateless person told me that she did not know the severity or significance of the issue until she tried to obtain her own identity card when she became eligible at the age of 12.[45] This stateless person had difficulty articulating the idea of statelessness, relying on her paralegal to help her.[46] Another stateless person stated they found out when someone came to their door during an election period to help the family fill out forms.[47] One NGO representative noted it was only when people interacted with paralegals regarding different social issues that they became aware of their status as stateless.[48]

The word "stateless" is not part of the vocabulary of stateless persons.[49] As one person explained, "People might talk more about difficulties of getting an identification card or passport. People talk in more practical and material terms when talking about deprivations of status or the pieces of paper they cannot get."[50]

A related problem is that even when people are aware that they do not have status, they go underground. As one NGO representative put it, "People don't understand the law and they have a fear of getting in trouble."[51] One academic stated, "There are some people who want to register their babies but don't know the process or don't prioritize because there are other survival needs."[52] This interviewee, troubled by the narrative that people are unaware, continued: "It is inaccurate to say people don't know the importance of registration when consequences are so acute and so present in their everyday lives. There is the fear of being detained and deported to a country you have never been. It is high in their consciousness."[53]

Normatively, the lack of awareness can be characterized in an alternative way — that stateless persons view themselves as citizens that lack documentation. For some, the need for legal recognition is triggered when encountering difficulties accessing different spaces in society. This makes sense given, as provided in Chapter 5, many stateless persons are in situ. It also explains why as discussed later, when the state, in this case Malaysia, claims they are foreign citizens, why non-citizenship labels are contested vociferously by stateless persons.

Language, Literacy, and Education

The barriers of language, literacy, and education manifest in two ways: the first is being required to research and understand what one needs to do in the citizenship application process; and the second is being required to obtain, read, and fill out documents and forms.[54]

One advocate stated, "Information is available on the JPN website regarding processes but because the families are also facing extreme poverty and limited access to education, there is a difficulty in accessing info."[55] At least two stateless individuals interviewed admitted that their lack of education impeded their ability to investigate how to get citizenship.[56] One NGO representative told me that they deal predominantly with Tamil speaking people who live and work in plantations in rural and remote locations and who, therefore, have no means of navigating the process without their paralegals' assistance.[57] All the advocates interviewed for this project attested to the fact that either they themselves, or persons working in their office, have assisted stateless persons with not only understanding the process, but obtaining and filling out documents. With or without assistance, one NGO representative stated, "A fair number of documents get sent back due to human error."[58]

The fact that children need citizenshIp to attend school has created a circular problem — stateless persons have no access to education and will, thus, have less ability to advocate for themselves. Of the stateless persons interviewed, twelve spoke of children being denied registration in public schools because they could not show proof of citizenship (a number of those interviewed consisted of families with two to five children unable to go to school).[59] Two families were able to afford private school which does not require citizenship for enrolment.[60] As one advocate commented, "there is a new generation of people … who can't get citizenship … This is a failure of the system. An epic crisis."[61]

Remote or Rural Locations

Many stateless persons, due to their remote location, are unable to access government offices to apply for citizenship.[62] One paralegal told me that, for one case, he drove for four hours to meet with someone who had asked him for help.⁶³ Another paralegal travelled to Sarawak to help 150 persons in an Iban community apply for citizenship. He said that "The location was two days travel away from the closest registration offices."⁶⁴

Even the existence of local offices does not guarantee access to services. As one lawyer put it, "Sometimes local offices don't do anything, so you have to travel all the way to the capital to go to the registration office."⁶⁵ One person explained that "People have restricted mobility because people fear getting arrested or harassed by police or immigration … Being able to physically get to the JPN is difficult."⁶⁶

Legal cases can also be heard in courts outside of the main cities. For example, one lawyer told me she travels to the "outskirt" courts with locations outside of the capital, and that appearing in front of these courts could be a disadvantage since the judges in remote locations are not familiar with the issues that stateless persons face.⁶⁷

Finally, stateless persons also have difficulty accessing consular or embassy services to obtain proof of citizenship. For example, many Indonesian migrant workers in the state of Sabah need to travel to an Indonesian consulate located, in some cases, a five-hour drive away.⁶⁸ While mobile registrations do occur, this interviewee stated that "due to limited personnel and resources, they can't catch everyone in a reasonable time."⁶⁹

Individual/Family Circumstances and Relations

As discussed in Chapter 5, who your family is can affect your ability to acquire citizenship. Beyond identifying who is family, a stateless person must depend on the cooperation of that family to provide documentation or assistance to apply for citizenship. For some stateless persons, this may be a hurdle that is insurmountable depending on the relationships and circumstances.

I talked to three stateless persons whose only familial link to citizenship was a deceased family member.⁷⁰ One person explained that while he is eligible for citizenship because his father is Malaysian, he is not close with his half siblings, the keepers of his deceased father's documents.⁷¹ Another person told me his deceased father lost all of his documents and while his father's death certificate indicates he is a citizen, this document was not accepted as sufficient for a citizenship application at the registrar.⁷² One NGO representative spoke of the strategies of helping people through family dynamics: "We provide counseling and advice in difficult family situations where members don't want to help others get documents or provide proof for citizenship applications."[73]

Documentation

Overwhelmingly, all stateless persons, legal professionals, and NGO advocates talked about how issues with documentation are inextricably linked to statelessness.[74] One NGO representative described this barrier as the "toughest one" for stateless individuals.[75]

Of the nineteen stateless persons interviewed, twelve discussed how they lacked necessary documentation to have a complete citizenship application.[76] Nine of the nineteen persons had sought help of legal professionals to get the necessary documentation.[77]

The complete absence of documentation for a stateless person signifies their invisibility.[78] As one NGO representative described in the case of a 70-year-old stateless person in detention, "There were no records of him. Officials took an ad out to see if anyone could vouch for him, but no one responded. It is like he doesn't exist."[79] Another NGO representative stated that sometimes they only knew of stateless persons because they reached out to them.[80] One NGO encounters persons born without documentation when the babies arrive in baby hatches they manage or when calls from the community bring to the NGO's attention a baby's need for a home.[81] The documentation that is commonly needed includes proof of birth, proof of marriage, school records, medical records, anything that shows an address, prenatal check-up books, or vaccination records for themselves and their family members.[82]

The Amorphous Requirement to Produce Documents

Stateless persons and advocates alike conveyed to us that there is immense confusion about what is required in citizenship applications. As one NGO representative stated, there are "[n]o clear guidelines for what sort of documentation is required."[83] One academic put it this way: "There is an inflexibility among documentary requirements … There is very little tolerance for people with an incomplete paper trail."[84] Stateless persons have been told that they need more documentation after they provide what was asked of them.[85] One NGO stated: "You go in with certain documentation but then you're told to get more."[86]

Providing an "Authentic" Document?

Even if one is able to obtain a document, that document may not be considered authentic.[87] Persons are tasked with notarizing or authenticating documents.[88] One person told me that, in registering his marriage, he had to have the marriage certificate translated and certified, and even after doing so, found that the document was rejected for being inauthentic even though it was genuine.[89] Customary marriage certificates are not considered valid[90] but without valid government identification (which one cannot obtain without citizenship), you cannot register a marriage, thus creating an unending problem of generational statelessness.[91] As well, death certificates are not considered a valid way to show citizenship of a parent.[92]

Starting with Nothing

Some people have difficulty acquiring documentation when they have nothing to begin with.[93] For example, parents who never registered births have difficulty proving that a birth occurred.[94] One NGO representative stated that stateless refugees such as Rohingya, Palestinians, and others have no hope of obtaining any kind of identification given they cannot return to their place of birth, but also because Malaysia is not issuing documentation to them.[95]

The Administrative Labour of Getting Documents

The act of obtaining documents is difficult. One stateless person stated that "Just obtaining a birth certificate is a fight [with a government official] …. Each step is a fight."[96] Some persons face barriers in locating an institution or person who can provide the documentation.[97] One academic, volunteering as a paralegal, stated that "It took months of trying to accumulate enough evidence to try to convince the education office to allow [a stateless boy] to go to school. We needed letters from his kampong [village] and the birth certificate of his grandmother because they didn't believe she was a citizen. We had to get her birth certificate verified by the [registration office]. It was a hassle."[98]

The Burden of Relying on Other People, Institutions or Family Members

In many cases persons have difficulty getting documentation because they must rely on other persons to produce that documentation.[99] One NGO representative explained that stateless persons need to get documentation from various persons such as health care staff, midwives, heads of villages, and persons who may have witnessed a birth.[100] Persons may not help unless there is a protest,[101] or it may be difficult because hospitals or institutions and/or records may no longer exist, or persons may not be willing to retrieve documents.[102] An NGO representative explained that where there is no birth record, "You have to find four witnesses somewhere to substantiate the child was born in Malaysia."[103] In other cases, persistence and insistence led to the discovery of records — for example when a paralegal demanded to speak to a director to complain, birth records appeared.[104] These accounts reveal the labour and resistance some stateless persons face when trying to obtain their documentation.

One lawyer described the problem as such: "Cases that require obtaining further documentation are difficult because they take up a lot of resources, time, money, and effort. Some of the problems are generational. It is hard to resolve when you are relying on different people and processes. People must make repeated trips to different people or offices and there is no guarantee they will be helped."[105] Sometimes people have waited too long and due to death, institutional or file closure, and other reasons, documentation is lost forever.[106]

Costs

Financial barriers present not only as fees for applications, but also as money paid to obtain documents, to authenticate and notarize them, for late registration, for DNA tests, or as legal fees, transportation fees, and costs associated with missed opportunities whether it means missed work, education or training or other opportunities.[107] These costs are so daunting that they sometimes prevent a stateless person from completing their application.[108] Further, if a family has multiple persons who are stateless, each person needs to take their independent legal path with its attendant costs.[109]

Intersection of Barriers

The documentation problem is compounded by other barriers for stateless persons. For example, one NGO representative stated that many of the stateless persons they were assisting are illiterate and do not speak the local language.[110]

The Confiscation, Issuance, or the Denial of Documentation Leads to Statelessness

This section discusses barriers particular to three types of documents that citizenship applications typically require: marriage certificates, birth certificates and DNA tests.

Marriage Certificates

As discussed in Chapters 4 and 5, statelessness can arise when a marriage was not registered or registered late rendering an "illegitimate" child ineligible to obtain citizenship from a Malaysian father. Six of the nineteen cases identified fit this scenario: Two of the six cases involved a parent whose divorce from a first marriage was not finalized and a second marriage did not occur until after the child was born;[111] one child was born before the parents were married;[112] one parent was told not to register the marriage until the child was born;[113] one family simply registered the marriage late, after the child was born;[114] and another family had not registered their marriage.[115] Overwhelmingly, the problem of the late or lack of marriage registration is faced by parents of interracial marriages, marriages that took place in a foreign country, and where the mother is not Malaysian.[116] As well, customary marriages are not considered valid.[117]

Birth Registrations

"Barriers to birth registration is a massive problem," said one NGO representative.[118] The first barrier is that it is not free; there are fees associated with registration at all stages, including late registration.[119] Second, the likelihood of birth registration depends on where people are born. There are registration drives and mobile clinics, especially in rural areas but they still do not reach everyone and do not occur very often.[120] One academic told me that while those who give birth in clinics and hospitals are given information about registration, this does not mean that registration will occur.[121] Those born in rural settings or outside of medical facilities have an even more difficult time. One NGO representative stated that birth registration used to occur in hospitals or police stations but now takes place at government offices that are not in locations convenient for those in rural settings and may be difficult to get to if one needs to take time off work, and bring two to four witnesses of the birth.[122]

For abandoned children, one NGO representative explained that "we make a police report so we can use it as a way to extract a birth certificate from the registration office," and often the birth certificate will list the baby as not a citizen.[123]

Birth Certificates

Many interviewees discussed how the request for a birth certificate, or the renewal of a birth certificate, the application for an identification card, or the adoption process led to birth certificates being deemed fraudulent, then confiscated. The consequent reissuance of the birth certificates resulted in a certificate that stated the person was not a citizen.

Chapters 4 and 5 have outlined how the birth certificate pronounces citizenship and is considered essential proof of entitlement to citizenship. One lawyer stated that the birth certificate is the gateway to citizenship, and it is the stateless person's burden to obtain it.[124]

This declaration of citizenship on a birth certificate is not a benign decision and yet it is treated as a clerical task. One NGO representative pointed out that clerical errors can be made and therefore can affect a person's future ability to retain, affirm, or acquire citizenship.[125] One lawyer provided that "when you request a new birth certificate, if they issue it, they sometimes purposely leave off citizenship or find that a person is not a citizen."[126] He surmised that "Sometimes insisting on [the issuance] of documentation is more counterproductive."[127] Another lawyer said clerks look for irrelevant information to reissue a certificate: "Once a birth certificate is issued, you can't look behind it. The NRD increasingly demands to see who the parents are or whether there are other opportunities for citizenship [in other countries]."[128]

For adopted children, birth certificates are a site where they are made stateless. Under the Adoption Act, an adopted child's prior birth certificate is surrendered and a new one is issued, listing the adoptive parents.[129] In some cases, persons may have had birth certificates that listed them as a citizen but then have them taken away.[130] Adopted children whose adoptions were not completed through formal channels and where children and/or their parents did not realize birth certificates may not be genuine are often rendered stateless. When these children try to obtain Identification Cards at the eligible age of twelve, registration offices confiscate birth certificates, replacing them with new certificates that indicate they are not a citizen.[131]

DNA Tests

Parents of stateless children who wish to use their parental link as the legal reason for a child's conferral of citizenship must prove they are the biological parent of the child unless they have formally adopted the child. Acquiring a DNA test is difficult given the costs and the time it takes to acquire the results. Even when a DNA test result has been obtained, it may not be enough. One NGO representative told me that "Sometimes registration offices will not accept private DNA tests but only ones affiliated with government ministries."[132]

Scams, Corruption, and Black Markets

Among my own family, friends, and the people I interviewed, I heard how things could be bought. An NGO representative said that "There is corruption within the NRD."[133] Another NGO representative said that "I've heard of cases where people bribed officials."[134] Another NGO representative told me that "I heard you can become a citizen if you pay 100,000RN."[135]

Others were victims of scams. For example, one paralegal encountered persons who paid "consultants" for help obtaining citizenship.[136] He said that "These consultants did not submit any application, help them obtain documents or fill out forms. They just took the money and disappeared."[137] Another person told me about a person who "paid [a government official] under the table and got cheated."[138]

Several people also told me about the existence of informal baby markets and adoption that was facilitated with the assistance of corrupt civil servants and the creation of fraudulent documents.[139] Where parents engaged with the informal economy to adopt a child, some do not realize their documents are fraudulent until years later.[140] In tackling this problem however, the government strips citizenship from innocent children rendering them stateless and does not enforce the law against agents, or those engaging in this informal market.[141] One interviewee said that "The child always pays the consequences and all just for convenience."[142]

Several advocates told me that the existence of fraudulent documents has been used as a rationale for stripping citizenship from children deemed foreign.

Multiple Preliminary Legal Steps

Stateless persons, in some cases, must go through multiple legal processes to obtain necessary documentation:[143] divorce, marriage (both the process of getting married and registering the marriage), adoption,[144] and legitimization or declaration of parentage.[145] This involved labour but also made people feel like a foreigner. One father said, "I am treated like a fraud. I feel my own child is not treated like my own."[146]

In one case, a parent told me that he first divorced his first wife; then married his second wife in Indonesia; registered his marriage both in Indonesia and in Malaysia; and then finally obtained a lawyer to legally adopt his biological child.[147] Despite completing these steps, he said that "It still led nowhere."[148] In this specific case, the child was born before the marriage was registered and could not acquire citizenship from the father (details of which are discussed in Chapter 4).[149]

Several interviewees explained the reasons why multiple legal processes were needed. One lawyer stated, "In [some] communities, adoptions were done informally. Where there was an abandoned child or someone wanted to give a child to someone, they did it without formalizing things."[150] An NGO representative agreed: "There are very interesting relationships in plantations. The community is happy to take care of someone who is not related to them, for example, when a parent passes on ... There are no documents for this."[151]

Still another barrier is that even where there is one family with multiple persons who are stateless, each person must proceed with a separate legal action, and the cases are not consolidated on request.[152]

Access to Legal Services

The legal system is so complicated that stateless persons seek assistance from others when they attempt to navigate it.[153] They usually approach members of Parliament and/or their staff,[154] paralegals,[155] lawyers,[156] or advocates.[157] As one NGO representative stated, "[Assistance] is vital to the process. [Paralegals] help with day-to-day challenges ... with documentation ....They assist people from beginning to end; take them step-by-step and hand-in-hand."[158]

While some families can afford legal services,[159] many cannot and rely on lawyers who do pro bono work.[160] Lawyers we talked to confirmed that there are just a few lawyers who do pro bono to serve social justice issues. Many stateless persons, especially those in rural communities, cannot afford a lawyer. Sometimes, NGOs chip in to help with costs. Legal Aid does not cover these cases, and self-represented people are not capable of navigating the system alone or of paying legal fees.[161]

Barriers at the Counter with Street-Level Bureaucracy

Complicated and Inconsistent Application Processes

Interviewees confirmed that across Malaysia, there is no uniform process or standard list of requirements or forms. One advocate said, "I have experience in four different states and each locality has different requirements. There is no standard form ... The process is not clear. The websites are not clear ... they are not consistent from place to place ... It is hard to advise people."[162] A stateless person stated, "I have received very different services from different officers. I was told I didn't need to translate Arabic documents and that photocopies were okay from one and then when I submitted these documents, another officer told me the opposite."[163] One paralegal told me, "Policies change all the time. Before, customary marriage certificates from churches were allowed but not anymore."[164] One lawyer said, "Cases are harder to resolve when you are relying on different people and processes."[165]

Guards at the Counters: Unwillingness of Administrative Delegates to Assist

Twelve of nineteen stateless persons told me government employees do not want to help.[166] All the advocates interviewed concurred. One advocate told me that "It is like trying to run through a brick wall."[167] An NGO representative said, "Officers are deliberately unhelpful."[168] Another said that "Frontline staff are not trained well. They look down on people. If we accompany people, we get more response but if people go alone, they don't get very far. They make remarks about the person openly that are sometimes discriminatory."[169] And another NGO representative stated that "Sometimes they seem helpful, but they really are not."[170] One person told me, "We sent invitations to workshops but they are never attended by government staff. There have been trainings but sometimes one training is not enough ...When you ask why they didn't register this person, we don't get a clear answer."[171] One NGO representative stated that when a person goes to a government office, "it does not mean they will get the service or treatment they expect. We get complaints. People get stopped, denied."[172] Another NGO representative said that sometimes it is a waste of time to go to a registrar.[173] One NGO representative told me that "They behave like they are doing you a favour and disrupting their work ... They refer, defer to other offices, people, delay, and push people around. There is no consideration for people."[174] One news outlet, Free Malaysia Today, reported in 2023 that administrative decision makers are also not following judicial decisions.[175]

Withholding of Information

Government officers actively withheld information.[176] One person stated, "They just kept telling us only one step at a time at each place; they won't tell you what happens next. There is no information and no list given. They were being deliberatively uncooperative."[177] Officers would not give an overview of the whole process or what were all the requirements needed to complete an application.[178] Another applicant was told to provide a copy of a marriage certificate. When the certificate was provided, the government official then told the applicant to get it certified. The applicant was upset that they were not told to do this at the outset.[179] Another stateless person told me that every time they went to the registrar, they were told to produce something new that had never been mentioned before.[180] One NGO representative described the problem as follows: "There is a lot of trial and error. You submit it and it gets kicked back saying incomplete."[181] Another NGO representative said, "They respond and don't tell us why the applications are not complete or why the applications are not granted ... They are just told to try again."[182]

Giving Erroneous Advice

The most disturbing accounts I heard were those of government officials giving erroneous information. A parent recounted that "At one point they told us to adopt our own child and to take an ad out in the paper to make sure no one would claim the child. This is ridiculous."[183] Others confirmed this,[184] with one asking, "Why should I have to do that? The child is my biological child ... I know some people do it just to get citizenship, but I think it perpetuates the problem and makes things worse. It makes it seem like the child is not deserving in the first place."[185] Interviewees stated that even if children were adopted, the conferral of citizenship would not be a guarantee.[186]

Erroneous advice can lead to significant outcomes. One person said he was denied registration of his marriage because his wife was not present, even after he explained to the government official that his wife, who was not a Malaysian citizen, was pregnant and was ordered bed rest by a doctor.[187] The official advised that this applicant could wait and register his marriage after the baby is born. However, since the child was born out of wedlock (because the marriage was not registered before the child's birth), the child did not acquire citizenship from his father.[188] This applicant expressed anger that he was misled about the timing of the marriage registration and the consequences of that delay, and felt this advice was given deliberately.[189]

Lack of Meaningful Response to Follow-Up Inquiries

Many interviewees indicated that attempts to follow up on their citizenship applications by phone or in person with staff at government offices were met with quick dismissals and a standard response that applicants need to wait for their applications to be processed.[190] Officials do not appear to look into their application but provide an oral standard response to just wait.[191] Some are told by government officials that they will put in a request for further information and they will get back to the applicant but often, the applicant does not hear back.[192] Sometimes, government offices do not answer the phone.[193] Stateless persons are also told to go to a different office to obtain information.[194] One advocate assisting stateless persons told me, "I try to follow up with cases once a month. They are tired of me. They don't have anything to tell us."[195] One lawyer stated, "Follow up on cases does not lead to success … In one case, the adoptive mother has been waiting four years."[196]

Denying Access to Borang (Forms)

As Chapter 4 explains, there are different kinds of citizenship applications (and the associated forms) depending on where your legal entitlement lies: (a) by operation of law; (b) by registration; or (c) by naturalization.

A disturbing theme that emerged in interviews was how government officials decided which application forms to give to applicants and the active denial of certain forms to stateless persons. Some stateless persons didn't know which form to ask for or what form fit their personal circumstances.[197] Six of the nineteen persons I interviewed stated they were given the wrong application form, denied a specific form, or had to fight vigorously for a form to be given.[198] Many advocates confirmed their experiences.¹⁹⁹ One person told me that "It was a fight to get the proper application form. Government officials will give out the blue, yellow, or green forms but purple is rare."²⁰⁰ This person's experience was confirmed by their paralegal who stated the form was only given after he insisted.²⁰¹ One NGO representative stated, "… civil servants will not tell you what you need to know and will give out the wrong forms or not give out forms."²⁰² The case law confirms these experiences as in the case of Lew Yee Hong.²⁰³

At a registration rally I attended, I witnessed the denial of forms even when specifically requested. I followed one stateless person after she received legal advice to ask for "Form 14" because her current application (already submitted) using "Form 19" was not appropriate. When the applicant asked for "Form 14," the government officer warned the applicant that if she submitted a second application, she could be "blacklisted." When questioned about how and why a person would be blacklisted, the officer didn't appear sure of what would happen. She simply stated she could not give out Form 14. Despite repeated requests, the officer refused to give the applicant the requested form. When a law student intern came to the counter to request Form 14, the officer continually refused to hand out the form despite the law student articulating why the applicant needed Form 14 under the law. It was only after a member of Parliament came to the counter and engaged in a heated argument with the official that the form was given to the applicant.²⁰⁴

One lawyer said, "There are barriers to get the proper forms and to be recognized in the category you are under."²⁰⁵ Another lawyer stated, "You have to fight for it. It is a real struggle. This is even after we intervene ourselves so you can imagine the level of struggle. Imagine if someone goes alone, they will be chased away."²⁰⁶ Stateless persons frequently discussed the difficulty of getting Article 14 applications and how government officials readily gave, if at all, Article 15A applications, implying that applicants did not have automatic entitlement, under operation by law, to citizenship but needed to seek discretionary relief.

Face and Race

There is much scholarship on how the administrative system can be experienced differently by certain racialized persons,²⁰⁷ and how the racial identity of the bureaucrat or the client as well as the context and politics informing how race is mediated in these institutions affects one's experience at a government counter.[208] The next two sections discuss how race informed interactions stateless persons had with persons at government counters.

Differential Treatment at the Counter Due to Race

Chapter 4 describes how Malaysian citizenship law discriminates based on gender and race while Chapter 2 provides historical background as to why this occurs. One advocate described this context as follows: "Discrimination is heavy. You experience that. People refer to each other by ethnicity first … Malay, Chinese, Indian."[209]

Four of the nineteen stateless persons spoke of how government officials made comments to them about their race or the legitimacy of their application due to their race.[210] One stateless person stated, "When I was applying for my IC [Identity Card], the government official said I did not look like my mom. She asked to look at my birth certificate and said it was wrong and took it away."[211] She was given a new birth certificate that stated she was not a citizen. This decision was based solely on the government official's observation that the stateless person (who was ethnically Chinese Filipino) did not look like her Chinese mother. Another stateless person said, "A government official told me I don't look Malaysian. But I am Malaysian."[212] This experience has been documented in case law as well. In the case of Lim Kai Lin, the court stated, "Upon attaining the age of 12 she applied for her identity card. Her application was held up by the NRD when the official noticed that her appearance and her skin colour did not resemble Hwa who claimed he was her biological father."[213]

At least one person justified discrimination as a proxy to finding fraudulent birth certificates given to people who had adopted children through informal channels.[214] Some of the people I interviewed were uncomfortable with the idea that race may play a role, proclaiming they did not see discrimination in the front office[215] or that one could only speculate.[216] Despite doubts about the role of race, the same interviewees acknowledged, "[civil servants] make remarks about the person openly that are sometimes discriminatory. There is an internal classification of people that is discriminatory."[217] One academic provided, "It is hard because the law itself and the procedures read colorblind."[218]

On balance, the majority of interviewees felt that race played a significant role in whether someone is able to get citizenship. As one academic acknowledged, "discrimination enters into micro-level interactions with government officials."[219] Another advocate stated unequivocally that "There is definitely discrimination."[220] An NGO representative said:

> I am hearing more and more discrimination against the Chinese population when it comes to obtaining documentation. Race plays a big role. There is a lack of rule of law and an apathy of NRD officers that they can get away and treat applicants with discrimination. There is very little opportunity for applicants to assert their rights.[221]

Another NGO representative said of government officials that "They view people as not Malay or not acting Malay and then deem them not a citizen. How do you ascertain when you look at a person? They are merging race, ethnicity, and citizenship. They are treated like illegals."[222] One interviewee said to me personally, "You look Chinese. Because of your background, you wouldn't be considered Malay" and concluded, "Race is an issue. It's political."[223]

A point of note is that most civil servants are Malay. One lawyer said, "There is ingrained discrimination going on. I have witnessed differential treatment when accompanying people to registration. Ninety-five percent of civil servants are Malay and are not sympathetic. Stateless cases are disproportionately not Malay."[224] An NGO representative stated, "The civil service is full of Malays … The civil service doesn't reflect the demographics of society. Officers are deliberately unhelpful when it comes to citizenship applications."[225]

One paralegal told the story of how a boy's grandmother, who was not only a citizen but Indigenous of the Dusun people, went to a school to appeal for her grandson to be admitted into the school despite the fact he was stateless. During the meeting, the education officer accused the grandmother of "faking documents and faking [being] Dusun." The staff at the school questioned why the grandmother's accent sounded Indonesian and why she did not enrol her grandson in an informal educational centre for migrant workers. The interviewee called this encounter "shocking" and said that the staff "had a clear anti-immigrant attitude."[226]

These overt racist experiences are contrasted with cases of Malay stateless who were able to resolve their cases easily. One lawyer told me,

"I know of one strange case where a stateless Malay girl grew up as a Buddhist but once it was revealed that her father was a Muslim, she was given citizenship even though her parents were not married. There is preferential treatment for some."[227]

I witnessed differential treatment with a stateless person I met at the registration rally I observed. This applicant was Muslim and was met with helpful and friendly service from an officer who did not appear to have the same approach with a different non-Muslim applicant at the same rally. This officer accepted the application even though the marriage certificate was only in Arabic; told her it was not necessary to get it translated; and accepted it as proof of her marriage despite the fact it was from a religious or customary ceremony, waiving the requirement to obtain a civil marriage certificate. The officer also accepted photocopies of the child's birth certificate rather than asking to review the originals.[228] When I spoke with lawyers and paralegals at the registration rally about this case, they provided their view that you canot discount the role race and religion play in the kind of service you may receive at the counters. One paralegal told me that "It is an issue of preference. Malays and Muslims are given higher priority. It is a racial policy. Malays have priority in anything and everything."[229] He confirmed, "In my experience, no Malay Muslim has issues with citizenship even if there is late registration."[230] Another lawyer relayed the differences experienced by stateless persons this way, "Currently, all of my cases are Chinese which involve intermarriage with Thai, Cambodian, Filipino … The practice is that the government asks people to get citizenship from other countries. They are treating them like foreigners."[231]

These experiences confirm findings in other research. Juliet Pietsch and Marshall Clark write that "The disproportionate representation of Malays in administration has reinforced special treatment of Malays in various areas" and that "the ethnic structure of Malaysian citizenship has meant that citizens are treated differently within Malaysia's institutions, resulting in systemic and institutional racism."[232] Sin Yee Koh, quoting a person interviewed for her research, provides: "Like you go to government offices, you don't speak Malay, you get the cold shoulder … I just don't think that what we feel is important … the thing is, fundamentally you are still different. You are still known as Chinese."[233]

Race as Proxy for Fraud and Foreign

As discussed in Chapter 4, the fact that birth certificates list whether a person is a citizen or not means that civil servants have the power to confer or deny citizenship. One of the factors that civil servants rely on is race. As one NGO representative stated, "There is a discriminatory practice of preventing [birth] registrations for some groups of people."[234] This NGO attempts to pre-empt any discriminatory decision-making by providing proof that the Malaysian father is the biological father of the child. This approach acknowledges the practice among government officials that any "foreignness" or non-Malay characteristics, features or perceptions of the applicants can be used against them to deny citizenship. Advocates have adopted strategies to try to disturb these findings.

The overt assessment by government officers as to the race of an applicant for citizenship has been bolstered by government policy aimed at cracking down on persons with fraudulent documents. One lawyer described this policy as follows: "The JPN had introduced a policy of red-flagging children who either didn't look like their parents or their skin colour didn't match."[235] In this lawyer's opinion, it was a good policy to implement since he felt that "it was good to crack down on clinics and agents who obtained [fake] birth certificates for children instead of the parents going through a formal adoption process."[236] At the time of the field study, no one could tell me that any clinic, agent, or medical professional was reprimanded for their role in creating false documents. As one NGO representative told me, "they are not targeting agents or educating people about baby selling or doing any prevention work. Instead, they are just revoking citizenship from children who were sold. They are punishing innocent children as a means of deterring parents while corrupt civil servants are making money off of this."[237]

One lawyer said people are "treated like foreigners."[238] She explained that "The ironic thing is that some of them get their red ICs [Identification Cards] which signify they are permanent residents, and the back of the card identifies the person's country of origin which states Malaysia. Why are they getting this [red IC] if they are Malaysians to begin with?"[239]

Lack of Transparency in Discretionary Decision-Making

One lawyer said, "The problem is that the issue rests with the Minister of Home Affairs."[240] One NGO representative concurred: "The Minister makes decisions and it is completely out of our control."[241] Another NGO representative put it this way: "I believe there should be certain parameters for this. You can't wake up one day and feel good and sign but tomorrow tear up the application. It seems arbitrary. No one knows when things will be approved and why."[242] One person felt that "The JPN and the Home Minister is a black box. It is hard to get insight into the decision-making process and why some are successful and others not. Maybe it is not a logical or rational process in how applications are treated. I have not seen one family go from step one to being able to hold an IC."[243]

Ghosting: Lack of Reasons

Several interviewees told me that when their applications were denied, there were no reasons given.[244] Where reasons were given, such as insufficient information or documents provided or incomplete application, there was no indication of what was missing.[245] The lack of reasons compounds the disappointment, especially after a long wait. One NGO representative stated in relation to a decision that came after three years: "People don't know how to improve on the next application."[246] Another NGO representative stated, "There is no explanation. We are just told to try again."[247] Jennifer Raso writes that "Reasons for administrative decisions are central to public law doctrines and theories of governance. Not only does a reason-articulating practice indicate whether the process used to reach an administrative decision was fair, but the reasons themselves suggest whether a decision is, in substance, acceptable."[248]

Politicization of the Conferral of Citizenship

Everyone we interviewed admitted that political will is an issue. One NGO representative stated, "The issue is a bit heated …. The government fears the floodgates. They feel that if it opens up 15A applications that it will lead to a large population of people coming."[249] Interviewees described statelessness as "a touchy issue"[250] where politicians want "communities excluded or beholden to them"[251] or simply do not want to approve applications of those deemed foreigner.[252] People I spoke to agreed that "policies change with Ministers"[253] with a previous Home Minister more willing to grant applications than the current one,[254] and that elections garnered more conferrals to gain votes.[255] As explored in Chapter 7, politicians will also engage in public gifts of citizenship to show they are serving constituents.[256] One lawyer reasoned that the floodgates argument is illogical "given that those that are actually foreigners would not be eligible for 15A applications but would have to apply to naturalize" affirming this as a reason to stop people from discovering the true reasons why applications are denied.[257] An NGO representative indicated, "We are always told that they need to look at it on a case-by-case basis. There is no political will to deal with this in a systemic manner. The government will not talk about policy …. They don't understand that they [stateless persons] are already here and belong here and are Malaysian."[258]

Time

The time it takes to gather and fill out the necessary forms and documentation, to leave one's workplace, to get to a government office, and to wait in line is immense for a stateless person. As Emens notes, "Admin seems to many people like wasting time" but takes one away from opportunities to use that time differently."[259]

Imagining how time is experienced through administrative tasks demonstrates how the government counter becomes a barrier for stateless persons, but also invites one to think about how the state values and uses time as a tool to construct the ghost citizen. As Elizabeth Cohen explains, "We implicitly accept that a state can and does legitimately command the time of its subjects … our sense of why this is so or what it means for a state to make illegitimate claims on the time of democratic citizens is relatively inchoate."[260] She discusses the importance of "making room in theories of justice for robust understandings of temporal justice" and to think about why we should not take for granted the state's imposition on our time and how the state deploys time to create assumptions that processes are neutral or objective.[261]

The entire process of attempting to obtain citizenship is lengthy. As one NGO representative stated, processes, whether it be for adoption or to acquire citizenship "can take years. Sometimes you will get rejected a few times and then you start again submitting new applications. Sometimes appeals lead nowhere. Some people submit three to four applications before they get citizenship."[262] An academic told me that "People wait years. I haven't seen one family go from step 1 to being able to hold an IC. Some processes take a very long time."[263] The following section highlights the myriad ways in which time serves to deny, deflect, and create foreign Others.

Lengthy Wait Times for Applications

All the stateless persons I interviewed who had submitted applications had to wait not just months but years.[264] Fifteen of nineteen stateless persons, at the time of the interview, had been waiting: two people had been waiting seven to eight years;[265] three had been waiting four to five years;[266] eight had been waiting two to three years;[267] and two others could not quantify and just said years.[268] One advocate said that "There are a lot of applications stuck in the minister's office … The applications are not rejected … They were never dealt with. It should not be at the mercy of one person where one person can decide the fate of a person. It is rule by man not rule of law."[269]

The length of the processing time varies, and it is not measured starting from the time an application is submitted, so the wait could be even longer.[270] Difficulties in building an application are discussed above. Lengthy wait times also exist in other kinds of proceedings that a stateless person needs to complete before submitting a citizenship application, including adoption processes.[271] The multiple processes and the wait times for each compounds the length of time it may take for someone to potentially acquire citizenship.[272]

The wait times experienced by stateless persons were echoed by advocates.[273] Common refrains were that it depended on the minister in power;[274] there are many cases where people not only lose hope but just give up;[275] that follow-up did not speed up the process or shed light on how long it would take.[276] The toll on stateless persons is heartbreaking. As one lawyer put it, "There are lots of costs and time involved and years pass by as children grow up, aging out of potential avenues to obtain citizenship."[277]

Multiple Citizenship Applications

Twelve of nineteen stateless persons I interviewed made multiple applications for citizenship.[278] Eight of the twelve persons made two applications and, at the time of the interview, all were still waiting for a decision.[279] One of the twelve persons had two active applications as the first application was submitted five years previously and no decision had been made; the stateless person felt that a new application may receive different attention.[280] One person, at the time of the interview, had submitted a fourth application,[281] and three persons had submitted their third application.[282] All twelve persons, at the time of the interviews, were awaiting an answer. The remaining stateless persons interviewed had submitted their first application. Making multiple applications is a common practice and it was widely understood that stateless persons need to make more than one application to be successful.[283] One NGO representative noted, "I have seen more than 100 cases. All had to make many applications."[284]

Lengthy Court Processes

Stateless persons also face long wait times when litigating citizenship application decisions. One lawyer told me:

> There are long delays at every step. When waiting, we talked to lots of officers about the status of the application. At least one year later, we got a response. It was rejected. We did another application, and it was rejected with no reasons. By then at least two years have gone by. It was resolved only by going to the High Court and then to the Court of Appeal. It was rejected at the Court of Appeal …. In another case we won at the Court of Appeal and it was sent back to the High Court to rehear the case. It is a lengthy process.[285]

Another lawyer spoke about how a judge's discretionary decision unduly lengthened the process:

> In one case I asked for a declaration of legitimacy as well as a declaration for citizenship. The judge asked me to withdraw the declaration for citizenship or he would not proceed with the declaration for legitimacy. I refused and the judge allowed all remedies except citizenship. The Court of Appeal allowed

citizenship and now the government is appealing this to the Federal Court. I'm not sure why the judge wanted to separate out the proceedings and lengthen this and why he denied the remedy even after giving the declaration of legitimacy. In another case, because I feared the judge wouldn't give us the declaration for legitimacy, I withdrew the prayer for citizenship.[286]

Another lawyer confirmed this judicial approach.[287]

In adoption cases, the process is lengthened because once the adoption process has completed, new birth certificates are issued but they list the child as not a citizen. One lawyer discussed how the extra step to judicially review the decision to list the child as not a citizen is costly and lengthy.[288]

Some NGO representatives told me that litigation is seen as a waste of time and money, with no little chance of success, and that the preferred strategy is to submit a new application.[289] Still, one NGO representative said they sometimes have no choice: "We knew that some cases could not be pursued further by the NRD. Some cases had been rejected multiple times, so we started to identify legal avenues."[290]

Time Is of the Essence for Children

As explained in Chapter 5, applying under Article 15(a) of the constitution requires one to be under 21 years of age. As one lawyer explained, "Time is especially worrying for those that want to qualify under 15(a). What if you time out and miss your chance?"[291] Children do age out of making an Article 15(a) application[292] and where children are involved, advocates try to submit applications as soon as possible but that may not be enough.[293]

Conjuring Ghost Citizens at the Government Counter

The encounters described by stateless persons in this chapter tell us how the administrative state socially constructs that person. Michael Lipsky writes that people go before street-level bureaucrats and "are transformed into clients" and assign them to categories for treatment, making these encounters social processes.[294] Unlike Lipsky's observations, stateless persons are often not processed at all; they are prevented from even entering the legal realm as a client. Government officials confiscate documents; reissue documents that declare persons as non-citizens; deny access to forms; refuse to take documents; deny assistance; and deliver erroneous advice. All this adds up to the denial of the status of the client. Stateless persons perceive these interactions not only as non-recognition of a citizen but as conferral of the label of foreigner. They are being ghosted at the counter. One stateless person commented, "I want to have a life. I don't have one."[295] A parent asked, "How can the government blame us for not sending our children to school when they do not even help our children?"[296] Another parent felt like his child was banished as "foreign" even though he was born in Malaysia to a Malaysian parent.[297] Stateless persons experience a policing of their birth certificates[298] and an administrative death.[299]

Conceptually we should reconsider the way we view the administrative state and how much deference we give to those operating in that legal realm. The experience of stateless persons should make us question the long-held judicial idea that deference should be given to the administrative state simply because of institutional design, or respect for the legislative branch of government. Having faith that the administration of law will operate as expected is not enough.[300]

Lawyers and legal scholars may point to the system of judicial review; where courts can review the decisions of government officials to see if they were made procedurally fair or whether the substantive decisions are reasonable or correct in law. There is much discussion in scholarly work and in the courts about the extent to which courts should intervene in administrative decision-making. Despite this, courts hear a small number of cases of judicial review and therefore courts provide little procedural protection for administrative decisions.[301] Further, how can one conceive of bringing a judicial review to a court arguing the denial of a form? How does one show that such a decision has been made? While it is beyond the scope of this book to explore legal remedies, other jurisdictions may offer options including administrative tribunals, ombudspersons, and others.[302]

The most significant experiences conveyed to me by stateless persons, their parents, and their advocates were the meetings they had with government officials. It is in speaking to a bureaucrat at the counter that they become stateless or are told they must be a ghost citizen. The counter, for them, is a site of disappointment, shock, and violent realization that their future has been upended. Their encounters speak to the many assumptions, mainly racial, that play an important role in their chances of being recognized as citizens.

Despite this, stateless persons and their families have shown a reluctance to accept what is being told to them or the negative answers they receive. They have shown grit, perseverance, and resilience. Their stories call for accountability, transparency, compassion, and honest dealings at the government counter. The multitude of retellings also reveal a systemic problem between stateless persons and the administrative state. The common experience at the government counter suggests that there is an overriding narrative of who are citizens and who are not and that this narrative is largely informed, as suggested in Chapter 2, by long-held colonial categories of racial communities. Since being rendered stateless at the counter is a widespread experience, attention must be paid at this legal site more. Seemingly public, the private discussions at the counter hide the state's active rejection of certain racialized persons from their community of citizens. As Shamsul A.B. writes, the modalities the state uses in the administration of government is "tailored to specific elements and needs on the administrative agenda" becoming "institutionalised and routinised in the day-to-day practice of colonial bureaucracy."[303] Further, Shamsul A.B. finds that there is "bureaucratic management of contemporary contestation regarding Malaysia's national identity"[304] and the current political agenda of the state "is contextualized within the existing legal-bureaucratic structures."[305]

Specious Blaming of Stateless Persons Not Doing the Administrative Work

In discussions leading up to the drafting of the Refugee Convention, the Belgian government stated that "the problem of statelessness is essentially different from that of refugees" and that "refugees are the victims of political regimes which violate freedom and human dignity, the fact that non-refugee stateless persons have no nationality is in most cases the result either of their own express wishes or of their negligence."[306] Similarly, the Israeli delegate distinguished between "persons who had lost their nationality by their own acts" and those, "who had lost it owing to circumstances beyond their control."[307] These views presuppose that citizenship is conferred whenever it is deserving. More problematically, it places undue burden and blame on stateless persons for their lack of citizenship.

Marginalized communities have long experienced the perception that they were the authors of their misfortune.[308] A powerful example in the statelessness context revolves around birth registration. This research project does not look deeply at the challenges of registering births but other scholars do so.[309] Amanda Cheong, for example, finds that NGO reports and other literature characterize the lack of birth registration as "a lot of victim blaming" and "it is inaccurate to say people don't know the importance of registration when consequences are so acute and so present in their everyday lives, and when you see they have tried everything to facilitate the process only to fail."[310] Birth registration is viewed as a development issue that requires resources rather than a political choice.[311] While this may be true to some extent, the stateless person's encounter with the state may show additional or other prevailing reasons for why births are not registered, and therefore why citizenship is not conferred. The discourse that the state and/or a marginalized community needs assistance and resources to register persons ignores the concerted efforts families make to try to regularize their status and the moves the state makes to thwart these efforts.

Beyond the way in which the stateless figure is constructed as lazy or unwilling subjects, another neglected aspect is how humiliating the experience of seeking service from government officials. Sara Ahmed writes that "when social problems are narrated as problems of will, they become a consequence of the failure of individuals to will themselves out of the situations in which they find themselves."[312] Kaitlyn Greenidge discusses the humiliation tied to some admin work by recalling her mother presenting food stamps at a checkout counter: "If you have ever had to deal with the bureaucracy of poverty, of having to prove over and over again to those in charge how fundamentally unworthy you are, you understand."[313]

Many stateless persons experience this shame and humiliation in a multitude of ways. For example, some parents have not told their children that they are stateless for fear of how it would affect their mental health or their interactions with others in their community.[314] Further, stateless persons recounted their experiences through tears, regret, and frustration, asking why they could not be treated like a community member or a fellow human being; they invariably expressed their surprise when they were treated like a foreigner or as someone who has committed fraud.[315]

Relational Theory: Improving State Interactions with Stateless Persons

Jennifer Nedelsky writes: "Legal attention to fair procedure can provide insights into how to structure bureaucratic power so that it enhances rather than undermines the autonomy of those who interact with it — for example, by ensuring that the voices of the most dependent are heard by decision makers."[316] Genevieve Cartier advocates for a "dialogic model" to conceive discretion as a dialogue in a constructive relationship, moving away from the exercise of discretion as an exercise of political power.[317] The challenge however, is how to translate this dialogic requirement and upset the imbalance of power between those in front of and those behind the government counter. But perhaps in shedding light on what happens in the administrative state we should shift the discussion to why recognition should be in the hands of the state. As discussed in Chapter 5, looking to relationality and ideas of kin in law, borrowed from Indigenous legal traditions, we can welcome further discussion on what kinds of recognition we should aspire to create and how we can build more dignity and respectful obligation with persons in our community marginalized by lack of citizenship.

SEVEN

THE SPECTACLE
Performing Citizenship and State Benevolence

The Performance

Throughout this book, stateless persons (and their experiences) are depicted as anonymous apparitions, ghostlike, unknown. This is done to protect their identities and their continual efforts to resolve their statelessness. In this chapter, I want to acknowledge the persons that embody that status by foregrounding the story of one previously stateless woman named Roisah.[1]

As I explained in Chapter 1, I am a child of a previously stateless person. My father was stateless until he immigrated to Canada.[2] He told me how statelessness made him feel unworthy, that he could never belong, and that he could be easily erased, discarded, or forgotten. His experience had a profound impact on his mental health and contributed to his desire to assimilate and blend into Canada. Throughout my time in the field, my family history was brought to the fore many times. When I interviewed a lawyer, she showed me a file involving a person that shared the same last name as me, spelled identically: Liew. It felt like an out of body experience.

Another emotionally fraught moment was when I revealed to an interviewee that my father was stateless. She looked at me and stammered, "Look at how far you've gone. How can anyone not see that no child deserves to be stateless. You are proof of how a child can thrive if they are given the right opportunities." Finally, at a registration rally, I remember being surrounded by a group of Chinese fathers who spoke my mother tongue, Hokkien. It saddened me to see people with whom I felt a kinship through language suffering as they were.

Photo Credit: Jamie Liew

It was only through this research, however, that I began to interrogate the behaviour of my father not only in his birthplace but here in Canada. I viewed his choice to take a chance to move across the continents as bold, risky, as an act of resilience and resistance, but his experience and existence here in Canada is one that I now view as a constant performance — demonstrating he is a good citizen through his public assimilation in his linguistic and cultural expression.

This chapter presents three considerations. The first is that this chapter attends to the methodology of critical race theory by providing one narrative of a previously stateless person in Malaysia. In this way, the chapter provides proof of what Gayatri Chakravorty Spivak calls the subaltern (the stateless figure) but one that is filtered through my Western-born and educated lens. The second is that this chapter discusses how various stateless persons exert control and agency in attempting to change their status while simultaneously being painted by some as either lazy or not doing the necessary work to acquire citizenship or even as deviant, wilful subjects that pose a challenge to the smooth governing of the state.[3] Like Pontianak and other ghostly figures in folk tales, ghosts interrupt, upset, mess up, frighten; they are wilful and wayward beings that we wish to eject from our lives. Finally, this chapter examines more closely these moments of disruption to suggest that the performance of becoming a citizen is one that reinforces the narrative of the postcolonial state; that there are those that belong and those that do not using the binary of foreigner and citizen. In moving through the stories of stateless persons and their journey to acquiring citizenship, we see not just resistance but also the necessary repudiation of identities (statelessness) to re-enact norms of citizenship that reproduce or reiterate the very power and racial relations that construct statelessness to begin with.[4] In this sense, this chapter borrows from Judith Butler's conception of how subjects are formed and produced through the constituted performativity of norms.[5] As Shompa Lahiri writes, "Just as Judith Butler has argued that parodic performance of gender undermines essentialized notions of sexual and gender difference, so equally race and class passing also threaten the stability of racial and class categorization."[6]

This chapter provides fodder for the discussion provided, in part, by Engin Isin, Daiva Stasiulis, and Abigail Bakan. Accordingly, citizenship is not stable, reliable or ideal but it is contestable, dynamic and negotiated and that citizenship is performed, practised through not only the exercising of citizenship rights but also through claiming a right to citizenship.[7] Much of the research of performative citizenship discusses cases of citizens and non-citizens claiming equal access to rights or recognition, but little of that discussion centres on those without citizenship.

Roisah's Loss of Citizenship

When I met Roisah, she was on the verge of adulthood. Once she turned 21, she would no longer be eligible to apply for citizenship in Malaysia as a child under Article 15 of the constitution. She initially presented as a shy and polite young woman who smiled easily. As I got to know her, Roisah showed me not only her positive outlook on life, but her determination, intelligence, bravery, and ability to articulate in a convincing manner.

Roisah's story is known because she chose to publicize her story. Her full name is Roisah bin Abdullah. "bin Abdullah" is a surname given to "illegitimate" children whose Muslim father is not married to their mother under sharia law.[8] Roisah has experienced stigma as an "illegitimate" and stateless child.

Roisah was born in Malaysia and was told by her late adoptive mother that her biological mother is Filipino. She has no information about her biological father. Roisah's adoptive parents divorced and are now deceased. They were unable to help her obtain citizenship when they were alive. Roisah didn't think to ask her adoptive mother, when she was alive, what the circumstances of her adoption were and so little is known about how she was adopted.

Roisah had a happy childhood and thought she was a citizen until she was 12 years old. As with many young Malaysians, at the age of 12, the rite of passage is to acquire your IC at the NRD. When she applied for her IC, the registrar told her that her birth certificate was fraudulent and confiscated it. Roisah told me the day she lost her citizenship, the government official told her she did not look Malaysian and did not look like her mother. Roisah stated that some people consider her Filipino even though she has never been to the Philippines, does not speak any Filipino language and has no connection or affinity to the Philippines. She has not tried to get a Filipino passport insisting, instead, that "Malaysia is my country." She said she felt different from her peers from that day forward.

Roisah was a Straight-A student. After losing her citizenship, Roisah was not admitted into the public school she had been attending. One of Roisah's teachers put her in touch with a paralegal known to help stateless children. Roisah learned that she needed permission from the District Department of Education to go to school. Since she was considered an international student, she also had to pay fees of around 120RN (40CAD) per year for primary school and 240RN (80CAD) per year for high school. Her paralegal connected her with community services that helped pay for the school levies. Going to school kept Roisah grounded and focused on the future rather than dwell on her statelessness. When Roisah finished high school, she dreamed of going to university to become a teacher. She was not admitted to university because she was not a citizen and did not have an IC. Since graduating from high school at the top of her class, she has been living with an aunt for whom she does odd jobs. She feels guilty and said, "If I get an IC, I will get a decent job with good pay. It doesn't matter to me now even if I don't get to further my studies." Clearly, Roisah's struggle to obtain citizenship has dampened her ambition.

Roisah and her paralegal, over the next decade, worked on obtaining citizenship. The paralegal accompanied her through various administrative tasks, including the acquisition of a birth certificate. Roisah expressed frustration at the administrative labour: "Even just trying to get a birth certificate, we had to fight with an officer at the NRD."

Roisah was issued a new red birth certificate that listed her as a non-citizen. Since she was not a citizen, she was referred to the Ministry of Home Affairs to apply for citizenship.

Roisah needed her adoptive parents to formally adopt her which was a process her paralegal assisted her with. Both her parents were Malaysian and so Roisah anticipated that it would not be difficult for her to obtain citizenship. After a formal adoption was finalized, a citizenship application was submitted. At the time of her interview with me, Roisah told me: "I'm still waiting. It's been 8 years since I sent in the application." The paralegal, as well as Roisah, did follow up with government officials but was repeatedly told to just wait.

Roisah was one of the first stateless persons I interviewed in Malaysia. She was eager and willing to tell me her story, after having done so publicly and repeatedly for some time. She was articulate and bright, stating that she understands what needs to be done but does not understand why it has not been. According to her, "It is frustrating because I have studied the constitution and it is unfair."

Federal Court Hearing

On March 6, 2018, there was a hearing scheduled at the apex court in Malaysia involving six stateless claimants. Roisah attended since she felt this hearing would inform her future. When I approached Roisah and her paralegal outside the courtroom, they told me Roisah received a negative decision on her citizenship application. Her paralegal said they were going to submit another application to the registrar. Roisah was sad but remained hopeful.

The hearing was postponed after a request was made by counsel of one of the stateless individuals to consolidate matters and to postpone due to illness. Roisah was disappointed. She wanted the hearing to have occurred to move things along, and did not understand why it was delayed. Roisah told me that she felt she had a lot riding on this legal proceeding since she might benefit from the court's ultimate findings.

Roisah's Day Trip to Putrajaya

Given that Roisah was on the verge of becoming a legal adult, she had very little time and her legal team felt that other tactics needed to be used.

On March 21, 2018, I accompanied Roisah and her legal team to personally appeal to the Minister of Education and the Minister of Home Affairs. At the time, the Deputy Prime Minister in Malaysia was also the Minister of Home Affairs. Roisah's lawyer told me that she had faxed a letter indicating she and Roisah would be coming on this date, invited the minister to offer alternative dates, and clearly stated that no response was a confirmation of an appointment.

A convoy of us drove 40 kilometres from Kuala Lumpur to Putrajaya. In one car was Roisah, her lawyer, her paralegal and me. A member of Parliament of an opposition party came in a separate car. Putrajaya, or more affectionately PJ, is a planned government city. While Kuala Lumpur is still the capital of Malaysia, and remains the home to Parliament, the Agong (monarch or head of state), and foreign embassies, Putrajaya became home to the ministries and the administrative arm of the state in the 1990s. When we arrived in PJ, it felt like I had entered a large, gated community with modern, twentieth-century architecture. The buildings were large and could double as museums, palaces, or places of worship. The streets and the layout were clean, orderly, and impressive. The scene gave a sense that government work was important, taken seriously, and done properly. "Putra" in Sanskrit means "prince" and "jaya" means "success" or "victory." Ironically, this felt like a façade given it was the site of much failure, chaos, and disappointment for many stateless persons.

Our first stop in Putrajaya was to meet with Zuraida binti Kamaruddin, a Member of Parliament. In January 2018, she was a "Woman Chief" of the political party, Parti Keadilan Rakyat (PKR) or the People's Justice Party. After the election in May 2018, the PKR became part of the ruling coalition in Malaysia and Zuraida binti Kamaruddin became the Minister of Housing and Local Government. Zuraida binti Kamaruddin is quoted in a news article about Roisah: "I found that this is a genuine case and she had been denied a citizenship. I was willing to adopt her if that would help. So, I applied and got a court order to be her adoptive parent. That's how it started."[9] She accompanied us to meet with the Home Minister.

When we arrived at the Ministry of Home Affairs, staff claimed that no correspondence had been received and that the minister was not present. Roisah's team worked the phones and discussed strategy. Roisah's lawyer received phone calls and text messages from a staff member of the Home Minister saying that he was in a different location, and that if Roisah came to where he was, he would make a public announcement in front of media that she would be conferred citizenship. Roisah's lawyer could be heard speaking loudly into the phone asking if Roisah's IC was in the minister's hands and that Roisah would only agree to meet with him and take photos in front of media if she would get her IC on arriving. The Minister would not confirm this and Roisah's lawyer kept demanding a closed-door meeting or confirmation that the IC would be there. Throughout the day, the minister's staff repeatedly called and texted Roisah's lawyer to ask Roisah to join him in a public announcement.

Roisah's lawyer told me that in the past, the minister did photo ops with stateless children telling the public that they would be granted citizenship but that after the news covered the story, no citizenship was granted, and the media did not follow up with the story. Roisah's lawyer said she did not want to see Roisah used by a politician that, in an election year, would benefit from looking beneficent with a young, studious stateless girl without absolute confirmation that her citizenship was granted. During these conversations, Roisah was silent, and her paralegal comforted her saying that this was the best way to proceed so that she does not fall into a trap where the minister would have the upper hand and have no incentive to give her citizenship. He explained that once the photo was taken, they would have nothing to bargain with. Roisah understood and agreed but she was losing hope that anything would be achieved that day. After some time, the Deputy Secretary General from the minister's office agreed to meet with Roisah and her team.

Prior to the meeting, the team explained to Roisah and me that the strategy was to listen but not to settle for an offer that would mean Roisah could go to university but without conferral of citizenship. They emphasized that this was not enough, that citizenship was the goal.

At the meeting, the Deputy Secretary General's staff were defensive. Staff claimed that their office had been trying to get a hold of Roisah for an interview, but they could not reach her. Both Roisah and her paralegal confirmed no contact had been made by the Ministry of Home Affairs and that he had personally followed up with the JPN or NRD every few months

Advocates filling out forms at the registrar: Latheefa Koya, lawyer (left front), N. Surendran, Member of Parliament at the time and lawyer (left back), Roisah bin Abdullah (centre), Sathiya Kebajikan, paralegal (right front). Photo Credit: Jamie Liew.

and was told that there had been no movement on her application. Staff requested a new application be completed. Roisah's lawyer asked why this was necessary given that an application was already in the system. The Deputy Secretary General insisted and provided personal assurance that it would be brought to the minister in the afternoon. Staff of the Deputy Secretary General indicated that Roisah's guardian needed to be present and Zuraida binti Kamaruddin gave assurances that she would be a guardian or sponsor and would submit any paperwork as long as the processing of this paperwork did not hold up the citizenship application processing. Staff assured the team that the citizenship application would be processed even if the guardian application was not fully processed.

Roisah was ushered to the registrar to submit yet another application. Forms were filled out and photos were taken. The Deputy Secretary General's staff accompanied Roisah's team throughout the process and took the application that was to be brought to the minister.

After the application was taken from Roisah, we all went for lunch. Before we could leave however, Zuraida binti Kamaruddin took a photo with Roisah. Roisah's lawyers answered questions for the assembled media representatives.

After lunch, staff of the Deputy Prime Minister called Roisah's lawyer to ask whether Roisah was on her way to meet the Home Minister, but Roisah's lawyer told them she would not return until her citizenship application was approved and her IC in hand. A staff member of the Home Minister then sent Roisah a message directly through WhatsApp asking her to come and meet with the minister face-to-face. Roisah, after consulting with her lawyer, replied asking if her IC was with the minister. She received no response.

Back at the waiting room, Roisah's team was informed that her application was with the minister. Roisah and the team waited for the rest of the afternoon hoping that a positive decision would be the outcome. At the end of the day, Roisah received a WhatsApp message from staff of the Home Minister indicating that she had missed her chance to meet with the minister. Roisah, on instruction from her lawyer, replied asking for further clarification. The team surmised that Roisah would not be getting any decision that day, let alone a positive decision.

Roisah bin Abdullah (left) and Zuraida binti Kamaruddin, Member of Parliament (right). Photo Credit: Jamie Liew

Roisah explained to me that she was disappointed and found the Deputy Secretary General and her staff's attitude hostile toward her. She was shocked they accused her of not being in touch with the registrar. She was surprised by how flippantly they were talking about her situation in front of her and that her presence did not deter the aggressive

Media scrum: Sathiya Kebajikan, paralegal (left front), N. Surendran, Member of Parliament and lawyer (left); Roisah bin Abdullah (centre left), Latheefa Koya, lawyer (centre right). Photo Credit: Jamie Liew

tone during the meeting. When asked what she would do if she did get her citizenship that day, Roisah said she would jump up and down. At the end of the day, it seemed clear that her application would not be approved. She was crestfallen but stoic, maintaining hope that a decision may come in the next few days. Sitting next to Roisah in the SUV on the drive back to Kuala Lumpur, I wondered whether the time spent in shuffling Roisah around the government counters and lobbies in Putrajaya was worth it and what it cost her. I was merely a witness and the experience had drained me. What was it doing to her?

Appeasing Roisah's Wilful Disobedience

Three occurrences of the day deserve particular attention. The first relates to the repeated requests made of Roisah to pose in a photo with the Minister of Home Affairs in exchange for a verbal public announcement that citizenship would be conferred. The warning from Roisah's lawyer that agreeing to pose for the photo would not likely lead to a conferral of citizenship is a direct result of the previous experiences of stateless persons seeking ICs.[10]

The requested photo op was intended as the government's public performance; this specific request was meant to appease public outcry and calls to resolve Roisah's case. The public promise embodied in the photo op (had it taken place) was also meant to nullify Roisah's display of disobedience. Roisah was treated as an impatient person who was not willing to wait for her application to be processed or as a recalcitrant applicant unwilling to accept the state's finding that she is the foreigner. The public declaration that she is a citizen was meant as a device used to placate the wayward figure of the stateless. It provides a commitment that is "non-performative"[11] and obscures the institutionalization of statelessness. As Sara Ahmed explains, citing Judith Butler, "Non-performatives describes the 'reiterative and citational practice by which discourse' *does not produce* 'the effects that it names.'"[12]

The second incident that should be examined occurred during the meeting with government officials, when Roisah was accused of not responding to requests for interviews. This claim, contested by Roisah and her legal team, may aim to paint Roisah as the author of her own misfortune, as someone who is not meeting the basic requirements or criteria for her citizenship application. The accusation shifted focus to Roisah's actions or inaction, instead of the state's inaction to process her application or the state's action to deny her previous application. This narrative — that Roisah did not respond in a timely manner — operates to situate Roisah as undeserving of citizenship because of her own doing; it depicts her as disobedient and dishonest in her dealings with the state.

The final incident of interest was the request by government officials to submit another citizenship application even though Roisah had already submitted one. Government officials discounted the administrative labour Roisah had already endured in submitting an application and again, shifted focus to the applicant's actions rather than to state (in)action.

Roisah Granted Citizenship

I left Malaysia in April 2018 but kept in touch with Roisah and her lawyer. As I left, I remember thinking that Roisah was now 21 and that if things were not going to be resolved soon, she could be stateless forever. Roisah was granted citizenship almost one year after I left, on March 28, 2019. It was a result of persistent efforts to lobby politicians outside of the administrative and legal system as well as a sustained media campaign.

We may never know exactly why Roisah was granted citizenship but there are several factors, in my opinion, that make Roisah a compelling public case wherein the state could be seen as benevolent and as willing to tackle the issue of statelessness in a palatable way.

The first factor is Roisah's academic record. Her scholarly profile as a Straight-A student assisted her cause, depicting her as an ideal citizen, hardworking, and smart. Her academic success was brought out as proof that she is deserving of citizenship. Roisah resembled the "model minority."

The second factor is Roisah has *masuk Melayu* or has "become Malay." As discussed in Chapter 2, *masuk Melayu* is Malay for "become Malay" and refers to the modelling or assimilation of persons by adopting the three pillars of Malay identity: language, culture, and religion. Donning a hijab, her image is that of a pious Muslim woman. This aided Roisah in demonstrating that she was an ideal citizen in a state where a majority observe the tenets of Islam. She speaks Malay fluently. Further, having lived in Malaysia all her life, she is not only familiar with Malay culture but can glide easily through the customs and practices of the state.

The third factor is the difficulty of identifying Roisah's origins. There is no certainty as to the identification of Roisah's parents and therefore her true ethnic, racial, or cultural roots remain undetermined. This allowed her to *masuk Melayu* where she did not have to shed a previous or originating identity.

The Model Minority

Very few news articles covered all aspects of Roisah's journey to obtaining citizenship but many focused on the fact that she was a studious and bright student as evidenced by her grades. For example, one news report stated: "Roisah made headlines last year when, despite obtaining a Cumulate Grade Point Average (CGPA) of 3.68 in the STPM [Sijil Tinggi Persekolahan Malaysia or Malaysian Higher School Certificate] examination in 2017, was unable to study at a public university due to her status."[13] Another provided: "The STPM top student of Sekolah Menengah Kebangsaan (Perempuan) Kapar, Klang who scored 3As, 1B was previously reported to have difficulties in furthering her studies as she had no identification documents."[14] The multiple reports focusing on Roisah's academic success may seem like a benign description but her performance as a top student played an important role in modelling citizenship. She was not the first to be described mainly as "a hardworking student."[15] As recently as 2023, news reports continually characterized stateless persons deserving of citizenship as studious.[16]

Borrowing from scholarly work on the stereotype of a model minority of Asian Americans, I argue that Roisah's performance and demonstration that she is worthy of citizenship acts to perpetuate the conditions that continually deny citizenship to persons with genuine and effective links to Malaysia. Freida Wong and Richard Halgin describe the "model minority" as "successful minorities who have quietly moved to the pinnacle of success in various contexts through hard work and determination" often used for Asian Americans despite the fact they are not a homogenous group. They discuss how it puts pressure on persons to perform well while masking difficulties faced in doing so.[17] Scholars agree that the model minority is a prevalent stereotype that focuses on success stories of Asian Americans, producing a colour-blind discourse that obscures the operation of racial power, protecting it from challenge, and permitting ongoing racialization via racially coded methods.[18] As "praiseworthy citizens," some persons were "conscripted into the manufacture of a certain narrative of national racial progress premised on the distinction between 'good' and 'bad' minorities."[19] More than just being an "assimilated Other," being a "model minority" meant a more subtle yet profound "metamorphosis," an "integral" character in the nation-state that helped create race classifications or define race relations.[20]

Performing the good student role is one way in which stateless persons have been able to slip from the stateless space into the citizen space, but it comes at a cost: it reinforces the framework that constructs the stateless person in the first place. The conferral of citizenship to model citizens fortifies the notion that stateless persons must do particular work to "earn" citizenship rather than viewing them as kin or de facto citizens and promotes racial categorizations by awarding those willing to perform. The figure of the model citizen hides structural barriers that stateless persons face in making claims for citizenship, obscuring the racial and discriminatory processes that prevented them from obtaining citizenship in the first place. As Yuko Kawai explains in the American context, "depicting Asian Americans as the model minority simultaneously serves downgrading other racial minorities as 'problem' minorities."[21] In the statelessness context, depicting some stateless persons as "model citizens" serves to construct other stateless persons as not desirable citizens. As Gary Okihiro explains, the model minority serves to construct the passive and malleable as well as the threatening figure.[22] By acting as the model student, Roisah helps to perpetuate and fetishize the racialized category of the ideal citizen,[23] allowing sharp boundaries to be defined so as to identify "who is clearly within and who is clearly beyond it."[24] Roisah's performance as an excellent student feeds meaning into the state narrative that stateless persons can be both: a threat to the state and able to graduate to become a citizen.

Roisah's academic achievements were touted as trophies to be admired; they signalled a reason for why she should be conferred citizenship. In my interview with Roisah, she herself places importance on her academic record: "Not all Malaysians can contribute to society and I have shown them that I can. It's unfair that I am not even given a chance."

Roisah *Masuk Melayu*, Becomes Malay

Engin Isin posits that "how people perform citizenship plays an important role in contesting and constructing citizenship." The malleability and flexibility of Roisah's identity allowed her to penetrate the permeable boundary of citizenship by enacting not only the markers of ideal citizen but also performing the struggle and acting as an object of a social struggle.[25] Roisah did this not only through her multiple and persistent applications for citizenship, but her presence at the Federal Court hearing, her willingness to engage with media, her lobbying the Home Minister and her insistence that she would not participate in any photo op without proof of citizenship in her hands. Her "resistance" that took the shape of wanting to be accepted as a stateless person illustrates not only the struggle necessary in negotiating citizenship but reveals the tenacity and resilience of stateless persons. As Judith Butler writes, performativity involves the "moment in which a subject — a person, a collective — asserts a right or entitlement to a liveable life when no such prior authorization exists, when no clearly enabling convention is in place."[26] Roisah has asserted, from the moment her birth certificate was taken away from her, that she was a citizen of Malaysia. She "constituted herself" as a citizen.[27] In this way Roisah performed what Butler calls a "performative contradiction" when she was "excluded from the universal, and yet belongs to it nevertheless, speaks from a split situation of being at once authorized and unauthorized."[28] Roisah demonstrated that "citizenship is defined not just by having these rights, but also by *claiming* them."[29]

Aside from claiming, Roisah has also performed the ideal citizenship. *Masuk Malayu* is a mode of performing citizenship. Roisah has deployed strategies of mimicry, passing, or even assimilation to cross from the stateless space into that of citizenship.

Assimilation explains the process by which immigrants adapt to new environments by exchanging their ethnic and cultural behaviours for the practices of the receiving society.[30] As immigrants interact with dominant groups in the state, distinctions fade and newcomers become similar to those in the dominant group.[31] Scholars assert there is no consensus among theorists on what migrant integration means; that the different theories of assimilation have come under criticism for their normative and nativist assumptions leading to reformulations of the concept and also debates on trajectories of assimilation — be it an upward or downward path.[32] Assimilation has, however, been described as a performance to project an outer self that resembles the dominant population as a protective strategy rather than the actual exchange of ethnic and cultural behaviours of the previous identity for the new; that hostile laws against migrants push immigrants to adopt an assimilatory presentation of self to pass as the dominant group.[33] The concept of assimilation as a strategy then can be seen as a means to exercise agency, overcome perceived limitations or realize life projects.[34] In this sense, this approach to understanding assimilation borrows from the concepts of mimicry and passing to highlight the performance stateless persons may undertake to gain the recognition that they are, indeed, kin.

Homi Bhabha writes that "mimicry is like camouflage, not a harmonization of repression of difference, but a form of resemblance, that differs from or defends presence by displaying it in part, metonymically."[35] Elaine Ginsberg explains that passing "implies such an individual crossed or passed through a racial line or boundary — indeed *trespassed* — to assume a new identity, escaping the subordination and oppression accompanying one identity and accessing the privileges and status of the other."[36] She also looks at the complex reasons for such a performance, "And although the cultural logic of passing suggests that passing is usually motivated by a desire to shed the identity of an oppressed group to gain access to social and economic opportunities, the rationale for passing may be more or less complex or ambiguous and motivated by other kinds of perceived rewards."[37]

In the case of Roisah, meeting the three pillars of Malay citizenship of language, culture, and religion, allowed her to pass as Malay. Shompa Lahiri notes that "passing is usually motivated by a desire to shed the identity of an oppressed group to gain access to social and economic opportunities"; however, in the case of stateless persons, passing could be a way to gain the status of citizen. As well, as noted by Lahiri, there may not be a deliberate decision or a calculated impulse. In the case of Roisah, having been adopted by a Malay family, raised with the Malay language, culture, and religion (Islam), she "mimics" or "passes" because of the "accident" of where she landed as an abandoned and adopted child. Indeed, one could argue that Roisah did not necessarily assimilate but is a product of Malay culture despite the racial and ethnic identities assumed or imposed on her because of her face.

Roisah herself believes she is Malaysian. Still, for many, the adoption of a racial identity can be particularly useful especially where there is a benefit attached, as it has been for other postcolonial migrants.[38] Lahiri finds that the class and education markers of respectability for migrants wanting to "pass" helped overcome the questions of racial identity.[39] Ginsberg explains that aside from visible physical characteristics, language, religion, and other markers can inform racial categories.[40] Roisah, in mimicking Malayness, "exploited" the familiar, gaining imagined proximity, provoking contestations to her belonging. Roisah's experiences thus illustrate the "fluid nature" of identity.[41] As Nurfadzilah Yahaya finds in her own research, minorities may help fuel the entrenchment of European colonial legalities to gain benefits for themselves.[42] The performance of a certain kind of citizenship helps entrench a particularized racial citizenship.

The Benevolent State

Roisah's acquisition of citizenship was accompanied by reports of the generosity of the Malaysian government.[43] One news report acknowledged: "Finally, after several applications were rejected, stateless and outstanding student Roisah Abdullah received her Malaysian citizenship today."[44] One news outlet reported that "Roisah, who will turn 22 next month, called today's news an early birthday present. 'Yup, yes, absolutely, this is truly a big gift,' she told reporters here."[45]

In another news report, Roisah expressed what this meant in practical terms for her: "'The first thing I want to do after getting my MyKad [IC] is to open a bank account and then apply for an LRT travel pass,' Roisah said brimming with excitement."⁴⁶ The news account also noted that "accessing affordable healthcare was one of the many problems that she had faced." Roisah was quoted as saying:

> Seeking medical treatment was difficult because I could only go to private facilities and it was not cheap. I couldn't take part in any activities which required an identification card. I couldn't even apply for a drivers' licence. When I was in secondary school, I had to pay a levy of 240RN every year, because I did not have any documentation.⁴⁷

Another news report stated: "Looking bright and cheerful, Roisah said she could not wait to enjoy the facilities provided for Malaysians including access to healthcare services, opening a bank account and obtaining a driving licence."⁴⁸

Roisah's case is not an isolated or unusual one. When I discussed the ad hoc act of benevolence with interviewees, many agreed that the resolution of individual stateless cases sometimes needed political pressure and ultimately the conferral of citizenship was seen not as a legal or administrative process but a political one.⁴⁹ One lawyer said that success comes with getting the attention of high-level politicians: "The PM [Prime Minister] will sometimes gift citizenship documents to individuals when it should be given as of right."⁵⁰ Another lawyer put it this way:

> Everything is delegated through a political connection. This system has broken down … Connections to politicians can make a lengthy wait shorter for applications. Political will is the problem. You see cases where they will give status but not across the board. For example, they will settle a case just so it doesn't set a precedent.⁵¹

One NGO representative said, "People tell me that if I get to the Deputy PM, he will give it. Yeah, maybe. It's like if you know someone then you can get somewhere. The problem is that the process is not transparent. If you know someone, suddenly the boxes get ticked."⁵² Another NGO representative spoke about some specific cases: "Some people are able to get citizenship if they have connections with the government. I noticed when matching babies with police officers or military officers, they found it easier to obtain citizenship for adopted children. The experience of success is informal, inconsistent, and anecdotal."[53]

One NGO representative did not see a problem with using political connections, stating that "If it is a political treat or not, people just have to do what they have to do to survive in Malaysia. If you can take advantage of a situation to get political interest in your case, you can get it done and get the right documentation. It is one avenue to access."[54] Another said that "You have a higher chance if you know someone and are able to get answers sooner or easier."[55] And another NGO representative stated: "Don't go to the JPN because they are resistant. They just deny you. Go higher up to the director general or secretary general....I make everyone go through the proper channels, line up and apply, but I don't have faith in the system."[56] She elaborated, "Sometimes we go [to the registration office] as a group or with someone powerful like a minister otherwise it goes nowhere. Or [at the registration office] I speed dial someone higher up to get somewhere. We have to use our connections."[57]

The media reporting of Roisah's conferral of citizenship as an early birthday present, coupled with the description of the multitude of benefits accompanying her status has helped state agents depict themselves publicly as benevolent and compassionate. The narrative that the state is gifting citizenship to a deserving foreigner reinforces the current structures that create statelessness. Public discourse focused on the charity of the Home Minister masks the narrative that Roisah herself has given to the media: that she has from the beginning been a citizen of Malaysia. These performances allow the state to continue to cast stateless persons as Others, foreigners, migrants, and potentially undeserving and illegals — wayward figures that need to be dealt with on a case-by-case basis. This narrative that the state is being compassionate obscures the barriers and structures that have created statelessness and any critique or contestation on how the state is dealing with persons that claim to be its kin.

Further, the demonstration of this handout serves to allow the state to control the narrative; not only can this demonstration show them as being considerate, kind, and tolerant of new members of their society, but it also appeases, temporarily, contestations that the state is not doing anything about the issue of statelessness. It allows the state to benefit from the public appearance of acting, of tackling a societal problem in a concrete way. Roisah resembles one problem solved, one case where the state did act and showed its capacity to deal with an isolated case of statelessness.

Roisah has highlighted to media and has said in public that she is not a unique case. She is quoted as saying: "I am very grateful that I am finally a Malaysian citizen. But I am hoping that under 'Malaysia Baru' such problems no longer exist."[58] Sadly however, this ad hoc approach of solving individual cases has highlighted not only the ineffectiveness of seeking resolution through the administrative legal system, but how sometimes using public, political means and the media to gain attention is the only way to gain citizenship.

Roisah's experience demonstrates that the resolution of some cases is occurring outside of the administrative and legal venues, and contests the notion that "solving" statelessness necessitates legal reform.

Roisah's journey to citizenship is in some ways an anomaly because very few people are able to garner public attention and to put forth a narrative palatable for action. As discussed earlier in this chapter, many advocates believe that political lobbying and advocacy through connections in government is one key strategy in helping stateless persons, but many also know that it is no guarantee. Roisah's story centres the political tensions and factors that undergird the public circus including who is in government at the time, whether an election has been called, and what kinds of political points a politician can score with a particular community. Further, Roisah's public performances are only possible with the help of a team of lawyers and advocates connected to media and advising her on how to present herself, crafting a solid narrative of her worthiness. Acting as a contributing member of the economic and social community as well as her ability to pose as a Malay played an important role in justifying the ad hoc conferral of citizenship. Clearly, the state benefits from the performance of looking beneficent, capably tackling issues of statelessness.

Registration Rally

On Friday, January 26, 2018, I attended a registration rally in Georgetown, Penang. I have referred to my notes to help me recall my observations from this rally. During this rally, I also provided paralegal support by helping people fill out documentation.

Georgetown is on Penang Island and the historical core is a UNESCO World Heritage Site. It is fondly regarded as the food capital of Malaysia boasting the fusion of Malay, Chinese, Indian, and other cuisines in hawker stalls. I travelled to Penang with my Malay research assistant (RA), Nursyahirah Mohd Daud (Syaz), and then Canadian PhD student, Amanda Cheong. The palm plantations greeting us from the highways were in stark contrast to the deciduous forests I was used to seeing in Canada.

I was told prior to the trip by a lawyer who was helping organize the rally, that the rally was a regular occurrence in different parts of Malaysia, conducted by a political party or a member of Parliament, to aid people in submitting their citizenship applications, but also to provide a public site of protest to the state ignoring the plight of statelessness. Thus, while the rally was meant to provide paralegal support and to listen to constituents' complaints and experiences, the media was invited to witness the extent to which statelessness exists.

When we arrived at the registration office, there were throngs of people waiting in the government building lobby. I asked a number of people how they found out about the rally, and they noted they heard about it through WhatsApp, Facebook, and through direct text messages from friends, family, NGOs, and staff members of one of the different political parties. Several of us counted and collected information of around sixty people to triage persons and connect them with paralegal support. There was a group of lawyers, members of Parliament, paralegals, and students trained to provide advice and support for putting together applications. I helped a few people fill out their documentation, with the supervision and instruction of lawyers in attendance.

Before people were permitted to enter the registration office, an official came out into the lobby to inform everyone that the registrar was closed to everyone who does not have an appointment. Lawyers and MPs were visibly upset and argued with the administrative official. I did not hear what transpired but after the heated discussion, one lawyer told me they requested a meeting with the official's manager. A few minutes later, a manager came out, and after another heated discussion, everyone was moved to a waiting room.

The room was loud and chaotic. Children were crying, or being fed while adults were patiently waiting, chatting, and filling out documents. Paralegals, lawyers, and MPs provided advice and attended to persons

Registration rally at the registrar in Penang. Photo Credit: Jamie Liew.

at government counters flanked by plexiglass. I shadowed my RA, Nursyahirah Mohd Daud (Syaz), a law student working for a lawyer who helped organize the rally. I watched as she explained to people how to fill out forms, answered questions, and sought lawyers and MPs for further clarification. We waded through the crowds to direct people to others who were helpful. During this time, I co-conducted — with Amanda Cheong, a Canadian PhD student — a few interviews of stateless persons and their family members after obtaining consent.

One interaction stood out to me. One woman told my RA that she was told she could not apply for citizenship and was denied a form at a government counter. When the RA approached the counter with the woman, I could hear them arguing in Malay. My RA informed me that the officer was refusing to give the woman any form to apply for citizenship. After a heated exchange, the officer did hand over a form, but it was an Article 15 form for discretionary citizenship. My RA pushed the form back and asked for a different form — the Article 14 form for the automatic conferral mode of citizenship. The officer refused to give the Article 14 form and instead insisted she was giving the correct form. My RA was dutifully translating for me every so often. I could see my RA pointing at her phone and saw that she was pointing at the Malaysian Constitution, specifically Article 14, and explaining what it meant. She told me she was trying to explain why the woman was eligible for the Article 14 form. The officer disagreed. In frustration, my RA asked me to bring the MP who was organizing the rally to come to the counter. The MP, also a practising lawyer (in Malaysia, MPs don't get compensated with a full salary and often must supplement their income with another profession) came to the counter. He engaged in a heated discussion with the government official who refused to issue the Article 14 application. The MP then asked to see her supervisor at which point she pointed to a portrait on the wall behind her and said that the MP could take it up with him. The portrait was of the then Home Minister. Another government officer was pulled into the discussion, and after a few more minutes of argument, the Article 14 form was finally given.

After the form was given to the woman, my RA assisted the woman in filling it out. I asked why we could not just photocopy this form and make it widely available. My RA showed me the form. It was a carbon copy form that had its own unique identification number at the top. She explained to me that each form has its own serial number.

While the RA was assisting the woman to fill out this form, the MP and I discussed the difficulties people face in accessing the proper forms and how the officer operated as a gatekeeper. We talked about how many stateless persons may not realize there are different forms, and that the denial of a form may be an erroneous decision. We discussed how many people may not know they can challenge a government official, and how many people may have been deterred forever from pursuing their citizenship application from an encounter at the registrar.

This encounter troubled me and has been seared in my memory. I had heard, through prior interviews with stateless persons, that the encounter with administrative officials in various government counters was often hostile and unhelpful, but it was different witnessing it. Aside from the blatant denial of a form, I was taken aback at the antagonistic approach administrative officials used to communicate to persons they were serving. I do not speak Malay and so my observation was based on the tone and volume of a person's voice and the nonverbal gestures — including the shaking of one's head, the pointing, gesturing, the crossed arms, the rolling of the eyes. Although my RA was translating during the incident, it was a very rapid exchange, and I could tell that the woman at the centre of this struggle was extremely worried. She was speechless, letting the RA and MP do the talking, but her hands were clenched, and she looked frantically from one to the other at the people talking.

Form serial numbers were noted down by paralegals and volunteers and some applications were submitted. Others were told of what steps they needed to take before their application could be submitted. In one case, the person did not have his proof of marriage with him. However, this was not a lost opportunity since he was connected with a paralegal to help him acquire that document.

After the long lines of people dwindled to just a few, some people congregated in a waiting area to decompress. There, I met with a local MP in Penang and three Chinese fathers of stateless children. It was there in both English and Hokkien that I heard them express their frustrations with the government and the system. Sitting around the table, I felt like I was at a family gathering, listening to my uncles complain, waiting for food to be placed on the table. The men were Malay citizens, fathers of young children born of mothers who were not. They talked about their struggles getting their children into school and having their children recognized as legal persons.

Grassroots Resistance

Public narratives that stateless persons are responsible for their own plight persist. One news report stated that "The Home Ministry has acted irresponsibly by blaming the issue of stateless children on parents who did not register their marriages."[59] Another reported the Home Minister as saying that "the onus is on parents to ensure their children possess the necessary documentation for citizenship applications to prevent them from becoming stateless."[60] As discussed in Chapter 1, statelessness, with this lens, is seen as a development issue or technical problem of documentation where one need only attend to the administrative task of registering with the government.[61] The stories recounted throughout this book paint a different picture. Stateless persons are not simply wayward, entitled, lazy persons trying to cheat a system. In fact, the turn to media, to political pressure, to rallies, and the collective registration of citizenship applications shows an engaged polity of individuals who have morphed into not only communities of care or advocacy, but also an emerging social movement. For example, many parents of stateless children are organizing by forming communities and engaging in various advocacy activities as evidenced on one public Facebook group page.[62] As well, there is a growing number of NGOs and advocacy groups supporting stateless persons.[63] As this chapter demonstrates, this movement challenges oppressive circumstances and creates widespread public awareness of the existence of statelessness. There are diverse, public, and collective actions and activities stateless persons undertake deliberately to exercise agency to seek changes to their conditions.[64] These public performances are proof that state narratives should not be taken for granted.

EIGHT

THE GHOST CITIZEN
Believe in Ghosts: Unsettling Narratives of the Foreign Stateless

The Ghost Citizen

I stand in the place my auntie and uncle take me, on the edge of the Brunei River, facing the water village Kampong Ayer. They bring me here because the village where my father grew up, along the same river, no longer exists and appears in my mind only like an apparition. I know they are being kind and generous in showing me around this foreign site — a place I have never known. Still, it seems familiar to me. The smells, the language, the faces. It is like I have been here before. My auntie's and my uncle's stories keep me present and focused, and it is like they are taking turns presenting eulogies. In many ways, it is like a memorial, a harkening back to the life lived, an honouring of a shared past.

    My father often said his early life as a stateless person was a purgatory. Like him, many stateless people experience an administrative death, be it at birth, at a government counter later in life, or during an encounter with police or other state authorities. Stateless persons avoid the notice of governments when they work under the table to avoid detention and possible deportation. But at other times, they want to be seen, for example when they need health care, education, employment, housing, and belonging. Their apparitions confuse people, sometimes spooking them, and often igniting speculation and fear about who they are.

    Throughout my time in Malaysia and Brunei, I felt a common thread pulling me through each story told to me by stateless persons, their parents, and their advocates. Many felt that they were misunderstood and were wronged in their interactions and encounters with the state. Some opined there was something awry with the law, while others felt it was misinterpretation on the part of a decision maker. Still others expressed their feeling that it was political, that they were not wanted. Despite the denials, rejections, and hardships, many insisted they felt at home in Malaysia, that they were citizens and needed to correct their status. They felt they were being ghosted by their own state and gaslit about who they really were.

There are gaps and issues with the law that spells out who is entitled to citizenship. The strict interpretation of the law combined with the legal, procedural, or administrative decisions create statelessness. Decisions of all facets and at all points of the process felt determinative to stateless persons. The type of application form, the (mis)information about the process given by frontline government officials, the submission or refusal to take a paper application, the rejection or approval of an application, the reasons for or lack of any explanation, or the silence about or lack of response to applicants all highlight a problematic system built with legal and procedural barriers, but also a dysfunctional relationship between the state and some of its de facto citizens. These laws and their interpretation exclude "illegitimate" children born in Malaysia by non-citizen mothers who are not married to their Malaysian fathers. They omit adopted children who cannot trace or find their biological parents. They dismiss persons who may not "look" like Malaysians.

As documented in this book, the rejection of such persons as citizens occurs in a multitude of spaces: at the government counter by officials, on paper by the Ministry of Home Affairs, in the courts by judges, by the media, at schools by administrators, by professionals in medical facilities, and by the public in their daily interactions. In examining these spaces, a troubling pattern emerges. First, this book upsets the state narrative that statelessness is not an issue. For example, one NGO representative stated, "When you have a deputy prime minister who is also the Home Minister say there are no stateless people in Malaysia, you are starting in the middle of the ocean."[1] Many stateless people were born in Malaysia, have family, some generational links; they live their lives there, and are part of enduring and permanent communities. They have, as termed in law, "genuine and effective" links to the state they consider themselves citizens of. This book suggests that the denials are the vestiges of a British colonial history where racial categories were created, and ideas of a nation-state built on a dominant group's identity, language, culture, and religion.

It is not just the denial of citizenship that contributes to the administrative death experienced by a stateless person but also the deeming of stateless persons as foreign citizens of other states that complicates the stateless person's existence. In identifying persons as citizens of faraway states, stateless persons are denied the ability to call themselves stateless. They are being gaslit and the public is manipulated into thinking of them as wayward aliens who deviously made their way into Malaysia. Thus, they do not only experience a death, but a purgatory. They are in the in-between space. Like ghosts, they are neither alive nor dead.

The depiction of stateless persons as necessarily migrant and foreign justifies the state's rejection of citizenship applications. Stateless persons and their advocates were fully aware they were being made the Other often masked by conflating and confusing descriptions of them. One NGO representative said, "The concepts of statelessness and undocumented get conflated all the time in the public narrative and there is a big difference between the two."[2] According to her, how we talk about the issue matters because it risks rendering people as not belonging, as foreign, or as if they don't exist.[3]

By pointing to the mere possibility of the acquisition of citizenship in another state, stateless persons are deemed strangers and therefore not kin nor of the community. The factual findings made in a variety of legal settings — including in the administrative arm of government and the courts — are alarming, given that when stateless persons are found to be foreign citizens, there is no evidence furnished to substantiate that fact. Instead, decision makers are relying on speculation and taking judicial notice of the mere opportunity that may exist for a stateless person to obtain citizenship from an alternative state. The possibility of the making of a future application appears to lend weight to assumptions in law that there was a duty or obligation to exhaust all possible remedies which includes the exploration of citizenship elsewhere. This prerequisite or preliminary legal matter has increasingly become a procedural barrier to having one's citizenship application processed on its merits. The deeming of a person as a foreign citizen then renders stateless persons as not only foreigners but also claimants who come to the court or administrator without having done all the necessary work. Stateless people become ghost citizens of states they do not consider their own. The treatment of these persons as strangers and as unrelated to those that claim them to be of the community validates state action in ghosting stateless persons, ignoring and denying their citizenship applications and even actively thwarting efforts to obtain citizenship. The denial of citizenship to stateless persons who may have bonds with Malaysia renders them not only aliens but wayward foreign citizens who have strayed from their far-off home country. They are reduced to being mere strangers in the only home they have known, forced to live a life in limbo or the in-between. This is even more concerning given that many of the stateless persons documented in this research were children, innocently born into situations not of their own creation. This is despite the deep ties these children have to Malaysia via their Malaysian fathers, their Malaysian adoptive parents, their residence, their embedded life within Malaysia through work, school, and community.

The creation of ghost citizens occurs just as a foreign female figure is blamed, namely the mothers of stateless children who are citizens of other states. The mixed blood and heritage from the alien mother muddies the connections children have with a state and casts those children as potentially disloyal, deviant, strange, and ultimately unwanted. Their faces, marking a racial label imposed on them, justifies the conferral of ghost citizenship, taking away their claims of statelessness and their identity as kin of the state.

The construction of the ghost citizen makes sense if we think about how the making of citizens and, therefore, non-citizens flows from the nation-building project undertaken during pre- and postcolonial developments of states. In the Malaysian case, some stateless persons experience their administrative death through the overt identification of non-citizens on their face by a bureaucrat's perceiving race over the counter. This encounter resembles the underlying structures put in place during colonial times that were embedded in the Federal Constitution, the legal text that provides the conferral of citizenship in Malaysia. There is a differentiated recognition of citizenship and access to it arising out of the racial categorizations created during British colonial rule. Ultimately, this book argues that the occurrences of statelessness, therefore, are not just about creating the foreign figure but is also about the particular nation-state–building project around a dominant group's language, culture, and religion. Despite this, a stateless person can emerge from purgatory by performing or becoming Malay, *masuk Melayu*.

Experiences of ghost citizens contest assumptions that stateless persons are not doing the work to obtain their citizenship or that statelessness is necessarily a development issue. The encounters depicted throughout this research suggest that the overriding issue stateless persons are facing is the active or deliberate acts of the state to prevent, foil, impede, obstruct, frustrate stateless people from obtaining citizenship. This book also documents not only the labour and persistence of stateless persons, their families, and their advocates, but their innovative and brave strategies to confront the state. Further, many of the stateless persons and their advocates insisted on using legal processes or tactics that maintained their own narrative: that they are citizens and belong in Malaysia. In other words, a significant number of stateless persons and their advocates were adamant that they did not want to be naturalized citizens or be treated as though they were immigrating to Malaysia. Doing so would allow the government to continue casting them as Others and as foreigners. They challenge the need to seek citizenship elsewhere explaining that their ties in another country are fewer, lacking, or non-existent and, therefore, specious.

Implications of Recognizing Ghost Citizens

The ontology of the term ghost citizens allows us to think about statelessness and citizenship differently. First, understanding some stateless persons as ghost citizens allows us to recognize the labels imposed on stateless persons. These labels include foreigner, stranger, illegal, and deviant. Some stateless persons claim they are de facto citizens with genuine, long-standing, effective, and enduring connections to the state. The turn to deem them ghost citizens acts as a reminder to prioritize the experiences and voices of stateless persons and to highlight the impact of law and policy on them.

Second, the identification of stateless persons as ghost citizens gives us the language to upset or disturb narratives about stateless persons. Primarily, stateless persons are denied their own existence and are told that statelessness is a benign, minor, or isolated problem that should be dealt with on a case-by-case basis. The existence of ghost citizens allows us to point to deliberate state action to depict stateless persons as Others. Ghost citizens' lived experiences not only illustrate the conscious denial of the dignity and the very existence of stateless persons, but also how the sufferings of stateless persons are clearly known to those who have the power to eradicate statelessness.[4] The belief that if the state knew exactly what was going on it would make changes is contradicted by the experiences of stateless persons.[5]

Further, ghost citizens provide us with the language to call out questionable findings of facts made with little or no evidence. Recognizing how ghost citizens are constructed raises awareness of the problematic practices of taking judicial notice of one's presumed citizenship and the making of speculative findings about the assumed citizenship of a person. Given international law's definition of statelessness and its turn to legal conferral as proof of one's citizenship, this specious practice should be interrogated, critiqued, and challenged before it becomes more entrenched as a legal or state practice. Beyond the findings of fact, the praxis of finding ghost citizens also points to the problematic approach of demanding the preliminary step stateless persons must take for their applications to be examined on their merits. The steps stateless persons are directed to take include applying for citizenship in another country where there is only a slight opportunity for entitlement to citizenship. This requirement is characterized in law as exhausting one's remedies or seeking alternative remedies. Whatever the case, they are legal devices meant to distract a decision maker from the task at hand, which is to examine the claim before them. It makes the assumptions that all that is needed is the regularization of status with the "proper" state identified documents, and takes for granted the fact that alternative states will see such persons as their citizen and will welcome them.

The term ghost citizens should not be applied universally to all stateless persons or essentialize experiences of stateless persons. Using ghost citizens as an ontology should not contribute to further marginalize migrants who may or may not be stateless. Recognizing stateless persons as non-migrants should not provide fodder for the exclusion or ill treatment of migrants. The device of deeming stateless people ghost citizens is meant for us to consider the experience of some in situ stateless persons, those within their "own" or "home" country. Rather than dividing in situ stateless persons from migrant stateless persons, the conception of the ghost citizen invites further investigation as to the experiences of stateless persons within a variety of contexts and further thinking in identifying and understanding occurrences of statelessness. In doing so, the perspective of the stateless persons should be placed at the forefront.

The incidents of statelessness in situ are important to study and explore. There is an urgency to understanding the manufacturing of statelessness in postcolonial states that might not adhere to human rights regimes. The stripping of citizenship from Rohingya Muslims in Myanmar and the Assamese in India reveal a concerning trend of the creation of statelessness as a method to mark persons as not only Others but as foreigners. In these contexts, the turn to statelessness reinforces, encourages, and justifies the oppression experienced by these racialized communities and have led to disturbing state behaviour that is now being examined in international legal venues. The creation, maintenance, and justification for statelessness and understanding this process can inform how we may acquire evidence and prosecute international humanitarian crimes like genocide and forced displacement, for example.

Informing Theories and Conceptions of Citizenship

The conceptual device of the ghost citizen invites theorists, be they political, legal, or otherwise, to think about state-individual relations and citizenship differently. As Phillip Cole points out, statelessness is often seen as ancillary, tangential, or anomalous in theorizing citizenship.[6] First, this book invites theorists to ground their work in the experiences of stateless persons.

Second, putting stateless persons in the foreground may disturb current notions provided in theory and scholarship. For example, theorists have advocated for doing away with the territorial principle or birthright citizenship as modes to confer citizenship because these methods are arbitrary and contingent.[7] My conversations with stateless persons revealed that territoriality and birthright citizenship were seen as protections and anchors by which they rested their perceived membership in their community. Theorists may argue that this understanding of citizenship entitlement may flow from dominant discourses of enduring practices to mark persons as citizens via territorial links.[8] Stateless persons, however, may respond by saying that any articulation of a theory that diminishes opportunities for stateless persons to be given citizenship should be avoided given the harsh consequences. Further, as this book points out, state practice already devalues "genuine and effective" links, such as residence and place of birth. Should theory encourage such state practices?

Another example is where theorists have opined that the status of citizenship is not needed to access certain rights[9] or that citizenship can and should be disaggregated from its current rights and obligations.[10] However, as I have shown in this book, the lived experiences of stateless persons contest this. Many stateless persons, their parents, and their advocates communicated to me the importance of the status and how everything flows from it. Their sufferings and survival demonstrate a struggle to access basic rights, services, a future, and a life. Further, statelessness is not overstated but a violent, oppressive, and sometimes persecutorial existence, especially in the case of in situ statelessness where the rejection, denial or exclusion is felt more deeply because of the genuine and effective links such persons have in the place of their birth or residence.

Theories around citizenship should also be grounded in the experiences of stateless persons, especially as the research relates to racialized minorities in postcolonial contexts. As Lindsey Kingston puts it bluntly, "statelessness isn't a politically neutral occurrence that happens in a vacuum or could impact anyone; statelessness affects *certain* people because they were deemed unworthy of membership and rights protection in their community."[11] Indeed, in forming theories regarding states and citizenship, race is often absent in the discussion. Charles Mills states that "We would expect that those who have historically been the beneficiaries of racial injustice would tend to have less interest in exploring the topic than those who have been its victims."[12] Mills finds that the construction of theory as raceless is pervasive. Tendayi Bloom writes that while "Liberalism's founding fathers developed theories that explicitly justified racialized exclusions of certain people from consideration — and indeed supported extremes of treatment of people thereby excluded" there were some that rallied against this.[13] This book therefore puts forward a particular apparition of the stateless person; that in situ stateless people are necessarily racialized, "Othered" and deemed foreign due to their inability to blend or perform through the currency of the dominant group's language, culture, or religion. Further, the research here calls for a more careful attentiveness to not only stateless persons but racialized persons.

Along these lines, this book also invites future work to further investigate the construction of the "indigenous" or "native" person. As Kamal Sadiq points out, "the foundation of colonial rule relied on a graded, racialized, and hierarchical conception of membership to the imperial center. Each of these claims to territory and empire created a racial hierarchy of colonial subjects vis-à-vis one another."[14] Sadiq argues that "the legacies of divide-and-rule colonialism and subsequent emergent nationalism and majoritarianism gave rise to the legal tensions between *jus soli* (birthright) citizenship and *jus sanguinis* (blood based) citizenship."[15] Theories of citizenship should therefore not only be grounded in the stateless experience but also recognize the colonial vestiges of racial categorization and hierarchy in law and nation-building, and therefore how "indigeneity" is conceived and utilized.

In interrogating "indigeneity" however, this book does not discount or disavow pluralistic conceptions of citizenship and law and, in fact, encourages us to consult and investigate what lessons we can learn from Indigenous legal traditions from a variety of Indigenous communities. In this sense, the turn to ghost citizens serves as a call to explore the salience of relationships, especially those between states and individuals and the default turn to the state for recognition.

Jennifer Nedelsky writes that "Relationships are central to people's lives – to who we are, to the capacities we are able to develop, to what we value, what we suffer, and what we are able to enjoy."[16] She argues that the relationship dimension of human experience should be central to the concepts and institutions by which we organize our collective lives.[17] As Hadley Friedland writes in relation to Cree legal traditions, "each individual existing and inextricably connected within a network of relationships" informs legal thought and practice — this should inform the wider legal thought on how communities can and should be formed.[18] Examining interactions and fostering harmonious relationships necessitates a legal order that is more decentralized and less vertical. Val Napoleon has written about reconciliation between Canada and Indigenous peoples and shows that rethinking legal orders is about developing a flexible overall framework where all persons might be able to express and describe how laws apply to their present-day problems.[19] Zainab Amadahy states that "Understanding the world through a Relationship Framework … we don't see ourselves, our communities, or our species as inherently superior to any other, but rather see our roles and responsibilities to each other as inherent to enjoying our life experiences."[20] She claims that relationships create accountability and responsibility.[21] This book hopes to further these conversations and calls for conceptions of citizenship to be framed around relations and attending to them responsibly.

Fuelling Innovation

Much of the advocacy efforts have focused on tweaking nationality laws, ratifying the Statelessness Conventions, and turning to human rights principles. This book argues that while these efforts should be lauded, the weight given to law-as-text and a rights-based framework to diminish and prevent statelessness may be disproportionate for several reasons. First, there is little uptake in the human rights regimes espousing rights to citizenship by states with significant stateless populations.

Second, even where there is some lip service paid or adherence to the principles aspiring to prevent and reduce statelessness, such efforts are trumped by the state's prerogative to decide who are citizens. Ultimately, in a contest of rights in an unbalanced relationship, states claim that they have the last word on who its citizens are. Given the Westphalian configuration of states and borders in the world, there is little the stateless person can do to overcome this structural barrier and not much that human rights regimes may do for them.

Third, as the encounters in this book show, we cannot take for granted the idea that states will act in bona fide ways to change systems or resolve situations that produce statelessness. Instead, states may perform their adherence to the movement to eradicate statelessness through public statements and promises to amend laws, but the lived experiences of stateless persons illustrate that the occurrences of statelessness are predominantly off the text. They are experienced through the issuance of identity documents, over government counters, in courtrooms and in the public discourse about foreigners.

Along this thinking, the figure of the ghost citizen invites us to take our gaze off the law-as-text, and the typical legal venues as the primary place to ponder how statelessness occurs and how to resolve cases of statelessness. For example, in discussing Indigenous legal traditions, Darcy Lindberg writes:

> Such issues of "legitimacy" are a result of the dominance of legal positivism in Western legal thought … Eve Darian-Smith suggests that there is a tendency within Western legal systems to assume:

> (1)[t]hat legal meaning is found strictly within legal texts, reports, and documents, (2) that law is almost wholly addressed in formal legal arenas such as courtrooms, governmental assemblies and places of legal adjudication, (3) that law should be described in the vocabularies of European-based languages, primarily English, and (4) common law and civil law legal systems are preferred.[22]

As discussed throughout this book, the law is experienced in a multitude of ways and in various places for stateless persons, including in public discourse, at the government counter, and even in their faces and bodies. Critical race scholars have taught us to look at how law is experienced and what that experience tells us about law. The ghost citizen is poking at the façade of legality. In lifting the veil, we may uncover a nation-building project interested in maintaining the social positioning of a dominant group above other racialized groups.

This book does not provide complete answers for how to move past these barriers and, in fact, invites radical thinking about the harms of state structures and borders. This research invites innovation in rethinking the way we form our communities. In the interim, this book provides a starting point by increasing the understanding of the experiences and the manifestations of statelessness, especially among those who are in situ. Future work may investigate how we increase accountability and respect in state-to-person encounters and what role the rule of law can play in tempering the invocation of the state prerogative. In the courtroom, we can call out the concerning trend to make factual findings without firm evidence that stateless people are citizens elsewhere. At the government counter, we may look at increasing transparency and accountability and create ways to monitor interactions or venues for stateless persons to submit their complaints. We can also think about crafting and providing modes of interruption and interrogation in public discourse, policy, legal submissions, and in the everyday interaction that are meaningful for stateless persons in their interactions with the state. We can talk radically of ridding borders, state recognition, and indeed, the state as it exists now.

Rewriting Pontianak's Story

This book started with the retelling of an infamous folktale — the story of a maligned woman who became the ghost Pontianak. The tale of the ghost citizen, told in this book, is inspired by Pontianak. Like Pontianak, ghost citizens are feared, misunderstood, and unwelcome. Both tell tragic stories about loss, death, and a wayward existence. These ghosts are hard to purge despite many tactics used to expunge them from the world of the living.

In my version, Pontianak is stuck in the in-between and does not want to leave because she is searching for her baby so she can give them citizenship. The baby, like many children, is stateless because of their mother's race, foreign citizenship, and lack of marriage to their Malaysian father. The baby's mother is not around to substantiate their identity but Pontianak wants to be. Pontianak floats in purgatory, worrying about the child she has left behind and their fate. I rewrite the ending of the ghost story, showing Pontianak where her baby is sleeping to allow her to tuck a birth certificate, a passport, or a citizenship certificate in its swaddle. It is her last task to aid her baby in acquiring not only their identity but their citizenship. It is only after this act of love that Pontianak can stop haunting people in her search for her baby. She leaves the life of limbo and finally rests.

This is my hope for the millions of stateless persons, many of whom are children, all over the world. My hope is that the journey has begun for stateless persons to move from the precipice of the afterlife to the land of the living. I hold out for the possibility that stateless persons will be recognized as kin, and that we will work to reconfigure our communities and relations to each other with honesty, respect, and compassion.

APPENDIX

Table 1: Statelessness in Reported Case Law

Case Type	Number
Detention	3
Military service	1
Mixed marriages or relationships; lack of marriage registration; no marriage	11
Abandoned or adopted children	8
Pre-Independence	3
Issues with documentation, evidence or proof of entitlement to citizenship (not including abandoned or adopted children)	3
Family law – dna test to determine paternity	2
Change of religion on documentation	3
Other (including Indigenous citizenship)	2
Total	36

Table 2: Cases of Statelessness

	Case Type	Told By	Number
1	Pre-Independence	Lawyers	2
		NGOS	2
		Total	4
2	Issues with documentation, evidence, or proof of entitlement to citizenship (not including abandoned or adopted children)	Stateless persons	5
		Paralegals	1
		Lawyers	3
		Academics	1
		NGOS	1
		Total	11
3	Mixed marriages; lack of marriage registration; no marriage	Stateless persons	8
		Lawyers	10
		NGOS	2
		Total	20
4	Abandoned or adopted children	Stateless persons	3
		Lawyers	5
		NGOS	7
		Total	15

	Case Type	Told By	Number
5	Indigenous persons	Paralegals	1
		Academics	1
		Total	2
6	Migrants and refugees	Stateless persons	2
		Academics	2
		NGOs	4
		Total	8
	Total		60

Note: NGO = nongovernmental organization

Table 3: Stateless Persons Interviewed

Anonymous Indicator	Circumstances Leading to Statelessness	Parents	How Person Discovered Stateless Status	Ethnicity
1S	Chinese father had second relationship (no marriage) with Filipino woman.	Chinese father with Malaysian citizenship and Filipino mother.	13 years old when applying for the Identification Card	Chinese Filipino
2S	Mother lost identity documents (from pre-independence).	Malaysian citizens of Indian Tamil descent.	Has always known but tried to rectify as 24-year-old when attempting to register her own birth and obtain birth certificate	Indian Tamil
3S	Adopted.	Only knows birth mother is Filipino. Adopted parents both Malaysian citizens.	12 years old when applying for Identification Card	Malay
4S	Child born before marriage registered.	Malaysian father of Indian Tamil descent and Indonesian mother.	Parents knew since birth due to difficulties registering birth	Indian Tamil and Indonesian

Anonymous Indicator	Circumstances Leading to Statelessness	Parents	How Person Discovered Stateless Status	Ethnicity
5S	Adopted.	Speculates biological mother was Filipino. Adoptive Chinese parents are Malaysian citizens.	12 years old when applying for Identification Card	Half-Filipino
6S	Lost or no documents.	Father is Chinese and mother is Indian. Both deceased and were Malaysian citizens.	18 years old now. Has not been able to go to school for some time or take exams due to lack of identification and citizenship	Chinese Indian
7S	Parents came as migrants; born in Malaysia. Living in Malaysia for over 10 years.	Indonesian parents.	Has not been able to go to school. Attending private religious school funded by a political party	Indonesian
8S	Father a permanent resident of Malaysia for 39 years and mother is Indonesian. Migrated from Indonesia. All five children born in Malaysia.	Indonesian mother. Father does not know if he has Indonesian citizenship.	Five children have not been able to go to school	Indonesian
9S	Child was born before marriage was registered.	Father was Chinese with Malaysian citizenship (now deceased) and mother is Thai.	Had issues registering birth. Two younger siblings not stateless	Chinese Thai
10S	Child was born before parents were married.	Mother is Malaysian of Chinese descent and Father is Chinese.	Had issues registering child in school. Child not aware of stateless status	Chinese

Anonymous Indicator	Circumstances Leading to Statelessness	Parents	How Person Discovered Stateless Status	Ethnicity
11S	Child born after marriage registered.	Father is Malaysian of Chinese descent and mother is a foreigner (citizenship or race not known).	Found out child stateless when registering son's birth	Chinese and unknown
12S	Child born outside of wedlock. Father was still married to first wife and divorce not finalized before child born with second partner.	Father is Malaysian (Chinese) and mother is Chinese (China).	Found out when registering child's birth	Chinese
13S	Child born in Thailand of Malaysian father (Chinese) and Thai mother.	Father is Malaysian (Chinese) and mother is Thai.	Found out when brought daughter back to Malaysia and tried to register her birth	Chinese Thai
14S	Mother (30 years old) who is stateless and has two stateless children.	Mother's mother is of Indian descent but has Malaysian citizenship. On birth certificate, no information about father. Father unknown.	Had issues since birth certificate stated citizenship unknown. Mother's birth certificate clearly states mother is citizen	Indian
15S	63-year-old woman who has permanent residence but no citizenship.	Mother is Malaysian citizen (Indian descent). She has three siblings who have Malaysian citizenship.	Lost her birth certificate and was not able to get a new one	Indian

Appendix 181

Anonymous Indicator	Circumstances Leading to Statelessness	Parents	How Person Discovered Stateless Status	Ethnicity
16S	33-year-old woman who was not born in a hospital and not issued a birth certificate at birth (in 1985).	Father is Malaysian of Indian descent and mother was adopted; she did not possess a birth certificate or identity card.	Had no birth certificate until 2009. Could not get one since her mother did not have any documents. Four other siblings have citizenship despite having the same parents	Indian
17S	Adopted child who had acquired birth certificate from doctor's clinic (fraudulent document).	Chinese adoptive parents. Biological mother was Chinese and not married. Not sure what citizenship and ethnicity biological father was.	Parents unknowingly acquired fraudulent birth certificate from clinic when child was adopted. When child tried to get IC at 12, birth certificate was seized	Chinese
18S	Child's birth registered late because marriage registered late.	Father is Malaysian (Chinese) and mother is Indonesian from Bali.	Mother has been trying to register the child for some time but has been forced to wait	Chinese Indonesian
19S	Child born before marriage registered.	Muslim woman; got married abroad in Thailand and had a child before marriage was registered.	At registration rally because heard about it through political party communication	Malay Muslim

Table 4: Lawyers. Paralegals, NGO representatives, and Academics Interviewed

Anonymous Indicator	Profession	Encounters with Stateless Persons	Cases
Paralegals			
1PL	Day job is as an insurance salesperson but volunteers with local political office to help stateless persons	Had worked in a member of Parliament's office for a number of years where constituents came to ask for help to get citizenship. Has seen fifty cases in 9 years with only approximately 20% success rate. Brought many stateless persons to me to interview	**Case 1**: Woman is 7th child in a family who wanted to get married but could not because she had no documentation. After a lot of work obtaining documentation for the hospital she was born in, she was able to get identity documents
2PL	Previously an MP and now runs social services through state funded organization	Assists persons in catchment area in citizenship applications in Kuala Selangor. Travelled to Sarawak to assist 150 Iban people to obtain identity cards	
Lawyers			
1L	Public interest lawyer for an NGO	Statelessness cases come through community and political referrals	**Case 1**: Thai woman married a Malaysian man. At time of birth of child, parents were not married. Subsequently, mother left. Applied for citizenship but courts say citizenship follows mother if parents not married. Case at Federal Court now **Case 2:** Three generations of stateless persons: grandmother, daughter, and grandchildren. Grandfather dead. Settled outside of court after judge placed pressure on Attorney General to do so

Anonymous Indicator	Profession	Encounters with Stateless Persons	Cases
			Case 3: Parents are Malaysian (Indian descent) but children were born in India. Parents registered children late at the Embassy of Malaysia in India. The government challenged issue of citizenship all the way
Case 4: Child was abandoned and adopted by a family. Family engaged in an unofficial adoption and obtained fake papers. There was no information as to where the child came from. Adoption had to be done properly but citizenship not given in new birth certificate. Going through courts now
Case 5: Person born pre-independence to parents who have Malaysian citizenship but birth was not registered.
2L	Family law specialist who had clients seeking to adopt stateless persons	Clients asking for help to adopt or resolve citizenship issue. Also gives summary advice. In one case, had to advise and advocate to foreign embassies as to why a child does not have any documentation and why the child should still travel with the family	**Case 1:** Father was Malaysian and mother Thai. They had a customary marriage in Thailand but it was not legal anywhere. Mother disappeared and father came to lawyer to obtain legal rights over the child. Even though the child was his biological child, the lawyer proceeded to help father adopt child. When new birth certificate was issued, child was stateless. Decision on birth certificate was going to be challenged. Lost contact with client after lawyer asked client to obtain DNA evidence
Case 2: Father was Malaysian and mother was Chinese. Same situation where helping parents adopt child and trying to get new birth certificate that would say child is a citizen

Anonymous Indicator	Profession	Encounters with Stateless Persons	Cases
			Case 3: Church approached lawyer to help get Rohingya stateless child to Germany to obtain free medical treatment for a severe respiratory problem. There was no way of getting the baby to travel because she had no access to travel documents and United Nations High Commissioner for Refugees was not issuing the documents to attest the baby was a refugee. Baby stayed in Malaysia and received help through the Church. **Case 4**: Child born before parents married. Father is Malaysian (Indian descent) and mother is Thai. Helped with getting declaration of legitimacy. Four-year ordeal and child may not be able to go to school. Thai mother wants to go back to Thailand, but the child doesn't want to. Marriage is on the rocks
3L	Lawyer who does pro bono statelessness work.	With law firm; has done about ten pro bono cases and given a lot of summary advice.	Has done cases involving Malay Muslim, Chinese and Indian people. Right now, all cases deal with Chinese who have married foreign women from Indonesia, Thailand, Cambodia, and the Philippines. **Case 1:** Parents unmarried. Father was Malaysian citizen (Indian descent) and mother was Filipino but could not be traced (not in child's life). Originally had birth certificate that listed citizenship status but when tried to get passport, was issued another birth certificate that said not citizen. Application for citizenship denied and was appealed. High Court granted citizenship, and appeal by government was rejected.

Anonymous Indicator	Profession	Encounters with Stateless Persons	Cases
			Case 2: Father is Malaysian (Chinese descent) and mother is Filipino. Case where parents not married and despite DNA evidence, during legitimacy proceedings, judge commented that father should adopt the child even though child is biological child of father. Case heading to the Federal Court. **Case 3:** Adopted child with biological parents as father is Malaysian citizen and mother Indonesian. Case going through courts. **Case 4:** 30-year-old man whose father is Malaysian citizen (Indian descent) and mother unknown. There is no trace of the mother. Father raised him but unable to obtain citizenship despite DNA evidence.
4L	Lawyer doing work with an NGO assisting with stateless persons.	Mainly helped stateless children through adoption process.	**Case 1:** Child was born before parents were married (father is Malaysian citizen of Indian descent and mother is Indonesian). Applied for declaration of legitimacy for child. Forced to abandon relief of citizenship to get legitimacy. Now trying to obtain citizenship. **Case 2:** Child born before parents were married (father is Malaysian citizen of Indian descent and mother is Papua New Guinean). Not reported case. Legitimacy granted but not citizenship. Relief for citizenship withdrawn. Now applying for citizenship through registration office with declaration of legitimacy.

Anonymous Indicator	Profession	Encounters with Stateless Persons	Cases
5L	Lawyer who was approached by client with personal problem of stateless child.	Client came with family problem. Gives summary advice. Lots of cases don't go forward after lawyer gives advice.	**Case 1:** Abandoned child was adopted by Malaysian parents of Chinese descent. The clinic the child was adopted from gave the couple fake adoption papers unbeknownst to the parents. When the child applied for his Identification Card at the age of 12, he discovered stateless status. The child's birth certificate was deemed fraudulent, and child was issued new one stating child not citizen. Child red-flagged as registration office noted that child did not look Chinese. Decision on birth certificate was judicially reviewed successfully. This case attracted attention of other people and other clients came forward. **Case 2:** Two cases involving two siblings who are stateless. Adoptive parents Chinese. Birth certificates after adoption stated not citizens. Judicially reviewed decision and resolved.
6L	Lawyer who works pro bono with NGO on statelessness cases.	Heard someone talking about statelessness on a panel and approached NGO to help. NGO focuses on helping those of Indian descent obtain citizenship.	**Case 1:** Father is Malaysian (Indian descent) and married to an Indonesian woman. Mother left after child was born. Father was biological father but had no legal rights. Lawyer tried to have grandmother adopt child, but court denied the application because it would effectively make father and daughter siblings on paper. Proceeded to have father adopt the child even with DNA evidence indicating biological link.
7L	Lawyer who worked previously at firm that represented stateless persons.	Assisted senior lawyers.	See 5L for cases.

Appendix   187

Anonymous Indicator	Profession	Encounters with Stateless Persons	Cases
8L	Lawyer working with NGO on statelessness issues.	Has given a lot of summary advice to stateless persons and also represented some through courts. Advocating politically for stateless persons after learning from a political party of constituents asking for help.	**Case 1:** Adopted child whose father is of Malaysian (Chinese) descent and mother Thai. Going through courts now.
Academics and Researchers			
1A	Academic who researches international law.	Touches upon citizenship issues tangentially.	Citizenship is a politically sensitive issue.
2A	Academic who works with NGOs on statelessness issues.	Academic who researches and works with stateless populations.	**Case 1:** Spoke with Ambassador of the Philippines about a stateless woman who was a waitress with no documents. She was born in Malaysia and spoke no Tagalog. Was able to assist her in getting passport but issue with travelling because confusion as to why she did not have an entry stamp into Malaysia.
1PHD	PhD student.	Dissertation on stateless persons in Malaysia.	Interviewed 100 stateless persons mainly in Sabah. Confirmed that many cases arise out of persons not registering births, marriages, or having appropriate documentation.
NGOS			

Anonymous Indicator	Profession	Encounters with Stateless Persons	Cases
1NGO	International NGO.	Works predominantly on refugee issues and intersects with stateless refugees.	**Case 1:** Malaysian father and Papua New Guinean mother — see 4L. Engaged in mapping project of stateless persons of Indian descent in Malaysia. Identified the following as stateless: · Those working at plantations before Malaysian independence (mostly of Indian descent) · Baja Laut (nomadic population) · Filipino refugees · Migrant workers from the Philippines and Indonesia · Indigenous people
2NGO	NGO that helps street kids.	Helping kids and discovering they are stateless. Discovered there is a market for babies. Founder of NGO adopted a stateless child that could not be sold to anyone.	**Case 1**: Founder's child is an abandoned stateless baby who was sold to her. Daughter is 10 years old and still stateless today. **Case 2:** Two stateless kids with Malaysian father and Indonesian mother. Children were adopted. Biological father in prison and mother is untraceable. Adoptive mother could not handle kids and abandoned them. A US couple wanted to adopt but was prevented because only Muslims can adopt Muslim children. US couple converted. When applying for adoption, court denied the adoption to foreign couple based on fear that couple would just convert back to Christianity. US adoption was denied as well. Children now entering early teens.
3NGO	Former employee of a network of NGOs.	NGOs in network working with stateless persons.	**Case 1:** 70-year-old man in detention. See 7NGO. **Case 2**: Aware of cases of stateless persons of Filipino descent deported to the Philippines even though they never set foot there. People agree to getting deported because it is better than staying in detention. Some come back to Malaysia.

Note: NGO = nongovernmental organization

Anonymous Indicator	Profession	Encounters with Stateless Persons	Cases
4NGO	Representative of international organization.	Works predominantly with refugees.	Aware of stateless persons in detention. People get picked up because they don't have identification. Not everyone gets refugee document from United Nations High Commissioner for Refugees and that problem creates limbo and grey zones for people.
5NGO	International organization that works on statelessness.	Experience working with stateless persons.	International organization that worked with local organizations to conduct mapping exercises.
6NGO	Lawyer who started an NGO that is an umbrella group of children's organizations.	Engages in out of court advocacy work for stateless children. Refers cases to lawyers.	**Case 1:** Child born when parents were not married. Parents married for 10 years now, and child is now 12. Father is Malaysian (of Chinese descent) and mother Filipino. **Case 2:** Adoption of a child with no documents. Nothing known about father, and little know about mother. Declarations provided from people that the baby had been given over. Has not reached court yet. **Case 3**: Grandmother, mother, and child all stateless. Not actually stateless but lacking documents. Grandmother's husband got drunk and destroyed all documents. All were granted citizenship after they went to court. **Case 4**: Domestic worker from the Philippines had baby in Malaysia before she married. Status in limbo. Aware of stateless populations: · Filipinos in Sabah who lived in Malaysia for generations · Children of mixed marriages · Children born of parents before married with mixed nationalities · People of Indian descent who came to work in Malaysia before independence · Chinese children born of polygamous families where multiple marriages not legally recognized

Anonymous Indicator	Profession	Encounters with Stateless Persons	Cases
7 NGO	Civil society network engaged in advocacy, capacity building, research and awareness raising on several issues.	Focused on immigration detention and encountered stateless persons in detention or through work with organization in network.	**Case 1:** Boy abandoned by parents at Thailand-Malaysia border. Grew up in Malaysia and was detained at age 14 for two years; part of the time was spent in solitary confinement. Not able to track down parents. Was just picked up on a random check. Unsure if still in detention. **Case 2:** 70-year-old Chinese man detained. Had no documents and is not in government system despite saying he was born in Malaysia. Placed a newspaper ad trying to find someone to identify the man but no one came forward.
8 NGO	NGO deals with abandoned children.	Operates a baby hatch for abandoned children who are undocumented and therefore stateless.	For abandoned babies, when registering birth, their birth certificate defaults to not a citizen. **Case 1:** Personal story of NGO worker who adopted two kids born to a domestic worker from the Philippines. Malaysia did not give citizenship but was able to give citizenship from her own country in Europe. Aware of many cases of baby abandonment for specific reasons, some of which are as follows: · Foreign workers having children while in Malaysia · Women having children out of wedlock · Women too young to raise a child · Children rescued from baby-selling rackets
9 NGO	Network of many Muslim organizations that works on development and social and economic issues.	Works with refugees and migrants.	

Appendix

Anonymous Indicator	Profession	Encounters with Stateless Persons	Cases
10NGO	Founder of NGO that helps street children.	Encountered stateless children among children NGO services and adopted an abandoned baby that was being sold on the black market.	**Case 1**: Children adopted are stateless and NGO is still trying to get citizenship for them after many years.
11NGO	NGO that provides legal services to refugees, and community and empowerment programs.	Encountered through providing services for Rohingya refugees. Commented that United Nations High Commissioner for Refugees and government treats refugees as people using Malaysia as a transit point to other resettlement locations, however, many refugees don't see Malaysia as transit but as final destination.	**Case 1:** Rohingya woman in Malaysia since 1986. No hope of her getting citizenship. Has lived in Malaysia since she was five years old. Spoke in general about how Rohingya don't even realize statelessness and are just trying to survive.
12NGO	NGO that provides services to Indian Tamil community.	Encountered by providing services to community.	Mapping of Indian Tamils who are stateless and helping to register them.
13NGO	NGO that provides services to remote locations in Sabah.	Encountered in helping persons in Sabah.	Providing paralegal assistance to stateless in Sabah.

ENDNOTES

CHAPTER 1

1. Yuen Ben Lee Adrian, "The Villainous *Pontianak*? Examining Gender, Culture and the Power in Malaysian Horror Films," *Pertanika Journal of Social Sciences & Humanities* 24, 4 (2016): 1431. See also the work of Avery F. Gord, *Ghostly Matters: Haunting and the Sociological Imagination* (Minneapolis: University of Minnesota Press, 2008).
2. Adrian, "The Villainous *Pontianak*?" 1434.
3. Adrian, "The Villainous *Pontianak*?" 1440.
4. Adrian, "The Villainous *Pontianak*?" 1440.
5. The phrase "own country" comes from Article 12(4) of the International Covenant of Civil and Political Rights and is discussed in more detail in Chapter 3.
6. Interview with 1S. For this study, I anonymized the names of the participants and labelled them with a letter and number system where each person received their own number and then a moniker of S (stateless person or a family member of a stateless person), L (lawyer), PL (paralegal), A (academic), and NGO (nongovernmental organization).
7. Interview with 3S.
8. Interview with 2S.
9. Interview with 6NGO.
10. Interview with 1NGO.
11. See for example, Tretsetsang v Canada, 2016, FCA 175; Budlakoti v Canada, 2015, FCA 139; See also Daiva Stasiulis, "The Extraordinary Statelessness of Deepan Budlakoti: The Erosion of Canadian Citizenship Through Citizenship Deprivation," *Studies in Social Justice* 11, no. 1 (2017): 1.
12. bell hooks, *Teaching to Transgress: Education as the Practice to Freedom* (London: Routledge, 1994), 61.
13. See William Conklin, *Statelessness: The Enigma of the International Community* (Oxford: Hart Publishing, 2014), 67.
14. Conklin, *Statelessness*, 67.
15. John H. Currie, *Public International Law*, second edition, (Toronto: Irwin Law, 2008). See also Derek Croxton, "The Peace of Westphalia of 1648 and the Origins of Sovereignty," *The International History Review* 21, no. 3 (1999): 569. While many trace the beginning of the international world order as we know it today to the Peace of Westphalia, scholars acknowledge that the concepts of the state system and state sovereignty were not simply constructed and applied at this specific point. An interstate system that was already developing or in existence was sanctioned or confirmed out of necessity because of a consequence of negotiating peace and not as an endorsement of the idea of sovereignty. Croxton explains that the ideas of state sovereignty emerged as the dominant organizing function of the Peace of Westphalia because of the growing recognition of a historical fact that European states were organizing themselves in this way.
16. See, for example, Catherine Dauvergne, *Making People Illegal: What Globalization Means for Migration and Law* (Cambridge: Cambridge University Press, 2008);

Charles Taylor, "Nationalism and Modernity" in *The Morality of Nationalism*, eds. Robert McKim and Jeff McMahan (Oxford: Oxford University Press, 1997); Margaret Somers, *Genealogies of Citizenship: Markets, Statelessness and the Right to Have Rights* (Cambridge: Cambridge University Press, 1998).

17 Amar Bhatia, "Re-Peopling in a Settler-Colonial Context: The Intersection of Indigenous Laws of Adoption with Canadian Immigration Law," *AlterNative* 14, no. 4 (2018): 343.

18 Amar Bhatia, "We are All Here to Stay? Indigeneity, Migration, and 'Decolonizing' the Treaty Right to Be Here" *Windsor Yearbook of Access to Justice* 13, no. 2 (2013): 63.

19 See Rita Dhamoon, "A Feminist Approach to Decolonizing Anti-Racism: Rethinking Transnationalism, Intersectionality, and Settler Colonialism," *Feral Feminisms*, no. 4 (Summer 2015): 27; Andrea Smith, "American Studies without America: Native Feminisms and the Nation-State" *American Quarterly*, 60, no. 2 (2008): 311–12.

20 Dhamoon, "A Feminist Approach," 23; see also Bonita Lawrence and Enakshi Dua, "Decolonizing Antiracism" *Social Justice* 32, no. 4 (2005): 120.

21 Dhamoon, "A Feminist Approach," 23 (original emphasis); see also Lawrence and Dua, "Decolonizing Antiracism," 120.

22 Dhamoon, "A Feminist Approach," 30; see also Jodi Byd, *The Transit of Empire: Indigenous Critiques of Colonialism* (Minnesota: Minnesota University Press, 2011), 67.

23 Lawrence and Dua, "Decolonizing Antiracism," 123.

24 "Ending Statelessness," UNHCR, accessed August 15, 2023, http://www.unhcr.org/stateless-people.html.

25 "Ending Statelessness within 10 Years," UNHCR.

26 Gábor Gyulai, "Statelessness in the EU Framework for International Protection." *European Journal of Migration and Law* 14, no. 3 (2012): 279.

27 The Gambia v Myanmar, The International Court of Justice (ongoing).

28 Aslan Tajuddin, "Statelessness and Ethnic Cleansing of the Rohingyas in Myanmar: Time for Serious International Intervention," *Journal of Asia Pacific Studies* 4, no. 4 (2018): 442; Nyi Nyi Kyaw, "Unpacking the Presumed Statelessness of Rohingyas," *Journal of Immigration & Refugee Studies* 15, no. 3 (2017): 269.

29 Reece Jones, "Agents of Exception: Border Security and the Marginalization of Muslims in India," *Environment and Planning* 27, no. 5 (2009):879.

30 Jones, "Agents of Exception," 879; Tajuddin, "Statelessness and Ethnic Cleansing," 10; Kyaw, "Presumed Statelessness of Rohingyas," 10.

31 Phillip Cole, "Insider Theory and the Construction of Statelessness" in *Understanding Statelessness*, eds. Tendayi Bloom, Katherine Tonkiss, and Philip Cole (New York: Routledge, 2017), 258–61; Tendayi Bloom, *Noncitizenism: Recognizing Noncitizen Capabilities in a World of Citizens* (London: Routledge, 2018); Kelly Staples, *Retheorizing Statelessness: A Background Theory of Membership in World Politics* (Edinburgh: Edinburgh University Press, 2012).

32 Conklin, *Statelessness*; Michelle Foster and Hélene Lambert, *International Refugee Law and the Protection of Stateless Persons* (Oxford University Press, 2019); Paul Weis, *Nationality and Statelessness in International Law* (The Netherlands: Sijthoff & Noordhoff, 1979).

33 Carol Batchelor, "Transforming International Legal Principles into National Law:

The Right to a Nationality and the Avoidance of Statelessness," *Refugee Survey Quarterly* 25, no. 3 (2006): 8; Carol Batchelor, "Stateless Persons: Some Gaps in International Protection," *International Journal of Refugee Law* 7, no. 2 (1995): 232; Alice Edwards and Laura Van Waas, eds, *Nationality and Statelessness under International Law* (Cambridge: Cambridge University Press, 2014).

34 Patrick Hayden, "From Exclusion to Containment: Arendt, Sovereign Power and Statelessness," *Societies without Borders* 3, no. 2 (2008): 248.

35 Lindsey Kingston, "Worthy of Rights: Statelessness as a Cause and Symptom of Marginalisation" in *Understanding Statelessness*, eds. Tendayi Bloom, Katherine Tonkiss, and Philip Cole (New York: Routledge, 2017), 17; Lindsey Kingston, *Fully Human: Personhood, Citizenship, and Rights* (Oxford University Press, 2019); Katherine Tonkiss, *Migration and Identity in a Post-National World* (Palgrave Macmillan, 2013).

36 See, for example, Kristy Belton, *Statelessness in the Caribbean* (Philadelphia: University of Pennsylvania Press, 2017); Bridget Wooding, "Contesting Dominican Discrimination and Statelessness," *Peace Review* 20, no. 3 (2008): 366.

37 See, for example, Anne Brekoo, "Statelessness in the European Union," *Statelessness and Citizenship Review* 2, no. 1 (2020): 24; Catherine Sawyer and Brad Blitz, eds., *Statelessness in the European Union: Displaced, Undocumented, Unwanted* (Cambridge University Press, 2011); Laura van Waas, "Fighting Statelessness and Discriminatory Nationality Laws in Europe," *European Journal of Migration and Law* 14, no. 3 (2012): 243.

38 Rodziana Mohamed Razali, *Safeguarding Against Statelessness at Birth: International Law and Domestic Legal Frameworks of ASEAN Member States* (Singapore: Springer, 2023).

39 See for example, Elena Fiddian-Qasmiyeh, "On the Threshold of Statelessness: Palestinian Narratives of Loss and Erasure," *Ethnic and Racial Studies* 39, no. 2 (2016): 301; Danielle Jefferis, "Institutionalizing Statelessness: The Revocation of Residency Rights of Palestinians in East Jerusalem," *International Journal of Refugee Law* 24, no. 2 (2012): 202; Noa Gani and Amal Jamal, "Half-Statelessness and Hannah Arendt's Citizenship Model: The Case of Palestinian Citizens of Israel," *Mediterranean Politics* 27, no. 3 (2020): 391.

40 Deepak Singh, *Stateless in South Asia: The Chakmas between Bangladesh and India* (Sage Publications India, 2010); Subrata Sankar Bagchi, "The Great Betrayal: Potential Statelessness After Living Decades in Mother India," *International Journal of Hindu Science and Religious Studies* 1, no. 2 (2017): 122; Sanjay Roy, "Bangladeshi Refugees in India: Statelessness, Rehabilitation and Citizenship," *Year Book of International Humanitarian & Refugee Law* 2 (2002): 207; Anushka Sharma, "Contextualizing Statelessness in the Indian Legal Framework: Illegal Immigration in Assam," *Christ University Law Journal* 8, no. 2 (2019): 25.

41 See for example, A. K. M. Ahsan Ullah, "Rohingya Crisis in Myanmar: Seeking Justice for the 'Stateless,'" *Journal of Contemporary Criminal Justice* 32, no. 3 (2016): 285; Katherine Southwick, "Preventing Mass Atrocities Against the Stateless Rohingya in Myanmar: A Call for Solutions," *Journal of International Affairs* 68, 2 (2015): 137; Mahanam Bhattacharjee Mithun, "Ethnic Conflict and Violence in Myanmar: The Exodus of Stateless Rohingya People," *International Journal on Minority & Group Rights* 25, no. 4 (2018): 647; Syeda Naushin Parnini, Mohammad Redzuan Othman, and Amer Saifude Ghazali, "The Rohingya Refugee Crisis and Bangladesh-Myanmar Relations," *Asian and Pacific Migration Journal* 22, no.

1 (2013): 133; Arcana Parashar and Jobair Alam, "The National Laws of Myanmar: Making of Statelessness for the Rohingya," *International Migration* 57, no. 1 (2018): 94.

42 Solomon Oseghale Momoh, Hanneke van Eijken, and Cedric Ryngaert, "Statelessness Determination Procedures: Towards a Bespoke Procedure for Nigeria," *Statelessness & Citizenship Review* 2, no. 1 (2020): 86.

43 For example, Janepicha Cheva-Isarakul, "'Diagnosing' Statelessness and Everyday State Illegibility in Northern Thailand," *Statelessness & Citizenship Review* 1, no. 2 (2019): 214.

44 For example, Julia Hess, "Statelessness and the State: Tibetans, Citizenship and Nationalist Activism in a Transnational World," *International Migration* 44, no. 1 (2006): 79.

45 Susan Kneebone, Brandais York, and Sayomi Ariyawansa, "Degrees of Statelessness: Children of Returned Marriage Migrants in Can Tho, Vietnam," *Statelessness & Citizenship Review* 1, no. 1 (2019): 69.

46 See, for example, Nandita Sharma, *Home Economics: Nationalism and the Making of 'Migrant Workers' in Canada* (Toronto: University of Toronto Press, 2006); Nicola Yeates, *Globalizing Care Economies and Migrant Workers: Explorations in Global Care Chains* (New York: Palgrave MacMillan, 2009); Martin Ruhs and Bridget Anderson, *Who Needs Migrant Workers? Labour Shortages, Immigration and Public Policy* (Oxford University Press, 2010); Nicole Constable, *Maid to Order in Hong Kong: Stories of Migrant Workers*, second edition, (Ithaca, New York: Cornell University Press, 2007); Roland Sintos Coloma, Bonnie McElhinny, Ethel Tungohan, John Paul C. Catungal, and Lisa M. Davidson, eds., *Filipinos in Canada: Disturbing Invisibility* (Toronto: University of Toronto Press, 2012); Geraldina Polanco and Sarah Zell, "English as a Border-Drawing Matter: Language and the Regulation of Migrant Service Worker Mobility in International Labor Markets," *Journal of International Migration and Integration* 18 (2017): 267–89.

47 See, for example, Amy Nethery and Stephanie Silverman, eds., *Immigration Detention: The Migration of a Policy and its Human Impact* (London: Routledge, 2015); Mary Bosworth, *Inside Immigration Detention* (Oxford: Oxford University Press, 2014); Daniel Wilsher, *Immigration Detention: Law, History, Politics* (Cambridge: Cambridge University Press, 2012); Nicholas de Genova and Nathalie Peutz, eds., *The Deportation Regime: Sovereignty, Space and the Freedom of Movement* (Durham, London: Duke University Press, 2010).

48 See for example, Joseph Carens, "Aliens and Citizens: The Case for Open Borders," *The Review of Politics* 49 (1987): 251; Joseph Carens, *The Ethics of Immigration* (New York: Oxford University Press, 2013); Linda Bosniak, "Being Here: Ethical Territoriality and the Rights of Immigrants" in *Citizenship Between Past and Future*, eds. Engin Isin, Peter Nyers, and Bryan Turner, (London: Routledge, 2008); Cecilia Menjívar and Daniel Kanstroom, eds., *Constructing Immigrant "Illegality": Critiques, Experiences and Responses* (New York: Cambridge University Press, 2014); Catherine Dauvergne, *Making People Illegal: What Globalization Means for Migration and Law* (Cambridge: Cambridge University Press, 2008).

49 See for example, Shauna Labman, *Crossing Law's Border: Canada's Refugee Resettlement Program* (Vancouver: UBC Press, 2019); Nur Masalha, ed., *Catastrophe Remembered: Palestine, Israel and the Internal Refugees: Essays in Memory of Edward Said (1935–2003)* (New York: Zed Books, 2005); Matthew Gibney, *The Ethics and Politics of Asylum: Liberal Democracy and the Response to Refugees*

(Cambridge: Cambridge University Press, 2004); Natasha Saunders, *International Political Theory and the Refugee Problem* (Routledge, 2018); Megan Bradley, *Refugee Repatriation: Justice Responsibility and Redress* (Cambridge: Cambridge University Press, 2013).

50   For example, with regards to "denizens" see Rainer Baubock, "Changing the Boundaries of Citizenship: The Inclusion of Immigrants in Democratic Politics," in *From Aliens to Citizens: Redefining the Status of Immigration in Europe*, ed. Rainer Baubock (Vienna: Avery, 1994), 199–232; Tomas Hammer, *Democracy and the Nation State: Aliens Denizens, and Citizens in a World of International Migration* (Aldershot: Avebury, 1990).

51   Irene Bloemraad, "Does Citizenship Matter?" in *The Oxford Handbook of Citizenship*, eds. Ayelet Shachar, Rainer Bauböck, Irene Bloemraad, and Martin Vink, (London: Oxford University Press, 2017).

52   Bloom, *Noncitizenism*.

53   See for example, Kristy Belton, *Statelessness in the Caribbean* (Philadelphia: University of Pennsylvania Press, 2017); Bloom, *Noncitizenism*; Tendayi Bloom, Katherine Tonkiss, and Phillip Cole, eds., *Understanding Statelessness* (New York: Routledge, 2017); Edwards and van Waas, *Nationality and Statelessness*; Foster and Lambert, *International Refugee Law*; Kingston, *Fully Human*.

54   Thomas Hobbes, *Leviathan* (Cambridge: Cambridge University Press, 1991); Aristotle, *The Politics of Aristotle and the Constitution of Athens,* ed. S. Everson (Cambridge: Cambridge University Press, 1996).

55   Jean Jacques Rousseau, *On the Social Contract with Geneva Manscript and Political Economy*, ed. Roger D. Masters (New York: St Martin's Press, 1978).

56   J. G. A. Pocock, "The Ideal of Citizenship since Classical Times" in *Theorizing Citizenship*, ed. Ronald Beiner (Albany: State University of New York Press, 1995); Michael Walzer, *Spheres of Justice: A Defence of Pluralism and Equality* (New York: Basic Books, 1983). Generally, liberal political theory finds conflict in differences borne from individual interests and divergent moral perspectives and focuses on a relationship between individual or state where the state provides the principal universal identification ideal of citizenship. Republicanism finds problems arising from interdependence, domination, and collective self-government, and promotes ideals of civic virtue, autonomy, and nondomination.

57   Carole Pateman, *The Disorder of Women, Democracy, Feminism and Political Theory* (Cambridge: Polity Press, 1989).

58   Iris Marion Young, *Inclusion and Democracy* (Oxford University Press, 2000); Melissa Williams, *Voice, Trust and Memory: Marginalized Groups and the Failings of Liberal Representation* (New Jersey: Princeton University Press, 1998); Martha Nussbaum, *The Cosmopolitan Tradition: A Noble but Flawed Ideal* (Cambridge: Belknap Press, 2019).

59   Will Kymlicka and Wayne Norman, "Return of the Citizen: A Survey of Recent Work on Citizenship Theory," *Ethics* 104, no. 2 (1994): 352.

60   David Miller, *Citizenship and National Identity* (Cambridge: Polity Press, 2000); Anna Stilz, *Liberal Loyalty: Freedom, Obligation, and the State* (New Jersey: Princeton University Press, 2009).

61   Jürgen Habermas, *Between Facts and Norms: Contributions to a Discourse Theory of Law and Democracy* (Cambridge: MIT Press, 1996); Jürgen Habermas, *The Inclusion of the Other: Studies in Political Theory* (Cambridge: MIT Press, 1998).

62 Thomas Pogge, *World Poverty and Human Rights: Cosmopolitan Responsibilities and Reforms* (Cambridge, UK: Polity, 2002).
63 Arash Abizadeh, "On the Demos and its Kin: Nationalism, Democracy, and the Boundary Problem," *American Political Science Review* 106, no. 4 (2012): 867; Arash Abizadeh, "Democratic Legitimacy and State Coercion: A Reply to David Miller," *Political Theory* 38, no. 1 (2010): 121; Arash Abizadeh, "Democratic Theory and Border Coercion: No Right to Unilaterally Control Your Own Borders," *Political Theory* 36, no. 1 (2008): 37; Robert Goodwin, "Enfranchising All Affected Interests, and Its Alternatives," *Philosophy & Public Affairs* 35, no. 2 (2007): 40.
64 Margaret Moore, *A Political Theory of Territory* (New York: Oxford University Press, 2015).
65 Joseph Carens, *Culture, Citizenship and Community: A Contextual Exploration of Justice as Evenhandedness* (New York: Oxford University Press, 2000); Abizadeh, "On the Demos and its Kin"; Veit Bader, "Citizenship and Exclusion: Radical Democracy, Community and Justice," *Political Theory* 23, no. 2 (1995): 211.
66 Rainer Bauböck, "Stakeholder Citizenship: An Idea Whose Time Has Come?" (Paper commissioned by the Transatlantic Council on Migration for a meeting in Ballagio, Italy, April 2008), 2. https://www.migrationpolicy.org/sites/default/files/publications/Baubock-FINAL%5B1%5D.pdf.
67 Bauböck, *Transnational Citizenship*.
68 Bloemraad, "Does Citizenship Matter?" 524–25.
69 Belton, *Statelessness in the Caribbean*; Jillian Blake, "Race-Based Statelessness in the Dominican Republic" in *Understanding Statelessness*, eds. Tendayi Bloom, Kathering Tonkiss, and Phillip Cole (New York: Routledge, 2017), 102–13; Zahra Al Barazi and Jason Tucker, "Challenging the disunity of statelessness in the Middle East and North Africa" in *Understanding Statelessness*, eds. Tendayi Bloom, Katherine Tonkiss and Phillip Cole (New York: Routledge, 2017), 87–98; Oscar Gakuo Mwangi, "Statelessness, Ungoverned Spaces and Security in Kenya" in *Understanding Statelessness*, eds. Tendayi Bloom, Kathering Tonkiss, and Phillip Cole (New York: Routledge, 2017), 117–30; Jamie Chai Yun Liew, ""Homegrown Statelessness in Malaysia and the Promise of the Principle of Genuine and Effective Links," *Statelessness and Citizenship Review* 1, no. 1 (2019): 95; Subin Mulmi and Sara Shneiderman, "Citizenship, Gender and Statelessness in Nepal: Before and After the 2015 Constitution" in *Understanding Statelessness*, eds. Tendayi Bloom, Kathering Tonkiss, and Phillip Cole (New York: Routledge, 2017), 135–52; Phillip Cole, "Insider Theory and the Construction of Statelessness," 255–59.
70 Phillip Cole, "Insider Theory and the Construction of Statelessness" in *Understanding Statelessness*, eds. Tendayi Bloom, Katherine Tonkiss, and Phillip Cole (New York: Routledge, 2017), 255–59.
71 Phillip Cole, "Insider Theory and the Construction of Statelessness," 260.
72 Phillip Cole, "Insider Theory and the Construction of Statelessness," 260.
73 Bloom, *Noncitizenism*, 1.
74 Kingston, *Fully Human*, 6.
75 Staples, *Retheorising Statelessness*, 5.
76 Amar Bhatia, "Re-Peopling in a Settler-Colonial Context: The Intersection of Indigenous Laws of Adoption with Canadian Immigration Law," *AlterNative* 14, no. 4 (2018): 343.
77 Bloom, *Noncitizenism*, 6.

78 Bloom, *Noncitizenism*, 16.
79 Samantha Balaton-Chrimes, "Statelessness, Identity Cards and Citizenship as Status in the Case of Nubians of Kenya," *Citizenship Studies* 18, no. 1 (2014): 17.
80 Kamal Sadiq, "Postcolonial Citizenship" in *The Oxford Handbook of Citizenship*, eds. Ayelet Shachar, Rainer Bauböck, Irene Bloemraad, and Martin Vink, (London: Oxford University Press, 2017): 178.
81 Sadiq, "Postcolonial Citizenship," 180.
82 Sadiq, "Postcolonial Citizenship," 181.
83 Erin Aeran Chung, "Citizenship in Non-Western Contexts" in *The Oxford Handbook of Citizenship*, eds. Ayelet Shachar, Rainer Bauböck, Irene Bloemraad, and Martin Vink, (London: Oxford University Press, 2017): 432.
84 Hannah Arendt, *The Origins of Totalitarianism* (New York: Harcourt Brace Jovanovich, 1979), 56.
85 Hannah Arendt, *The Origins of Totalitarianism*, 56.
86 Hannah Arendt, *The Origins of Totalitarianism*, 56 (original emphasis).
87 David Owen, "Citizenship and Human Rights" in *The Oxford Handbook of Citizenship*, eds. Ayelet Shachar, Rainer Bauböck, Irene Bloemraad, and Martin Vink, (London: Oxford University Press, 2017): 247.
88 David Owen, "Citizenship and Human Rights," 248.
89 Michael Weinman, "Arendt and the Legitimate Expectation for Hospitality and Membership Today," *Moral Philosophy and Politics* 5, no. 1 (2018): 127.
90 Ayten Gundogdu, *Rightlessness in the Age of Rights* (London: Oxford University Press, 2015): 9.
91 Samuel Moyn, *Human Rights and the Uses of History*, second edition, (London: Verso, 2018).
92 See, for example, Bloom, *Noncitizenism*; Neil Walker, "The Place of Territory in Citizenship" in *The Oxford Handbook of Citizenship,* eds. Ayelet Shachar, Rainer Bauböck, Irene Bloemraad, and Martin Vink, (London: Oxford University Press, 2017): 554.
93 Chung, "Citizenship in Non-Western Contexts," 434. Chung writes: "the rights associated with liberal democratic citizenship in the West are not necessarily guaranteed for nationals in non-Western countries, even in established democracies."
94 Chung, "Citizenship in Non-Western Contexts," 434.
95 Kingston, *Fully Human*, 58.
96 Owen, "Citizenship and Human Rights," 258.
97 Linda Bosniak, "Status Non-Citizens," 322; Owen, "Citizenship and Human Rights," 260.
98 Kathleen Arnold, *Homelessness, Citizenship and Identity* (New York: State University of New York Press, 2004), 8.
99 Kathleen Arnold, *Homelessness, Citizenship and Identity*, 469 and 471.
100 Duncan Ivison, Paul Patton, and Will Sanders, "Introduction" in *Political Theory and the Rights of Indigenous Peoples*, eds. Ducan Ivison, Paul Patton, and Will Sanders (Cambridge: Cambridge University Press, 2000), 2.
101 Costas Douzinas, "The Paradoxes of Human Rights," *Constellations* 20, no. 1 (2013): 60–61.
102 Spade, *Normal Life,* 91.
103 Sara Ahmed, *Strange Encounters: Embodied Others in Post-Coloniality* (London: Routledge, 2000); Sherene Razack, ed., *Race, Space and the Law: Unmapping a*

White Settler Society (Toronto: Between the Lines, 2002); Arnold, *Homelessness, Citizenship and Identity*.

104 Kamal Sadiq, "When Being 'Native' is not Enough: Citizens as Foreigners in Malaysia," *Asian Perspective* 33, 1 (2009): 14–15; Aryn Martin and Michael Lynch, "Counting Things and People: The Practices and Politics of Counting," *Social Problems* 56, 2 (2009): 243–66.

105 See for example Laura Madokoro, *Elusive Refuge: Chinese Migration in the Cold War* (Harvard University Press, 2016) where she discusses how Chinese migrants resisted the label refugees, for example.

106 See, for example, Sara Ahmed, *Strange Encounters: Embodied Others in Post-Coloniality* (New York: Routledge, 2000); Rita Kaur Dhamoon, "Relational Othering: Critiquing Dominance, Critiquing the Margins," *Politics, Groups and Identities* 9, 5 (2019): 873; Mae Ngai, "Birthright Citizenship and the Alien Citizen," *Fordham Law Review* 75 (2006): 2521; Petra Molnar Diop, "The 'Bogus' Refugee: Roma Asylum Claimants and Discourses of Fraud in Canada's Bill C-31," *Refuge* 30, 1 (2014): 67; Megan Gaucher, *A Family Matter: Citizenship, Conjugal Relationships, and Canadian Immigration Policy* (Vancouver: UBC Press, 2018); Shauna Labman, *Crossing Law's Border: Canada's Refugee Resettlement Program* (Vancouver: UBC Press, 2020); Harsha Walia, *Border and Rule: Global Migration, Capitalism and the Rise of Racist Nationalism* (Halifax: Fernwood Publishing, 2021); Abigail Bakan and Daiva Stasiulis, *Negotiating Citizenship: Migrant Women in Canada and the Global System* (New York: Palgrave MacMillan, 2003).

107 Arnold, *Homelessness, Citizenship and Identity*, 7. See also Ngai, "Birthright Citizenship and the Alien Citizen," 2251

108 Alice M. Nah, "Negotiating Indigenous Identity in Postcolonial Malaysia: Beyond Being 'Not Quite/Not Malay,'" *Journal for the Study of Race, Nation and Culture* 9, 4 (2003): 511; Charles Hirschman, "The Making of Race in Colonial Malaya: Political Economy and Racial Ideology," *Sociological Forum* 1, 2 (1986): 330; Charles Hirschman, "The Meaning and Measurement of Ethnicity in Malaysia: An Analysis of Census Classifications," *The Journal of Asian Studies* 46, 3 (1987): 555; Timothy Daniels, *Building Cultural Nationalism in Malaysia* (New York: Routledge, 2005).

109 Barbara Andaya and Leonard Andaya, *A History of Malaysia,* third edition, (London: Palgrave, 2017).

110 A. B. Shamsul, "A History of an Identity, an Identity of a History: The Idea and Practice of 'Malayness' in Malaysia Reconsidered," *Journal of Southeast Asian Studies* 32, 3 (2001): 355.

111 Sandra Manickam, "Bridging the Race Barrier: Between 'Sakai' and 'Malay' in the Census Categorisations of British Malaya," *Asian Studies Review* 38, 3 (2014): 372; Hirschman, "Meaning and Measurement of Ethnicity in Malaysia".

112 Juliet Pietsch and Marshall Clark, "Citizenship Rights in Malaysia: The Experience of Social and Institutional Discrimination Among Ethnic Minorities," *Citizenship Studies* 18, 3 (2014): 303; Gabriel Chin, "Regulating Race: Asian Exclusion and the Administrative State," *Harvard Civil Rights-Civil Liberties Law Review* 37 (2002).

113 Harsha Walia, *Border and Rule: Global Migration, Capitalism and the Rise of Racist Nationalism* (Halifax: Fernwood Publishing, 2021): 2.

114 Ahmed, *Strange Encounters*, 22.

115 United Nations, "Sustainable Development Goals Agenda," *United Nations,* accessed August 15, 2023. https://www.un.org/sustainabledevelopment/develop-

ment-agenda/.

116 Jane Caplan and John C. Torpey (eds.). *Documenting the Individual Identity: The Development of State Practices in the Modern World* (Princeton: Princeton University Press, 2001); Mara Loveman, *National Colors: Racial Classification and the State in Latin America* (Oxford: Oxford University Press, 2014.); James Scott, *The Art of Not Being Governed: An Anarchist History of Upland Southeast Asia* (New Haven: Yale University Press, 2009); James Scott, *Seeing Like a State: How Certain Schemes to Improve the Human Condition Have Failed* (New Haven: Yale University Press, 1999); Colin Bennett and David Lyon, *Playing the Identity Card: Surveillance, Security and Identification in Global Perspective* (New York: Routledge, 2008).

117 Marion Fourcade and Kieran Healy, "Classification Situations: Life-Chances in the Neoliberal Era," *Accounting, Organizations and Society* 38 (2013): 559–72.

118 Margaret Franz and Kumarini Silva, "Theorizing Belonging Against and Beyond Imagined Communities" in *Migration, Identity, and Belonging: Defining Borders and Boundaries of the Homeland*, eds. Margaret Franz and Kumarini Silva (New York: Routledge, 2020).

119 Geoffrey C. Bowker and Susan Leigh Star, *Sorting Things Out: Classification and Its Consequences* (Cambridge: The MIT Press, 1999); Pierre Bourdieu, Loic Wacquant, and Samuel Farage, "Rethinking the State: Genesis and Structure of the Bureaucratic Field," *Sociological Theory* 12, 1 (1994): 1–18.

120 Caplan and Torpey, *Documenting the Individual Identity*; Scott, *The Art of Not Being Governed*; Scott, *Seeing Like a State*.

121 Caplan and Torpey, *Documenting the Individual Identity*.

122 Caplan and Torpey, *Documenting the Individual Identity*; Benedict Anderson, *Imagined Communities: Reflections on the Origin and Spread of Nationalism* (London: Verson, 1991); Amanda Cheong, "Immigration and Shifting Conceptions of Citizenship: The Case of Stateless Chinese-Bruneians in Canada" in *New Chinese Migrations: Mobility, Home, Inspirations*, eds. Yuk Wah Chan and Sin Yee Koh (New York: Routledge, 2018), 191–206.

123 Jamie Chai Yun Liew, "We Must Not Allow Stateless People to be Made Outsiders," April 29, 2022. https://theglobeandmail.com/opinion/article-we-must-not-allow-stateless-people-to-be-made-outsiders/.

124 Heba Gowayed, *Refuge: How the State Shapes Human Potential* (Princeton: Princeton University Press, 2022):151.

125 Kimberly Kay Hoang, *Dealing in Desire: Asian Ascendancy, Western Decline and the Hidden Currencies of Global Sex Work* (University of California Press, 2015), 23.

126 Hoang, *Dealing in Desire*, 23

127 Hoang, *Dealing in Desire*, 24.

128 Linda Lumayag, "A Question of Access: Education Needs of Undocumented Children in Malaysia," *Asian Studies Review* 40, 2 (2016): 1.

129 Avyanthi Azis, "Urban Refugees In Graduated Sovereignty: The Experiences of the Stateless Rohingya in the Klang Valley," *Citizenship Studies* 18, 8 (2014): 839.

130 Greg Accialioli, Helen Brunt, and Julian Clifton, "Foreigners Everywhere, Nationals Nowhere: Exclusion, Irregularity and Invisibility of Stateless Bajau Laut in Eastern Sabah, Malaysia," *Journal of Immigration & Refugee Studies* 15, 3 (2017): 232.

131 "Ending Statelessness in Malaysia," UNHCR, accessed August 13, 2023. https://unhcr.org/ending-statelessness-in-malaysia.html.

132 Rodziana Mohamed Razali, Rohaida Nordin and Tamara Joan Duraisingam, "Mi-

gration and Statelessness: Turning the Spotlight on Malaysia," *Pertanika Journal of Social Sciences & Humanities* 25, S (2015): 19.
133 Raymond Mah and Chloe Hwa, "Citizenship for Adopted Children — A Malaysian Perspective," *Mah Weng Kwai & Associates*, January 10, 2013. https://mahwengkwai.com/citizenship-for-adopted-children-a-malaysian-perspective/. This blog discusses the unreported case of Lee Chin Pon; Rodziana Mohamed Razali, "Addressing Statelessness in Malaysia: New Hope and Remaining Challenges," (Working Paper No 2017/9, Institute on Statelessness and Inclusion, 2017).
134 Catherine Allerton, "Contested Statelessness in Sabah, Malaysia: Irregularity and the Politics of Recognition," *Journal of Immigrant & Refugee Studies* 15, 3 (2017): 251.
135 Allerton, "Contested Statelessness in Sabah," 251.
136 Allerton, "Contested Statelessness in Sabah," 251.
137 Allerton, "Contested Statelessness in Sabah," 251 (original emphasis).
138 Catherine Allerton, "Impossible Children: Illegality and Excluded Belonging Among Children of Migrants in Sabah, East Malaysia," *Journal of Ethnic & Migration Studies* 44, 7 (2018): 1081.
139 See for example, Catherine Allerton, "Statelessness and the Lives of the Children of Migrants in Sabah, East Malaysia," *Tilburg Law Review* 19, 1–2 (2014): 26; Avyanthi Azis, "Urban Refugees in a Graduated Sovereignty: The Experiences of the Stateless Rohingya in the Klang Valley," *Citizenship Studies* 18, 8 (2014): 839; Linda Lumayag, "A Question of Access: Education Needs of Undocumented Children in Malaysia," *Asian Studies Review* 40, 2 (2016): 1.
140 See for example, Allerton, "Children of Migrants in Sabah"; Azis, "Urban Refugees in a Graduated Sovereignty"; Lumayag, "A Question of Access: Education Needs of Undocumented Children in Malaysia."
141 Allerton, "Contested Statelessness in Sabah"; Regional Conference on Stateless / Undocumented Children in Sabah Kota Kinabalu, Sabah, Malaysia, Tenaganita (Organization), Asia-Pacific Mission for Migrants, Christian Conference of Asia. Urban Rural Mission, *Acting Today for Tomorrow's Generation* (Kuala Lumpur: Tenagita, 2006); Nando Sigona, "Everyday Statelessness in Italy: Status, Rights, and Camps," *Ethnic and Racial Studies* 39, 2 (2016): 263.
142 Rita Kaur Dhamoon, "Relational Othering: Critiquing Dominance, Critiquing the Margins" *Politics, Groups and Identities* 9, 5 (2019): 2.
143 *1954 Convention Relating to the Status of Stateless Persons*, 28 September 1954, 360 UNTS 117 (entered into force 6 June 1960), article 1.
144 *Convention Relating to the Status of Refugees*, 28 July 1951, 189 UNTS 137 (entered into force 22 April 1954), article 1(A)(2).
145 *Convention against Torture and Other Cruel, Inhuman or Degrading Treatment or Punishment*, 10 December 1984, 1465 UNTS 85 (entered into force 26 June 1987).
146 Department of Statistics Malaysia, *Population Distribution and Basic Demographic Characteristic Report 2010* (Census Report, August 5, 2011). https://www.dosm.gov.my/v1/index.php?r=column/ctheme&menu_id=L0pheU43NWJwRWVSZklWdzQ4TlhUUT09&bul_id=MDMxdHZjWTk1SjFzTzNkRXYzcVZjdz09.
147 Mari Matsuda, "Looking to the Bottom: Critical Legal Studies and Reparations" *Harv CR-CL Rev* 22 (1987): 323.
148 Nandita Sharma, *Home Rule: National Sovereignty and the Separation of Natives*

      and Migrants (Durham, NC: Duke University Press, 2020), 37.
149 Renisa Mawani, *Across Oceans of Law: The Komagatu Maru and Jurisdiction in the Time of Empire* (Duke University Press, 2018): 153.
150 Mawani, *Across Oceans of Law*, 154.
151 Mawani, *Across Oceans of Law*, 156.
152 Mawani, *Across Oceans of Law*, 157.
153 Mawani, *Across Oceans of Law*, 157.
154 Katja Swider, "Why End Statelessness?" in *Understanding Statelessness*, eds. Tendayi Bloom, Katherine Tonkiss, and Philip Cole (New York: Routledge, 2017): 193.

CHAPTER 2

1 Frederic Bouchon, "Truly Asia and Global City? Branding Strategies and Contested Identities in Kuala Lumpur," *Place Branding and Public Diplomacy*, 10 (2014): 6.
2 Nasser Hussain, *The Jurisprudence of Emergency: Colonialism and the Rule of Law* (Ann Arbor: University of Michigan Press, 2003): 3.
3 Piyel Halder, *Law, Orientalism and Postcolonialism: The Jurisdiction of the Lotus Eaters* (London: Routledge, 2007).
4 Edward Said, *Culture and Imperialism* (New York: Vintage, 1994).
5 Jean Lave and Etienne Wenger, *Situated Learning: Legitimate Peripheral Participation* (Cambridge: Cambridge University Press, 1991).
6 See for example, Nandita Sharma, *Home Rule: National Sovereignty and the Separation of Natives and Migrants* (Durham: Duke University Press, 2020); Harsha Walia, *Border & Rule: Global Migration, Capitalism, and the Rise of Racist Nationalism* (Halifax: Fernwood Publishing, 2021).
7 See for example Irfan Ahmad, *Islamism and Democracy in India: The Transformation of Jamaat-E-Islami* (Princeton, NJ: Princeton University Press: 2009); Barak Kalir, *Latino Migrants in the Jewish State: Undocumented Lives in Israel* (Bloomington: Indiana University Press, 2010); Yasemin Soysal, "Limits of Citizenship: Migrants and Postnational Membership in Europe and the Nation State" in *Citizenship, Nationality and Migration in Europe*, eds. David Cesarani and Mary Fulbrook, (London: Routledge, 1994).
8 Roxanne Wheeler, *The Complexion of Race: Categories of Difference in Eighteenth-Eentury British Culture* (Philadelphia: University of Pennsylvania Press, 2000); Frank Reeves, *British Racial Discourse: A Study of British Political Discourse About Race and Race-Related Matters* (New York: Cambridge University Press, 1983).
9 Shamsul A. B., "Ethnicity, Class, Culture, or Identity? Competing Paradigms in Malaysian Studies" *Akademika* 53 (1998): 33.
10 Maria-Eugenia Merino and Cristian Tileaga, "The Construction of Ethnic Minority Identity: A Discursive Psychological Approach to Ethnic Self-Definition in Action," *Discourse and Society* 22, 1 (2011): 86; Kanchan Chandra, "What is Ethnic Identity: A Minimalist Definition." In *Constructivist Theories of Ethnic Politics* (New York: Oxford University Press, 2013).
11 Benedict Anderson, *Imagined Communities: Reflections on the Origin and Spread of Nationalism* (London: Verson, 1991): 5.
12 Anderson, *Imagined Communities*, 6.
13 Margaret Franz and Kumarini Silva, "Theorizing Belonging Against and Beyond Imagined Communities" in *Migration, Identity, and Belonging: Defining Borders*

and *Boundaries of the Homeland*, eds. Margaret Franz and Kumarini Silva (New York: Routledge, 2020): 2.

14 Geoffrey Benjamin, "On Being Tribal in the Malay World" in *Tribal Communities in the Malay World: Historical, Social and Cultural Perspectives*, eds. Geoffrey Benjamin and Cynthia Chou (Leiden and Singapoer: Institute of Southeast Asian Studies/International Institute for Asian Studies, 2002). For example, Geoffrey Benjamin argues that the term "tribal" is more appropriate because the term "indigenous" does not fully capture the social and political issues that attach to certain populations in Malaysia. As well, as discussed in this chapter, some communities have preferences for the exact term they want to be called rather than those foisted upon them through historical or official (political) means.

15 Alice M. Nah, "Negotiating Indigenous Identity in Postcolonial Malaysia: Beyond Being 'Not Quite/Not Malay,'" *Journal for the Study of Race, Nation and Culture* 9, 4 (2003): 514; Kay Anderson, "The Idea of Chinatown: The Power of Place and Institutional Practice in the Making of a Racial Category," *Annals of the Association of American Geographers* 77, 4 (1987): 580.

16 Nah, "Negotiating Indigenous Identity in Postcolonial Malaysia"; Anderson, "The Idea of Chinatown."

17 Nah, "Negotiating Indigenous Identity in Postcolonial Malaysia"; Anderson, "The Idea of Chinatown."

18 Nah, "Negotiating Indigenous Identity in Postcolonial Malaysia."

19 Nah, "Negotiating Indigenous Identity in Postcolonial Malaysia."

20 Barbara Watson Andaya and Leonard Y. Andaya, *A History of Malaysia*, third ed. (London: Palgrave, 2017), 55; Timothy Daniels, *Building Cultural Nationalism in Malaysia* (New York: Routledge, 2005), 19; Charles Hirschman, "The Making of Race in Colonial Malaya: Political Economy and Racial Ideology," *Sociological Forum* 1, 2 (1986): 333.

21 Hirschman, "The Making of Race in Colonial Malaya," 333.

22 Hirschman, "The Making of Race in Colonial Malaya," 333.

23 Hirschman, "The Making of Race in Colonial Malaya," 336.

24 Hirschman, "The Making of Race in Colonial Malaya," 337.

25 Daniels, *Building Cultural Nationalism in Malaysia*, 22. Daniels finds that Chinese migrants worked in British and Chinese owned plantations and tin mines organized under Kongsi dialect associations with Chinese merchants and shopkeepers working in the colonial distribution networks, wholesale and retail trade, and tax collecting. Indian migrants, Daniels finds, worked in plantations and in urban infrastructure projects and notes that "dark-skinned" persons were seen as "a docile, menial laborer or 'coolie.'"

26 Nah, "Negotiating Indigenous Identity in Postcolonial Malaysia," 515; Sharmani Patricia Gabriel, "'After the Break': Re-Conceptualizing Ethnicity, National Identity and 'Malaysian-Chinese' Identities," *Ethnic and Racial Studies* 37, 7 (2014): 1214.

27 Nah, "Negotiating Indigenous Identity in Postcolonial Malaysia." 515–16.

28 Nicholas Dodge, "The Malay-Aborigine Nexus Under Malay Rule," *Bijdragen tot de taal-, land- en volkenkunde / Journal of the Humanities and Social Sciences of Southeast Asia* 137, 1 (1981): 3.

29 Nah, "Negotiating Indigenous Identity in Postcolonial Malaysia," 515–16.

30 Andaya and Andaya, *A History of Malaysia*, 112; Daniels, *Building Cultural Nationalism in Malaysia*, 22. These regional groups included the Bugis, Achenese,

Minangkabau, and Jawi Peranakan, among others
31 Daniels, *Building Cultural Nationalism in Malaysia*, 22.
32 Daniels, *Building Cultural Nationalism in Malaysia*, 22.
33 Daniels, *Building Cultural Nationalism in Malaysia*, 22.
34 Hirschman, "The Making of Race in Colonial Malaya," 456–57.
35 Dodge, "The Malay-Aborigine Nexus Under Malay Rule."
36 Andaya and Andaya, *A History of Malaysia*, 112; Daniels, *Building Cultural Nationalism in Malaysia*, 22.
37 Shamsul A. B., "A History of an Identity, an Identity of a History: The Idea and Practice of 'Malayness' in Malaysia Reconsidered," *Journal of Southeast Asian Studies* 32, 3 (2001): 357.
38 See for example Collin E. R. Abraham, *Divide and Rule: The Roots of Race Relations in Malaysia* (Kuala Lumpur: INSAN, 1997); Kua Kia Soong, "Racial Conflict in Malaysia: Against the Official History," *Race & Class* 49, 3 (2008): 33; Shamsul A. B.,, "Ethnicity, Class, Culture, or Identity?"; Anthony Milner, *The Invention of Politics in Colonial Malaya* (Melbourne: Cambridge University Press, 1994); Anthony Reid, "Understanding Melayu (Malay) as a Source of Diverse Modern Identities," *Journal of Southeast Asian Studies* 32, 3 (2001): 295.
39 Daniels, *Building Cultural Nationalism in Malaysia*, 23.
40 Hirschman, "The Making of Race in Colonial Malaya," 356.
41 Hirschman, "The Making of Race in Colonial Malaya," 356..
42 Hirschman, "The Making of Race in Colonial Malaya," 356. He explains that the "colonial government 'managed' the plural society by trying to maintain the Malay feudal social structure in the countryside and a 'temporary' immigrant population working in the mines, plantations and cities" while atop all of this "perched the European elites who ruled and reaped enormous economic gains."
43 Sandra Manickam, "Bridging the Race Barrier: Between 'Sakai' and 'Malay' in the Census Categorisations of British Malaya," *Asian Studies Review* 38, 3 (2014): 372. See also Charles Hirschman, "The Meaning and Measurement of Ethnicity in Malaysia: An Analysis of Census Classifications," *The Journal of Asian Studies* 46, 3 (1987).
44 Manickam, "Bridging the Race Barrier," 372.
45 Manickam, "Bridging the Race Barrier," 372.
46 Nah, "Negotiating Indigenous Identity in Postcolonial Malaysia," 516.
47 Nah, "Negotiating Indigenous Identity in Postcolonial Malaysia," 516; Hirschman, "The Making of Race in Colonial Malaya," 333.
48 Shamsul A. B., "A History of an Identity, an Identity of a History," 357.
49 Shamsul A. B., "A History of an Identity, an Identity of a History," 357.
50 Shamsul A. B., "A History of an Identity, an Identity of a History," 361.
51 Juliet Pietsch and Marshall Clark, "Citizenship Rights in Malaysia: The Experience of Social and Institutional Discrimination Among Ethnic Minorities," *Citizenship Studies* 18, 2 (2014): 307.
52 Shamsul A. B., "A History of an Identity, an Identity of a History," 364.
53 Shamsul A. B., "A History of an Identity, an Identity of a History," 364.
54 Daniels, *Building Cultural Nationalism in Malaysia*, 28.
55 Gabriel, "'After the Break,'" 1213. See the following for examples of Chinese and Indigenous communities trying to advocate for equal positioning: Kua Kia Soong, *National Culture and Democracy* (Petaling Jaya: Kersani, 1985); Lim Kit Siang,

Malaysia: Crisis of Identity (Petaling Jaya: Democratic Action Party, 1986); Francis Loh Kok Wah, "Modernization, Cultural Revival and Counter-Hegemony: The Kadazans of Sabah in the 1980s" in *Fragmented Vision: Culture and Politics in Contemporary Malaysia,* eds. Fracis Loh Kok Wah (Sydney: Allen and Unwin, 1992), 225–53. For examples on Islamic resurgence in Malaysia, Jomo KS and Ahmad Shabery Cheek, "The Politics of Malaysia's Islamic Resurgence," *Third World Quarterly* 10, 2 (1988): 843; Alias Mohamed, *Malaysia's Islamic Opposition: Past, Present and Future* (Kuala Lumpur: Gateway Publications, 1991).

56 Pietsch and Clark, "Citizenship Rights in Malaysia," 306; Bhikhu Parekh, "British Citizenship and Cultural Difference" in *Citizenship,* ed. G. Andrews, (London: Lawrence and Wishart, 1991), 183–204.
57 Pietsch and Clark, "Citizenship Rights in Malaysia," 306.
58 Pietsch and Clark, "Citizenship Rights in Malaysia," 306.
59 Daniels, *Building Cultural Nationalism in Malaysia*, 30.
60 See for example, *Federal Constitution of Malaysia,* 31 August 1957, amended 20 July 1995, articles 161(b)(a), (b); Yogeswaran Subramaniam, "Ethnicity, Indigeneity and Indigenous Rights: The 'Orang Asli' Experience," *QUT Law Review* 15, 1 (2015): 71–77.
61 Rusaslina Idrus, "From Wards to Citizens: Indigenous Rights and Citizenship in Malaysia," *Political and Legal Anthropology Review* 33, 1 (2010): 90.
62 Idrus, "From Wards to Citizens," 90.
63 Idrus, "From Wards to Citizens," 90.
64 Kamal Sadiq, "When Being 'Native' is not Enough: Citizens as Foreigners in Malaysia," *Asian Perspective* 33, 1 (2009): 14–15.
65 Robert Arakaki, "2008 Malaysian Election: The End of Malaysia's Ethnic Nationalism?" *Asian Politics and Policy* 1, 1 (2009): 79; See also Pietsch and Clark, "Citizenship Rights in Malaysia," 308.
66 Sadiq, "When Being 'Native' is Not Enough": 8.
67 Shamsul A. B., "A History of an Identity, an Identity of a History," 357.
68 Hirschman, "The Making of Race in Colonial Malaya," 331–32.
69 Department of Information, *Demography of Population,* Government of Malaysia, (2016). https://malaysia.gov.my/portal/content/30114.
70 Sin Yee Koh, "How and Why Race Matters: Malaysian-Chinese Transnational Migrants Interpreting and Practicing Bumiputera-Differentiated Citizenship," *Journal of Ethnic and Migration Studies* 41, 3 (2015): 532.
71 Shad Saleem Faruqi, *Document of Destiny: The Constitution of the Federation of Malaysia* (Petaling Jaya: Star, 2008), 93.
72 Shamsul A. B., "Nations-of-Intent in Malaysia" in *Asian Forms of the Nation,* eds. Stein Tonnesson and Han Antlov, (London: Curzon, 1996), 323.
73 Shamsul A. B., "A History of an Identity, an Identity of a History," 364.
74 Gabriel, "'After the break," 1214.
75 Indigenous Working Group on Indigenous Affairs, "Malaysia," IWGIA, accessed August 15, 2023. https://www.iwgia.org/en/malaysia.html.
76 Mahmood Mamdani, *Neither Settler nor Native: The Making and Unmaking of Permanent Minorities* (Boston: Harvard University Press, 2020), 2–17.
77 Yogeswaran Subramaniam, "Ethnicity, Indigeneity and Indigenous Rights," 71; See also Leonard Y. Andaya, "Orang Asli and the Melayu in the History of the Malay Peninsula," *Journal of the Malaysian Branch of the Royal Asiatic Society* 75, 1

(2002): 23; Saroja Dorairajoo, "The Orang Asli of Peninsular Malaysia: Aborigine but Yet Not Bumiputera" (Master's dissertation, Cornell University, 1996).
78 Sadiq, "When Being 'Native' is Not Enough," 5.
79 To explore more on the Chinese in Southeast Asia, see for example Tan Chee Beng, "Nation-Building and Being Chinese in a Southeast Asian State: Malaysia" in *Changing Identities of the Southeast Asian Chinese Since World War II*, eds. Jennifer Cushman and Wang Gungwu, (Hong Kong: Hong Kong University Press, 1988).
80 Gabriel, "'After the break,'" 1211.
81 Gabriel, "'After the break,'" 1211.
82 Gabriel, "'After the break,'" 1211.
83 Nah, "Negotiating Indigenous Identity in Postcolonial Malaysia," 520.
84 Nah, "Negotiating Indigenous Identity in Postcolonial Malaysia," 520.
85 Gabriel, "'After the break,'" 1213.
86 Nah, "Negotiating Indigenous Identity in Postcolonial Malaysia," 520.
87 Gabriel, "'After the break,'" 1215.
88 Gabriel, "'After the break,'" 1215.
89 Gabriel, "'After the break,'" 1215.
90 Gabriel, "'After the break,'" 1215.
91 Gabriel, "'After the break,'" 1215 (original emphasis).
92 Gabriel, "'After the break,'" 1215.
93 Julie Chernov, "Plural Society Revisited: Chinese-Indigenous Relations in Southeast Asia," *Nationalism and Ethnic Politics* 9, 3 (2003): 104.
94 Gabriel, "'After the break,'" 1216.
95 Nah, "Negotiating Indigenous Identity in Postcolonial Malaysia," 519–20; see also Timothy Norman Harper, *The End of Empire and the Making of Malaya* (Cambridge: Cambridge University Press, 1999).
96 Nah, "Negotiating Indigenous Identity in Postcolonial Malaysia," 520; see also Gabriel, "'After the break,'" 1212; Tan Chee Beng, "Nation-Building and Being Chinese in a Southeast Asian State: Malaysia" in *Changing Identities of the Southeast Asian Chinese Since World War II,* eds. Jennifer Cushman and Wang Gungwu, (Hong Kong: Hong Kong University Press, 1988), 56.
97 See also Koh, "How and Why Race Matters," 536, where she provides a summary of historical racial tensions.
98 Nah, "Negotiating Indigenous Identity in Postcolonial Malaysia": 520.
99 Gabriel, "'After the break,'" 1214; see also Kok Wah Loh, Phang Chung Hyap, and Johan Saravanamuttu, *The Chinese Community and Malaysia-China Ties: Elite Perspectives* (Tokyo: Institute of Developing Economies, 1981), 72.
100 Gabriel, "'After the break,'" 1214. For more on cultural citizenship, see Aihwa Ong, "Cultural Citizenship as Subject-Making: Immigrants Negotiate Racial and Cultural Boundaries in the United States," *Current Anthropology* 37, 5 (1996): 737; Aihwa Ong, *Flexible Citizenship: The Cultural Logics of Transnationality* (Durham, NC: Duke University Press, 1999).
101 *Federal Constitution of Malaysia,* 31 August 1957, amended 20 July 1995, article 160.
102 Nah, "Negotiating Indigenous Identity in Postcolonial Malaysia," 521.
103 Nah, "Negotiating Indigenous Identity in Postcolonial Malaysia," 521 (original emphasis).

104 Koh, "How and Why Race Matters," 531. For more on Chinese in Southeast Asia, see Wang Gungwu, "The Study of Chinese Identities in Southeast Asia" in *Changing Identities of the Southeast Asian Chinese since World War II*, eds. Jennifer Cushman and Wang Gungwu, (Hong Kong: Hong Kong University Press, 1988), 1–22; See also Theodora Lam and Brenda S. A. Yeoh, "Negotiating 'Home' and 'National Identity': Chinese Malaysian Transmigrants in Singapore," *Asia Pacific Viewpoint* 45, 2 (2004): 141; Patrick Pillai, *People on the Move: An Overview of Recent Immigration and Emigration in Malaysia* (Kuala Lumpur: Institute of Strategic and International Studies, 1992).

105 Koh, "How and Why Race Matters," 538.

106 Koh, "How and Why Race Matters," 538.

107 Koh, "How and Why Race Matters," 542.

108 Koh, "How and Why Race Matters," 542.

109 Koh, "How and Why Race Matters," 546.

110 Subramaniam, "Ethnicity, Indigeneity and Indigenous Rights," 73

111 Subramaniam, "Ethnicity, Indigeneity and Indigenous Rights," 71-72.

112 Subramaniam, "Ethnicity, Indigeneity and Indigenous Rights," 71.

113 Subramaniam, "Ethnicity, Indigeneity and Indigenous Rights," 71. See also Robert Knox Dentan, Kirk Endicott, Alberto G. Gomes, and A. B. Hooker, *Malaysia and the Original People: A Case Study of the Impact of Development on Indigenous Peoples* (Boston: Allyn and Bacon, 1997); Anthony Williams-Hunt, "Land Conflicts: Orang Asli Ancestral Laws and State Policies" in *Indigenous Minorities of Peninsular Malaysia: Selected Issues and Ethnographies*, ed. Razha Rashid, (Kuala Lumpur: Intersocietal and Scientific, 1995), 36–47.

114 Subramaniam, "Ethnicity, Indigeneity and Indigenous Rights," 73–74; Colin Nicholas, "Organizing Orang Asli Identity" in *Tribal Communities in the Malay World: Historical, Cultural and Social Perspectives*, eds. Cynthia Chou and Geoffrey Bengamin, (Institute of Southeast Asian Studies/International Institute for Asian Studies, 2002), 119.

115 Subramaniam, "Ethnicity, Indigeneity and Indigenous Rights," 84.

116 Subramaniam, "Ethnicity, Indigeneity and Indigenous Rights," 87.

117 Nah, "Negotiating Indigenous Identity in Postcolonial Malaysia," 523–24.

118 Subramaniam, "Ethnicity, Indigeneity and Indigenous Rights," 87.

119 Subramaniam, "Ethnicity, Indigeneity and Indigenous Rights," 88.

120 Nah, "Negotiating Indigenous Identity in Postcolonial Malaysia," 527.

121 Nah, "Negotiating Indigenous Identity in Postcolonial Malaysia," 527.

122 For example, Margaret Roff, *Politics of Belonging: Political Change in Sabah and Sarawak* (Kuala Lumpur: Oxford University Press, 1974); Peter Searle, *Politics in Sarawak, 1970-1975: An Iban Perspective* (Kuala Lumpur: Oxford University Press, 1983); Jayum A Jawan, *The Iban Factor in Sarawak Politics* (Serdang: Pernibit Universiti Pertanian Malaysia, 1993); Alice M Nah, "(Re)mapping Indigenous 'Race'/Place in Postcolonial Peninsular Malaysia," *Geografiska Annaler Series B: Human Geography* 88, 3 (2006): 285.

123 Interview with 1S, appendix in Chapter 5, Table 2, January 28, 2018.

124 Sadiq, "When Being 'Native' is Not Enough," 6: "In 1999, I was standing in a queue at the immigration office in the Malaysian state of Sabah (East Malaysia) when I noticed Malaysian students from Peninsular Malaysia (West Malaysia) filling out immigration forms. We were providing the same biographical details, such as our

name, sex, age address, race, and residential status, and were going through the same immigration procedures, yet I was an international visitor to Sabah and they were Malaysian citizens. The experience seemed counterintuitive to the common view of Malaysia as an integrated multiethnic union … Sabah was treating citizens and foreigners on an equal footing when it came to internal movement within the country."

125 Sadiq, "When Being 'Native' is Not Enough," 11–12.
126 Sadiq, "When Being 'Native' is Not Enough," 12.
127 Sadiq, "When Being 'Native' is Not Enough," 12.
128 Sadiq, "When Being 'Native' is Not Enough," 12.
129 Sadiq, "When Being 'Native' is Not Enough," 20–21.
130 James Chin, "Second-Class Bumiputera? The Taming of the Dayak and Kadazandusun of East Malaysia" in *Misplaced Democracy: Malaysian Politics and People*, ed. Sophie Lemière (Petaling Jaya: Strategic Information and Research Development Centre, 2014): 109.
131 Chin, "Second-Class Bumiputera?" 117.
132 Chin, "Second-Class Bumiputera?" 124. For more on "universal citizenship" see Iris Marion Young, "Polity and Group Difference: A Critique of the Ideal of Universal Citizenship," *Ethics* 99, 2 (1989): 250.
133 Shamsul A. B., "A History of an Identity, an Identity of a History," 331–32. For more on the concept of "imagined communities" see Benedict Anderson, *Imagined Communities: Reflections on the Origin and Spread of Nationalism* (London: Verso, 1983); Partha Chatterjee, *The Nation and Its Fragments: Colonial and Postcolonial Histories* (Princeton: Princeton University Press, 1993).
134 Shamsul A. B., "A History of an Identity, an Identity of a History," 345–46. For more on the political and social history of Malay nationalism, see William Roff, *The Origins of Malay Nationalism* (Kuala Lumpur: University of Malaya Press, 1967); Anthony Milner, *The Invention of Politics in Colonial Malaya* (Melbourne: Cambridge University Press, 1994).
135 Leo Chavez, *Shadowed Lives: Undocumented Immigrants in American Society*, third edition (Wadsworth Cengage Learning, 2013); William Flores, "Introduction: Constructing Cultural Citizenship" in *Latino Cultural Citizenship: Claiming Identity, Space and Rights*, eds. William Flores and Rina Benmayor (Boston: Beacon Press, 1997); Renato Rosaldo, "Cultural Citizenship in San Jose, California," *Polar* 17 (1994); Renato Rosaldo, "Cultural Citizenship, Inequality and Multiculturalism" in *Latino Cultural Citizenship: Claiming Identity, Space, and Rights*, eds. William Flores and Rina Benmayor, (Boston: Beacon Press, 1997).
136 Linda Bosniak, *The Citizen and the Alien* (Princeton: Princeton University Press, 2006), 88.
137 See for example, Luis Moreno, "State and Stateless Nationalism, Old and New Diversities, and Federal Governance" in *The Multicultural Dilemma: Migration, Ethnic Politics and State Intermediation*, ed. Michelle Williams (Abingdon: Routledge, 2013).
138 For more on nationalism see Rogers Brubaker, "In the Name of the Nation: Reflections on Nationalism and Patriotism," *Citizenship Studies* 8, 2 (2004): 115; Nazaruddin Hj Mohd Jali, Ma'rof Redzuan, Asnarulkhadi Abu Samah, Ismail Hj Mohd Rashid, *Malaysian Studies: Nationhood and Citizenship* (Petaling Jaya: Pearson Prentice Hall, 2003); Eleonore Kofman, "Citizenship, Migration and the

Reassertion of National Identity," *Citizenship Studies* 9, 5 (2005): 453; David Miller, *Citizenship and National Identity* (Malden, MA: Polity Press, 2000).

139 Chee-Beng Tan, "Indigenous People, the State and Ethnogenesis: A Study of the Communal Associations of the 'Dayak' Communities in Sarawak, Malaysia," *Journal of Southeast Asian Studies* 28, 2 (1997): 279.

140 David Pearson, "Theorizing Citizenship in British Settler Societies," *Ethnic and Racial Studies* 25, 6 (2002): 989; Sharma, *Home Rule*.

CHAPTER 3

1 Alice Edwards and Laura Van Waas (eds.) *Nationality and Statelessness under International Law* (Cambridge: Cambridge University Press, 2014): 1.

2 Mark Manly, "UNHCR's Mandate and Activities to Address Statelessness" in *Nationality and Statelessness*, eds. Alice Edwards and Laura van Waas (Cambridge: Cambridge University Press, 2014): 95.

3 UN Ad Hoc Committee on Statelessness and Related Problems, *First Sesssion: Summary Record of the Second Meeting*, published 26 January 1950, E/AC.32/SR.2, para 2.

4 Manly, "UNHCR's Mandate," 99–111.

5 Manly, "UNHCR's Mandate," 106.

6 Paul Weis, *Nationality and Statelessness in International Law* (Alphen aan den Rijn: Sijthoff & Noordhoff, 1979); William Conklin, *Statelessness: The Enigma of the International Community* (Oxford: Hart Publishing, 2014); Alice Edwards and Laura Van Waas, (eds.) *Nationality and Statelessness under International Law* (Cambridge University Press, 2014).

7 *1954 Convention Relating to the Status of Stateless Persons*, 28 September 1954, 360 UNTS 117 (entered into force 6 June 1960).

8 *1961 Convention on the Reduction of Statelessness*, 30 August 1961, 989 UNTS 175 (entered into force 13 December 1975).

9 *1954 Convention*, article 1.

10 Laura Van Waas, "The UN Statelessness Conventions" in *Nationality and Statelessness under International Law*, eds., Alice Edwards and Laura Van Waas (Cambridge University Press, 2014), 71–72.

11 Van Waas, "The UN Statelessness Conventions," 71–72.

12 International Law Commission, "Commentary to the Draft Articles on Diplomatic Protection with Commentaries," *Yearbook of the International Law Commission* 2 (2006).

13 Van Waas, "The UN Statelessness Conventions," 74–75.

14 Van Waas, "The UN Statelessness Conventions," 74–75.

15 Van Waas, "The UN Statelessness Conventions," 74–75.

16 Conklin, *Statelessness*, 141.

17 Conklin, *Statelessness*, 81.

18 Manly, "UNHCR's Mandate," 95–96.

19 Carol A. Batchelor, "Stateless Persons: Some Gaps in International Protection," *International Journal of Refugee Law* 7, 2 (1995): 232.

20 Carol A. Batchelor, "Stateless Persons," 232.

21 UNHCR, *Handbook on Protection of Stateless Persons under the 1954 Convention Relating to the Status of Stateless Persons*, United Nations High Commissioner for

Refugees, 2014, 16, para 37.
22 Van Waas, "The UN Statelessness Conventions," 81.
23 Conklin, *Statelessness,* 140–41.
24 UN Ad Hoc Committee on Statelessness and Related Problems, *United Kingdom: Draft Proposal of Article 1*, 17 January 1950, E/AC.32/L.2.
25 UN Ad Hoc Committee on Statelessness and Related Problems, *United Kingdom: Draft Proposal of Article 1*, 17 January 1950, E/AC.32/L.2.
26 Foster and Lambert, *International Refugee Law*, 40–46.
27 Foster and Lambert, *International Refugee Law*, 32, 41.
28 Carol Batchelor, "Stateless Persons: Some Gaps in International Protection," *International Journal of Refugee Law* 7 (1995); James Hathaway and Michelle Foster, *The Law of Refugee Status*, second edition (Cambridge: Cambridge University Press, 2014), 65.
29 Foster and Lambert, *International Refugee Law*, 32–33.
30 Foster and Lambert, *International Refugee Law*, 39.
31 *Universal Declaration of Human Rights*, 10 December 1948, UNGA 217 A(III) [*UDHR*].
32 *UDHR*, article 2.
33 *International Covenant on Civil and Political* Rights, 19 December 1966, 999 UNTS 171 (entered into force 23 March 1976) [ICCPR], article 12.
34 ICCPR, articles 12 and 16.
35 ICCPR, article 16.
36 ICCPR, for example, articles 2, 26.
37 ICCPR, article 16.
38 ICCPR, article 24.
39 *International Covenant on Economic Social and Cultural Rights*, 16 December 1966, 993 UNTS 3 (entered into force 3 January 1976) [ICESCR].
40 *Convention on the Rights of the Child*, 20 November 1989, 1577 UNTS 3 (entered into force 2 September 1990), article 3, 21 [CRC].
41 CRC, art 7.
42 CRC: art 8.
43 CRC: art 2.
44 International Convention on the Elimination of All Forms of Racial Discrimination, 21 December 1965, 660 UNTS 195 (entered into forced 4 January 1969) [ICERD].
45 ICERD: art 5(d)(iii).
46 ICERD: art 1.
47 The Institute on Statelessness and Inclusion, *The World's Stateless*, ISI, March 2020, 78. https://www.institutesi.org/worldsstateless.pdf.
48 Association of Southeast Asian Nations, "Member States," ASEAN, accessed August 16, 2023. https://asean.org/asean/asean-member-states/.
49 UN High Commissioner for Refugees, "States Party to the Statelessness Conventions," accessed August 16, 2023. https://www.refworld.org/docid/54576a754.html.
50 See for example, Michael Caster, "Eliminating Statelessness in Southeast Asia: ASEAN Can Take Some Reasonable Measures to Address the Plight," accessed August 16, 2023. https://thediplomat.com/2016/05/eliminating-statelessness-in-southeast-asia/.

51 "Malaysia Calls for ASEAN to Coordinate Aid for Rohingya at Myanmar Crisis Talks," *South China Morning Post*, December 19, 2016, https://www.scmp.com/news/asia/southeast-asia/article/3074423/myanmar-army-sues-reuters-news-agency-criminal-defamation.
52 Tani, "ASEAN Aims to Express 'Concern.'"
53 Tani, "ASEAN Aims to Express 'Concern.'"
54 Rodziana Mohamed Razali, *Safeguarding Against Statelessness at Birth*: International Law and Domestic Legal Frameworks of ASEAN Member States (Singapore: Springer, 2023), 142
55 ICCPR: article 24(3); CRC, articles 7(1)–(2); *Convention on the Elimination of All Forms of Discrimination against Women*,18 December 1979, 1249 UNTS 13 (entered into force 3 September 1981) [CEDAW], art 9(1); ICERD, article 1(3); *UDRH*, article 15.
56 Conklin, *Statelessness*, 157; *Vienna Convention on the Law of Treaties*, 23 May 1969, 1155 UNTS 331, (entered into force 27 January 1980), article 19(c).
57 Conklin, *Statelessness*, 153–54.
58 Conklin, *Statelessness*, 153–54.
59 Conklin, *Statelessness*, 154.
60 CRC, article 8(2).
61 ICCPR, article 2(3).
62 ICERD, article 2(1).
63 Organization of African Unity, *Convention Governing the Specific Aspects of Refugee Problems in Africa*, 10 September 1969, 1001 UNTS 45 (entered into force 20 June 1974), article 11(1), V.
64 Conklin, *Statelessness*, 155.
65 ICERD, article 1(2).
66 ICERD, article 1(3).
67 Conklin, *Statelessness*, 158: "The ramification of the limitation clauses is threefold. For one thing, a state's internal jurisdiction, not international standards, determine the 'vital interests' of the state. Second, it is domestic institutions that get to ascertain whether a stateless person has contradicted the state's vital interests. Third, executive action inside the reserved domain is not justiciable regarding nationality matters. Once again, the right to nationality and to legal personhood are conflated into internal state jurisdiction as representative of the international community's residuary."
68 ICCPR, article 24(3); CRC, articles 7(1)–(2); *CEDW*, article 9(1); ICERD, article 1(3); *UDHR*, article 15.
69 Peter J. Spiro, "A New International Law of Citizenship," *American Journal of International Law* 105, 4 (2011): 717, 718, 720; See also Case of the Yean and Bosico Children v The Dominican Republic (2008), Inter-Am Ct HR, (Ser C) No 130: para 140.
70 Spiro, "A New International Law of Citizenship," 722.
71 Nottebohm Case (Liechtenstein v Guatemala), (1955) ICJ Rep 4, 13.
72 *Nottebohm Case*, 13.
73 *Nottebohm Case*, 13.
74 *Nottebohm Case*, 16.
75 *Nottebohm Case*, 22–25.
76 *Nottebohm Case*, 23.

77 Case No A/18 [1984], 5 Iran–US Claims Tribunal Reports 251, para 5; "Claims of Dual Nationals in the Modern Era: The Iran–United States Claims Tribunal," *Michigan Law Review* 83, 3 (1984): 601; Abraham Kannoff, "Dueling Nationalities: Dual Citizenship, Dominant and Effective Nationality, and the Case of Anwar Al-Aulaqi," *Emory Law Review* 25, 3 (2011): 1390–1.
78 Charles N. Brower and Jason D. Brueschke, *The Iran–United States Claims Tribunal* (The Hague, Boston, London: Martinus Nijhoff 1998), 321.
79 John R. Dugard, Special Rapporteur, *First Report on Diplomatic Protection*, UN Doc, A/CN.4/506 (March 7 and April 20, 2000), para 106.
80 Robert Sloane, "Breaking the Genuine Link: The Contemporary International Legal Regulation of Nationality," *Harvard International Law Review* 50 (2009).
81 *Case No A/18* [1984], 5 Iran-US Claims Tribunal Reports, 251, 265–66.
82 Rubenstein and Lenagh-Maguire, "More or Less Secure?" 286–87.
83 ICCPR, article 12(4).
84 Marc Bossuyt, *Guide to the "Travaux Preparatoires" of the International Covenant of Civil and Political Rights* (Springer, 1987), 260; Commission on Human Rights, 5th Session (1949), 6th Session (1950), 1952 A/2929 Chapter VI: para 58–59.
85 Bossuyt, Guide to the Travaux Preparatoires, 261; Commission on Human Rights, 5th Session (1949), 6th Session (1950), 8th Session (1952), A/2929, Chapter VI: para 60.
86 Bossuyt, Guide to the Travaux Preparatoires, 262; Third Committee, 14th Session (1959), A/4299: para 17.
87 United Nations Human Rights Committee, Stewart v Canada, 58th Session, Annex, Communication No 538/1993, UN Doc CCPR/C/58/D/538/1993 [*Stewart*].
88 *Stewart,* para 2.1.
89 *Stewart,* para 2.2.
90 *Stewart,* para 2.2.
91 *Stewart,* para 3.4.
92 *Stewart,* para 3.4.
93 *Stewart,* para 5.1.
94 *Stewart,* para 5.3.
95 *Stewart,* para 9.3.
96 *Stewart,* para 12.4.
97 *Stewart,* para 12.4.
98 *Stewart,* para 12.5.
99 *Stewart,* para 12.5.
100 *Stewart,* para 12.8.
101 *Stewart,* para 18-19.
102 *Stewart,* para 20-21.
103 *Stewart,* para 20-21.
104 *Stewart,* para 21.
105 *Stewart,* para 22.
106 *Stewart,* para 22.
107 *Stewart,* para 23.
108 *Stewart,* para 25.
109 *Stewart,* para 26.
110 United Nations Human Rights Committee, Canepa v Canada, 59th Session, Annex,

Communication No 538/1993, UN Doc CCPR/C/59/D/538/1993, para 11.3 [*Canepa*].
111 United Nations Human Rights Committee, Madafferi v Australia, 81st Session, Annex, Communication No 1011/2001, UN Doc CCPR/C/81/D/1011/2001, para 9.6.
112 United Nations Human Rights Committee, Ilyasov v Kazakhstan, 111th Session, Annex, Communication No 2009/2010, UN Doc CCPR/C/111/D/2009/2010, 16, para 6 [*Ilyasov*].
113 *Ilyasov*, 14, para 9.
114 *Ilyasov*, 18, para 3.
115 *Ilyasov*, 20, para 3.
116 United Nations Human Rights Committee, Warsame v Canada, 102nd Session, Annex, Communication No 1959/2010, UN Doc CCPR/C/102/D/1959/2010 [*Warsame*].
117 *Warsame*, para 8.5.
118 *Warsame*, 20–24.
119 United Nations Human Rights Committee, Nystrom v Australia, 102nd Session, Annex, Communication No 1557/2007, UN Doc CCPR/C/102/D/1557/2007, para 7.4 [*Nystrom*].
120 *Nystrom*, 24, para 3.3.
121 *Nystrom*, para 3.4.
122 United Nations Human Rights Committee, Budlakoti v Canada, 122nd Session, Annex, UN Doc CCCPR/C/122/D/2264/2013 [*Budlakoti*].
123 *Budlakoti*.
124 Stacy Douglas, "Canada Must Give Deepan Budlakoti Back His Citizenship" *Ottawa Citizen,* October 28, 2019. https://ottawacitizen.com/opinion/douglas-canada-must-give-deepan-budlakoti-back-his-citizenship.
125 *Budlakoti*, para 9.3.
126 *Budlakoti*, para 9.3.
127 Douglas, "Canada Must Give Deepan Budlakoti Back His Citizenship."
128 Daiva Stasiulis, "The Extraordinary Statelessness of Deepan Budlakoti: The Erosion of Canadian Citizenship Through Citizenship Deprivation" *Studies in Social Justice* 11, 1 (2017): 1.
129 *Budlakoti v Canada*, 2015, FCA, 139.
130 United Nations Human Rights Committee, CCPR General Comment No 27: Article 12 (Freedom of Movement), Adopted at the 67th Session (2 November 1999) CCPR/C/21/Rev.1/Add.9: at para 19.
131 CCPR General Comment No 27, para 20.
132 CCPR General Comment No 27, para 20.
133 CCPR General Comment No 27, para 20.

CHAPTER 4

1 See for example Catherine Allerton, "Contested Statelessness in Sabah, Malaysia: Irregularity and the Politics of Recognition," *Journal of Immigrant & Refugee Studies* 15, 3 (2017): 251; Regional Conference on Stateless / Undocumented Children in Sabah Kota Kinabalu, Sabah, Malaysia, Tenaganita (Organization), Asia-Pacific Mission for Migrants, Christian Conference of Asia. Urban Rural Mission, *Acting*

Today for Tomorrow's Generation (Tenagita, 2006). This article also does not provide an overview of the rules of state succession, which may provide an explanation of how some people may not have acquired citizenship when Malaysia became independent. As I allude to earlier, even if state succession rules did confer citizenship, some simply did not obtain citizenship due to administrative and other legal barriers, which are discussed in other writing from this research project.

2. CCH & ADY v Pendaftar Besar bagi Kelahiran dan Kematian, Malaysia [2022] 1 MLJ, 71 (CYM).
3. *Universal Declaration of Human Rights*, 10 December 1948, UNGA 217 A(III) [*UDHR*].
4. *Convention on the Rights of the Child*, 20 November 1989, 1577 UNTS 3 (entered into force 2 September 1990), articles 3, 21 [CRC].
5. *1954 Convention Relating to the Status of Stateless Persons*, 28 September 1954, 360 UNTS 117 (entered into force 6 June 1960); *1961 Convention on the Reduction of Statelessness,* 30 August 1961, 989 UNTS 175 (entered into force 13 December 1975).
6. *Convention Relating to the Status of Refugees*, 28 July 1951, 189 UNTS 137 (entered into force 22 April 1954), article 1(A)(2) [*Refugee Convention*].
7. *International Convention on the Elimination of All Forms of Racial Discrimination*, 21 December 1965, 660 UNTS 195 (entered into forced 4 January 1969) [ICERD].
8. *International Covenant on Civil and Political* Rights, 19 December 1966, 999 UNTS 171 (entered into force 23 March 1976) [ICCPR].
9. *Convention against Torture and Other Cruel, Inhuman or Degrading Treatment or Punishment*, 10 December 1984, 1465 UNTS 85 (entered into force 26 June 1987) [CAT].
10. "Suhakam Wants Malaysia to Ratify Six Human Rights Conventions, Says Waytha Moorthy" *The Star*, August 21, 2018. https://www.thestar.com.my/news/nation/2018/08/21/suhakam-wants-malaysia-to-ratify-six-human-rights-conventions/.
11. Interview with 5L, Appendix in Chapter 5, Table 2, January 29, 2018.
12. Interview with 5L.
13. Interview with 6L, Appendix in Chapter 5, Table 2, January 30, 2018.
14. Interview with 4L, Appendix in Chapter 5, Table 2, January 23, 2018.
15. Than Siew Beng & Nor v Ketua Pengarah Jabatan Pendaftaran Negara & Ors, [2017] 8 CLJ 16 (Malaysia), para 16.
16. Lew Yee Hong & Anor v Ketua Setiausaha Kementerian Dalam Negeri & Ors, [2020] 1 CLJ 419 (Malaysia), para 13 [Lew Yee Hong]. See also Chan Tai Ern, and the Court of Appeal in Than Siew Beng.
17. *Adoption Act*, Malaysia, 1952 (revised 1981).
18. *Legitimacy Act,* Malaysia, 1961 (revised 1971).
19. *Federal Constitution of Malaysia*, 31 August 1957, amended 20 July 1995, article 14.
20. *Federal Constitution of Malaysia*, articles 15–18.
21. *Federal Constitution of Malaysia*, article 19.
22. *Federal Constitution of Malaysia*, article 22.
23. Interview with 3S, Appendix in Chapter 5, Table 2, March 6, 2018.
24. *Federal Constitution of Malaysia.*
25. *Federal Constitution of Malaysia,* schedule II part II section 1(a).

26 See for example, Yu Sheng Meng (A Child Represented by His Litigator, Yu Meng Queng) v Ketua Pengarah Pendaftaran Negara & Ors, [2016] 7 MLJ 628 (Asmabi Mohamad J) (High Court of Malaya) [Yu Sheng Meng, Child].
27 *Federal Constitution of Malaysia*, article 14(1)(b), schedule II part II section 1(a).
28 *Federal Constitution of Malaysia*, schedule II part II s 2(3).
29 See for example, Than Siew Beng & Anor v Ketua Pengarah Jabatan Pendaftaran Negara & Ors, [2015] MLJU 2059 (Unreported, High Court of Malaysia, Asmabi Mohamad J, 16 November 2015), 10–13; Than Siew Beng & Anor v Ketua Pengarah Jabatan Pendaftaran Negara & Ors, [2017] 5 MLJ 662 (David Wong, Badariah Sahamid and Harmindar Singh JJCA) (Court of Appeal).
30 See for example, interview with 5L.
31 *Federal Constitution of Malaysia*, article 15(A).
32 Interview with 2L, Appendix in Chapter 5, Table 2, February 5, 2018.
33 Haja Mohideen MK Abdul Rahman & Ors, [2007] 6 CLJ 662 (Malaysia), para 25 [Haja Mohideen].
34 Ahmad Mustakim Zulkifli, "Rights Group Blasts Home Ministry Over 'Indifference' to Citizenship Bids After Court Ruling" March 16, 2023, https://www.malaysianow.com/news/2023/03/16/rights-group-blasts-home-ministry-over-indifference-to-citizenship-bids-after-court-ruling.
35 Interviews with 1L, Appendix in Chapter 5, Table 2, January 9, 2018; interview with 2L, Appendix in Chapter 5, Table 2, February 5, 2018; interview with 3L, Appendix in Chapter 5, Table 2, January 22, 2018; interview with 4L; interview with 5L; interview with 6L; interview with 1NGO , Appendix in Chapter 5, Table 2, January 17, 2018.
36 Interview with 1L.
37 Interview with 2NGO , Appendix in Chapter 5, Table 2, January 23, 2018.
38 Interview with 2L.
39 *Haja Mohideen*, [2007] 6 CLJ 662: para 12.
40 Yong Lee Hua v Director of National Registration Sabah & Anor, [2011] 9 CLJ 125 (Malaysia) [Yong Lee Hua]; Chin Kooi Nah v Pendaftar Besar Kelahiran Dan Kematian, [2016] 1 CJL 736 (Malaysia) [Chin Kooi Nah]; Lim Kai Lin v Pendaftar Besar Kelahiran Dan Kematian, Malaysia, [2018] 1 LNS 1828 (Malaysia) [Lim Kai Lin]; Cho Chiang Huat v Pendaftar Besar Kelahiran Dan Kematian, Malaysia, [2019] 1 LNS 1463 (Malaysia) [Cho Chiang Huat]; Tan Lee Heng & Anor v Ketua Pengarah, Jabatan Pendaftaran Negara & Ors, [2019] 8 CLJ 865 (Malaysia) [Tan Lee Heng].
41 *Lim Kai Lin* [2018] 1 LNS 1828, para 2, 6.
42 *Haja Mohideen*, [2007] 6 CLJ 662, para 28.
43 Madhuvita Janjara Augustin (Suing Through Next Friend, Margaret Louisa Tan) v August Lourdsamy & Ors [2018] 4 CLJ 758 (Malaysia) [Madhuvita Janjara Augustin].
44 *Madhuvita Janjara Augustin*, para 5.
45 *Tan Lee Hengs,* [2019] 8 CLJ 865.
46 *Tan Lee Hengs*, para 3.
47 *Tan Lee Hengs*, para 18.
48 *Yong Lee Hua*, [2011] 9 CLJ 125; *Chin Kooi Nah*, [2016] 1 CJL 736; *Lim Kai Lin*, [2018] 1 LNS 1828; *Cho Chiang Huat*; *Tan Lee Heng*, [2019] 8 CLJ 865.
49 Ong Boon Hua & Anor v Menteri Hal Ehwal Dalam Negeri, Malaysia & ORs,

50   [2008] 5 CLJ 42 at paras 56–57 [Ong Boon Hua].
50   Ong Boon Hua.
51   Nalan Kunji Kanan v Secretary General of Ministry of Home Affairs, Malaysia [2017] 1 LNS 1712 (Malaysia) [Nalan Kunji Kanan].
52   *Nalan Kunji Kanan*, para 40.
53   *Yong Lee Hua*, [2011] 9 CLJ 125 at para 2 [*Yong Lee Hua*].
54   *Yong Lee Hua*, para 3.
55   *Yong Lee Hua*, para 10.
56   *Yong Lee Hua,* paras 13–14.
57   *Yong Lee Hua*, paras 16–19.
58   *Yong Lee Hua,* paras 16–19.
59   Foo Toon Aik v Ketua Pendaftar Kelahiran, [2012] 4 CLJ 613 (Malaysia) [Foo Toon Aik]; Yu Sheng Meng v Ketua Pengarah Pendaftaran Negara [2016] 1 CJL 336 (Malaysia) [Yu Sheng Meng]; Chin Kooi Nah v Pendaftar Besar Kelahiran Dan Kematian, [2016] 1 CJL 736 (Malaysia) [Chin Kooi Nah]; Pendaftar Besar Kelahiran Dan Kematian, Malaysia v Pang Wee See & Anor, [2017] 7 CLJ 33 [Pang Wee See]; Lim Kai Lin,[2018] 1 LNS 1828; Than Siew Beng & Nor v Ketua Pengarah Jabatan Pendaftaran Negara & Ors, [2017] 8 CLJ 16 (Malaysia) [Than Siew Beng]; Samuel Duraisingh v Pendaftar Besar Kelahiran, [2019] 1 LNS 1474 (Malaysia) [Samuel Duraisingh]; Cho Chiang Huat,[2019] 1 LNS 1463.
60   See for example, Chelsea Ng, "Judge Fixes Date to Hear Salman's Suit," *The Star* May 4, 2006, https://www.thestar.com.my/news/nation/2006/05/04/judge-fixes-date-to-hear-salmans-suit; "14-Year-Old Girl Gets Malaysian Citizenship After DNA Test," *The Star*, July 31, 2013, https://www.thestar.com.my/news/nation/2013/07/31/courts-yanesha-dna/; Chen Yih Wen, "Stateless Man from Sabah Finally Granted Citizenship," *The Star*, October 22, 2019, https://www.thestar.com.my/news/nation/2019/10/22/stateless-man-from-sabah-finally-granted-citizenship; Ida Lim, "Top-Scoring Roisah Stateless No More with Early Birthday Gift of Citizenship," *Malay Mail*, March 28, 2019, https://www.malaymail.com/news/malaysia/2019/03/28/top-scoring-roisah-stateless-no-more-with-early-birthday-gift-of-citizenshi/1737285.
61   Ida Lim, "Three Malaysia-Born Stateless Kids' Long Road to Citizenship Continues" *Malay Mail* February 14, 2019, https://www.malaymail.com/news/malaysia/2019/02/14/three-malaysia-born-stateless-kids-long-road-to-citizenship-continues/1722765.
62   Pang Wee See, [2017] 7 CLJ 33; Lim Kai Lin, [2018] 1 LNS 1828; Than Siew Beng; and Cho Chiang Huat; Samuel Duraisingh, [2019] 1 LNS 1474.
63   *Chin Kooi Nah*; *Yu Sheng Meng.*
64   *Foo Toon Aik*.
65   *Than Siew Beng*, para 17.
66   Interview with 6L.
67   Interview with 6L.
68   Ida Lim, "Malaysia-Born but Stateless, Three Kids Win Citizenship at Doorstep to Hearing," *Malay Mail*, February 14, 2019. https://www.malaymail.com/news/malaysia/2019/02/14/malaysia-born-but-stateless-three-kids-win-citizenship-at-doorstep-to-heari/1722883.
69   See Raymond Mah and Chloe Lim Yen Hwa, "Citizenship for Adopted Children: A Malaysian Perspective," *Mah Weng Kwai & Associates* (blog), January 10, 2013,

https://mahwengkwai.com/citizenship-for-adopted-children-a-malaysian-perspective/,in the case of Lee Chin Pon (unreported); Lim, "Malaysia-Born But Stateless."
70 *Foo Toon Aik.*
71 Yu Sheng Meng, [2016] 1 CJL 336; Chin Kooi Nah,, [2016] 1 CJL 736; Chan Tai Ern Bermillo,[2017] 1 LNS 1246; Mohamed Sadik Mohamed Ali & Anor v Menteri Dalam Negeri & Ors, [2017] 8 CLJ 442 (Malaysia) [Mohamed Sadik Mohamed Ali]; Madhuvita Jangara Augustin v Augustin Lourdsamy & Ors, [2018] 4 CLJ 758 [Madhuvita Jangara Augustin]; Samuel Duraisingh, [2019] 1 LNS 1474 [Samuel Duraisingh].
72 *Foo Toon Aik*, paras 2–3.
73 *Foo Toon Aik*, para 2.
74 *Foo Toon Aik*, para 3.
75 *Foo Toon Aik*, para 4.
76 *Foo Toon Aik*, para 4.
77 *Foo Toon Aik*, para 5.
78 *Foo Toon Aik*, para 6.
79 *Foo Toon Aik*, para 13.
80 *Adoption Act*, Malaysia, 1952 (revised 1981).
81 *Foo Toon Aik*, para 10–11.
82 *Foo Toon Aik*, para 10-11.
83 *Foo Toon Aik*, para 23.
84 *Foo Toon Aik*, paras 22-23, 25.
85 *Foo Toon Aik*, paras 22-23, 25.
86 *Foo Toon Aik*; *Cho Chiang Huat*, paras 2 and 24; *Pang Wee See*.
87 *Samuel Duraisingh*, para 98.
88 *Samuel Duraisingh*, para 110; *Than Siew Beng*, paras 31–8.
89 *Chin Kooi Nah*, para 29.
90 *Than Siew Beng*, para 18.
91 *Than Siew Beng*, para 18.
92 *Than Siew Beng*, para 18; Cho Chiang Huat: para 20.
93 Interview with 1L.
94 Interview with 3L.
95 Interview with 5L.
96 *Foo Toon Aik*; *Pang Wee See*; *Yu Sheng Meng*, para 10; *Chin Kooi Nah*, para 92; *Than Siew Beng*, paras 23–25; *Samuel Duraisingh*, para 6; *Cho Chiang Huat*, para 19.
97 *Chin Kooi Nah*, para 141.
98 *Chin Kooi Nah*, para 106; *Lim Kai Lin*, para 6; *Than Siew Beng*, para 36; *Cho Chiang Huat*, at para 2.
99 *Yu Sheng Meng*, para 13; *Samuel Duraisingh*, para 11.
100 CCH & Anor (on behalf of themselves and as litigation representatives of one CYM, a child) v Pendaftar Besar bagi Kelahiran dan Kematian, Malaysia, [2022] 1 MLJ 71 [CYM]; Ahmad Mustakim Zulkifli, "Rights Group Blasts Home Ministry Over 'Indifference' to Citizenship Bids After Court Ruling" March 16, 2023 https://www.malaysianow.com/news/2023/03/16/rights-group-blasts-home-ministry-over-indifference-to-citizenship-bids-after-court-ruling; Free Malaysia

Today, "Adoption Order Does Not Confer Citizenship, High Court Rules" Free Malaysia Today, March 16, 2023; Jamie Chai Yun Liew, "Case Note, CYM v Malaysia: Landmark Decision for Adopted Stateless Children has Little Traction Beyond Apex Court," Statelessness & Citizenship Review 5, 1 (2023): 100–04. https://www.freemalaysiatoday.com/category/nation/2023/03/16/adoption-order-does-not-confer-citizenship-high-court-rules/.

101 Haja Mohideen, [2007] 6 CLJ 662 at paras 1-6; Mohamed Sadik Mohamed Ali, [2017] 8 CLJ 442 at paras 3–5; Ramanoojum Muniandy & Ors v Ketua Setiausaha, Kementerian Dalam Negari & Ors, [2016] 5 CLJ 76 (Malaysia) [Ramanoojum Muniandy].
102 *Chan Tai Ern Bermillo*, [2017] 1 LNS 1246.
103 *Yu Sheng Meng*.
104 Madhuvita Jangara Augustin,[2018] 4 CLJ 758; Tan Lee Heng, [2019] 8 CLJ 865; Lew Yee Hong, [2020] 1 CLJ 419; Iwan Liaw v PP, [2019] 9 CLJ 780 (Malaysia); Jabatan Pendaftaran Negara v MEMK, [2020] 1 LNS 199 (Malaysia); Lim Jen Hsian & Anor v Ketua Pengarah Jabatan Pendaftaran Negara & Ors, [2017] 8 CLJ 412 (Malaysia) [Lim Jen Hsian].
105 *Lim Jen Hsian*, [2017] 8 CLJ 412.
106 *Madhuvita Jangara Augustin*.
107 *Lew Yee Hong*.
108 *Tan Lee Heng*, [2019] 8 CLJ 865; *Iwan Liaw*, [2019] 9 CLJ 780.
109 *Madhuvita Jangara Augustin*, para 4.
110 "Two Stateless Children Granted Citizenship," *The Star*, October 26, 2018. https://www.thestar.com.my/news/nation/2018/10/26/two-stateless-children-granted-citizenship; *Madhuvita Jangara Augustin*, [2018] 4 CLJ 758; *Lim Jen Hsian*, [2017] 8 CLJ 412.
111 *Madhuvita Jangara Augustin*; *Tan Lee Heng*; *Lew Yee Hong*; *Lim Jen Hsian*; *Haja Mohideen*; *Mohamed Sadik Mohamed Ali*.
112 *Iwan Liaw*.
113 *Chan Tai Ern Bermillo*; *Yu Sheng Meng*.
114 *Mohamed Sadik Mohamed Ali*, para 25.
115 *Haja Mohideen*, paras 12–26
116 *Ramanoojum Muniandy*, [2016] 5 CLJ 76: para 30.
117 *Ramanoojum Muniandy*, paras 25, 55.
118 *Ramanoojum Muniandy*, para 46.
119 *Federal Constitution*: section 17 in Part III of the Constitution
120 *Madhuvita Jangara Augustin*.
121 *Madhuvita Jangara Augustin*, para 55.
122 *Madhuvita Jangara Augustin*, paras 60–2.
123 *Madhuvita Jangara Augustin*, paras 63–6.
124 *Lim Jen Hsian,* [2017] 8 CLJ 412.
125 *Lew Yee Hong*, [2020] 1 CLJ 419, para 5.
126 *Lew Yee Hong*, para 5.
127 Ida Lim, "Anwar Cabinet Agrees to Enable Automatic Citizenship for Children Born Overseas to Malaysian Mums" *Malay Mail*, February 18, 2023, https://www.malaymail.com/news/malaysia/2023/02/18/anwar-cabinet-agrees-to-enable-automatic-citizenship-for-children-born-overseas-to-malaysian-mums/55523.
128 See for example, *Yu Sheng Meng*.

129 The Vibes, "LFL Calls Out 'Sickening' Proposed Amendments to Citizenship Law," *The Vibes,* June 24, 2023. https://www.thevibes.com/articles/news/95248/lfl-calls-out-sickening-proposed-amendments-to-citizenship-law.
130 *Federal Constitution of Malaysia*, 31 August 1957, amended 20 July 1955, s 1(e) of Part II of the Second Schedule.
131 *Chin Kooi Nah*, para 51.
132 *Cho Chiang Huat*, para 10.
133 *Samuel Duraisingh*, para 96; *Cho Chiang Huat*, para 37.
134 *Than Siew Beng*, para 27-30; *Ong Boon Hua*.
135 *Cho Chiang Huat*; *Than Siew Beng*; *Ong Boon Hua*; *Samuel Duraisingh*.
136 *Than Siew Beng*, para 35.
137 *Haja Mohideen*, [2007] 6 CLJ 662 at para 25.
138 Ramanoojum Muniandy, [2016] 5 CLJ 76.
139 *Haja Mohideen*; *Ramanoojum Muniandy*; *Mohamed Sadik Mohamed Ali*; *Yu Sheng Meng*; *Tan Lee Heng*; *Foo Toon Aik*; *Lim Jen Hsian*; *Chan Tai Ern Bermillo*; *Lew Yee Hong*; *Madhuvita Janjara Augustin*; *Chin Kooi Nah*; *Pang Wee See*; *Lim Kai Lin*; *Than Siew Beng*; *Samuel Duraisingh*; *Cho Chiang Huat*.
140 *Lim Jen Hsian*, para 10.
141 *Lim Jen Hsian*, para 10.
142 *Lim Jen Hsian*, para 40.
143 *Lim Jen Hsian*, para 40.
144 *Chan Tai Ern Bermillo*.
145 David Paciocco & Lee Stuesser, *The Law of Evidence, 4th ed* (Toronto: Irwin Law, 2005), 376.
146 *Paciocco and Stuesser*, 377.
147 See for example, *Foo Toon Aik*, para 27; *Pang Wee See*, para 42.
148 Haja Mohideen, [2007] 6 CLJ 662: para 25.
149 *Haja Mohideen*, para 20.
150 See Nalan Kunji Kanan, [2017] 1 LNS 1712; *Chin Kooi Nah*; *Lim Kai Lin*.
151 *Chin Kooi Nah*, paras 155, 158.
152 *Chin Kooi Nah*, para 158.
153 *Pang Wee See*, para 46.
154 *Lim Kai Lin*, para 10.
155 Interview with 3L.
156 Interview with 6L.
157 Interview with 5L.
158 Interview with 2NGO.
159 Interview with 1NGO, Appendix in Chapter 5, Table 3, January 17, 2018.
160 Interview with 1NGO.
161 Interview with 6NGO, Appendix in Chapter 5, Table 3, January 30, 2018.
162 Interview with 6NGO.
163 Kung Aik v Public Prosecutor [1970] 2 MLJ 174 (Malaysia) [Kung Aik]; Minister of Home Affairs v Chu Choon Yong & Anor, [1977] 1 LNS 71 (Malaysia) [Chu Choon Yong]; Kolandavaloo Ramasamy v Menteri Dalam Negeri et al., [2014] 1 LNS 806 (Malaysia); Iwan Liaw.
164 Interview with 7NGO, Appendix in Chapter 5, Table 3, January 28, 2018.
165 Interview with 7NGO.

166 Free Malaysia Today, "Detained children to be moved out of immigration depot," *Free Malaysia Today*, February 16, 2023. https://www.freemalaysiatoday.com/category/nation/2023/02/16/detained-children-to-be-moved-out-of-immigration-depot/.
167 Interview with 3L.
168 Interview with 3L.
169 Interview with 5L.
170 Interview with 5L.
171 Interview with 5L.
172 Interview with 4L.
173 Interview with 6L.
174 Interview with 12NGO, Appendix in Chapter 5, Table 3, February 6, 2018.
175 Interview with 3L; 12NGO
176 Interview with 8L, Appendix in Chapter 5, Table 2, March 23, 2018; Interview with 1NGO, Appendix in Chapter 5, Table 3, January 27, 2018.
177 Interview with 1NGO.
178 *Nalan Kunji Kanan*.
179 Interview with 2L.
180 Interview with 2L.
181 Interview with 6L.
182 Interview with 6L.
183 Interview with 6L.
184 Interview with 6L.
185 Interview with 8L, Appendix in Chapter 5, Table 3, March 23, 2018.
186 Interview with 6NGO; Interview with 8NGO, Appendix in Chapter 5, Table 3, February 26, 2018.
187 Interview with 2L.
188 Interview with 2L.
189 Interview with 4L.
190 Interview with 2L.
191 Interview with 12NGO, Appendix in Chapter 5, Table 3, February 6, 2018.
192 Interview with 12NGO.
193 Interview with 1NGO, Appendix in Chapter 5, Table 3, January 17, 2018.
194 Interview with 1NGO.
195 Interview with 6NGO.
196 Interview with 6NGO.
197 Ketua Pengarah Pendaftaran Negara, Malaysia et al v Navin Moorthy, Order dated 29 July 2015 (No K/P 730520-10-5805).
198 Gàbor Gyulai, "The Determination of Statelessness and the Establishment of a Statelessness-Specific Protection Regime" in *Nationality and Statelessness under International Law*, eds. Alice Edwards and Laura Van Waas (Cambridge: Cambridge University Press, 2014), 121.
199 Gyulai, "The Determination of Statelessness," 127, 137.
200 UNHCR, *Expert Meeting — Statelessness Determination Procedures and the Status of Stateless Persons*, December 2010 [Geneva Conclusions].
201 UNHCR, Geneva Conclusions, para 13; UNHCR, *Handbook on Protection of Stateless Persons*, para 89.
202 Gyulai, "The Determination of Statelessness," 138.

CHAPTER 5

1. "Ending Statelessness in Malaysia," UNHCR, accessed August 16, 2023. http://www.unhcr.org/en-my/ending-statelessness-in-malaysia.html.
2. "Statelessness," *Lawyers for Liberty*, https://www.lawyersforliberty.org/statelessness/.
3. Sally Engle Merry, *The Seductions of Quantification: Measuring Human Rights, Gender Violence, and Sex Trafficking* (Chicago: University of Chicago Press, 2016).
4. Merry, *The Seductions of Quantification*.
5. For example, interview with 8L, Appendix in Chapter 5, Table 2, March 23, 2018. 8L said they had clients that were fearful of coming to the attention of authorities until statelessness made it impossible to continue as children were denied education.
6. Interview with 8L.
7. Gàbor Gyulai, "The Determination of Statelessness and the Establishment of a Statelessness-Specific Protection Regime" in Alice Edwards and Laura Van Waas, eds, *Nationality and Statelessness under International Law* (Cambridge: Cambridge University Press, 2014), 118.
8. For example, Rodziana Mohamed Razali, Rohaida Nordin and Tamara Joan Duraisingam, "Migration and Statelessness: Turning the Spotlight on Malaysia" *Pertanika Journal of Social Science and Humanities* 23, S (2015): 19.
9. For example, Munguntan Vanar, "Sabah Seeks to Resolve Issue of Stateless People in the State," *The Star*, November 16, 2018, https://www.thestar.com.my/news/nation/2018/11/16/sabah-seeks-to-resolve-issue-of-stateless-people-in-the-state/; United Nation High Commissioner for Refugees, "UNHCR Welcomes Move by Malaysia to Grant Citizenship to Stateless Persons," *UNHCR, Malaysia*, August 15, 2018 https://www.unhcr.org/en-my/news/press/2018/8/5b73e54d4/unhcr-welcomes-move-by-malaysia-to-grant-citizenship-to-stateless-persons.html.
10. Nandita Sharma, *National Sovereignty and the Separation of Natives and Migrants* (Durham, NC: Duke University Press, 2020).
11. See Tendayi Bloom, Katherine Tonkiss, and Phillip Cole, eds., *Understanding Statelessness* (New York: Routledge, 2017); Mely Caballero-Anthony, Priyanka Bhalla, and Pau Khan Khup Hangzo, *The Many Faces of Statelessness*, NTS Alert Report, issue 2 (NTS Centre, February 2010), http://www.rsis.edu.sg/wp-content/uploads/2014/07/NL100228_NTS_Alert_Feb2010_Issue2.pdf. The report discusses stateless persons in their habitual residence.
12. Ayelet Shachar defines this term as membership based on an individual's genuine connection to the state.
13. *Federal Constitution of Malaysia*, 31 August 1957, amended 20 July 1955: s 14(1).
14. *Federal Constitution*, ss 16, 16A.
15. Interview with 1NGO, Appendix in Chapter 5, Table 3, January 17, 2018; interview with 4NGO, Appendix in Chapter 5, Table 3, January 17, 2018; see also "Ending Statelessness in Malaysia," UNHCR, http://www.unhcr.org/en-my/ending-statelessness-in-malaysia.html.
16. Interview with 1NGO, Appendix in Chapter 5, Table 3, January 17, 2018; interview with 4NGO, Appendix in Chapter 5, Table 3, January 17, 2018; interview with 6NGO, Appendix in Chapter 5, Table 3, January 30, 2018.
17. Interview with 1NGO; interview with 4NGO; interview with 6NGO.

18 Interview with 1NGO; interview with 4NGO; interview with 6NGO.
19 Interview with 1NGO; interview with 4NGO; interview with 6NGO.
20 See Razali, Nordin, and Duraisingam, "Migration and Statelessness," 5 citing Barisan Nasional, *Malaysian Indian Blueprint* (Policy Report, 2018).
21 Interview with 3A, Appendix in Chapter 5, Table 2, January 25, 2018; Ruben Sario, "Small Filipino Community Makes Big Impact on Sabah's Landscape," *The Star*, September 16, 2017. https://www.thestar.com.my/metro/metro-news/2017/09/16/small-filipino-community-makes-big-impact-on-sabahs-landscape/; interview with 2A, Appendix Table 3, April 9, 2018; interview with 13NGO, Appendix in Chapter 5, Table 3, April 9, 2018.
22 See for example, Greg Acciaioli, Helen Brunt, and Julian Clifton, "Foreigners Everywhere, Nationals Nowhere: Exclusion, Irregularity, and Invisibility of Stateless Bajau Laut in Eastern Sabah, Malaysia," *Journal of Immigrant & Refugee Studies* 15, 3 (2017): 232–49. There has been some research in this area.
23 Interview with 2S, Appendix in Chapter 5, Table 2, January 28, 2018.
24 Interview with 3NGO, Appendix in Chapter 5, Table 2, January 18, 2018.
25 Interview with 6NGO; Interview with 1L, Appendix in Chapter 5 Table 2, January 9, 2018.
26 Interview with 1L, Appendix in Chapter 5, Table 2, January 9, 2018.
27 Catherine Allerton, "Contested Statelessness in Sabah, Malaysia: Irregularity and the Politics of
Recognition," *Journal of Immigrant & Refugee Studies* 15, 3 (2017): 257; Catherine Allerton, "Statelessness and the Lives of the Children of Migrants in Sabah, East Malaysia," *Tilburg Law Review* 19, 1–2 (2014): 26; Razali, Nordin, and Duraisingam, "Migration and Statelessness."
28 Interview with 6S, Appendix in Chapter 5, Table 2, March 20, 2018.
29 Interview with 14S, Appendix in Chapter 5, Table 2, March 21, 2018.
30 Interview with 15S, Appendix in Chapter 5, Table 2, March 21, 2018.
31 Yu Sheng Meng, Child (A Child Represented by His Litigator, Yu Meng Queng) v Ketua Pengarah Pendaftaran Negara & Ors [2016] 7 MLJ 628; Foo Toon Aik, (Suing on His Own behalf and as Representative of Foo Shi Wen, Child) v Ketua Pendaftar Kelahiran dan Kematian, Malaysia [2012] 9 MLJ 573 (High Court of Malaya); Lee Chin Pon & Anor v Registrar-General of Births and Deaths (Unreported, Application for Judicial Review No R1-25-343-08, High Court of Malaya, 16 December 2009) (Malaysia); Leong Peng Kheong & Anor v Registrar-General of Births and Deaths (Unreported, Application for Judicial Review No 25-102-05/2014 and 25-103-5/2014, High Court of Malaya, 29 July 2015) (Malaysia); Than Siew Beng & Anor, v Ketua Pengarah Jabatan Pendaftaran Negara & Ors [2015] MLJU 2059 (Unreported, High Court of Malaya) (Malaysia); Than Siew Beng & Anor v Ketua Pengarah Jabatan Pendaftaran Negara & Ors [2017] MLJ 662 (Court of Appeal) (Malaysia); Chin Kooi Nah (Suing by Herself and as Next of Kin to Chin Jia Nee, An Infant) v Pendaftar Besar Kelahiran dan Kematian, Malaysia [2016] 7 MLJ 712 (High Court of Malaya); (Malaysia) Pendaftar Besar Kelahiran dan Kematian, Malaysia v Pang Wee See [2017] 3 MLJ 308 (Court of Appeal, Malaysia).
32 Interview with 10NGO, Appendix in Chapter 5, Table 2, March 16, 2018.
33 Interview with 8NGO.
34 Interview with 1L; interview with 5L, Appendix in Chapter 5, Table 2, January 29, 2018.

35 Interview with 3S, Appendix in Chapter 5, Table 2, March 6, 2018.
36 Interview with 5S, Appendix in Chapter 5, Table 2, March 5, 2018.
37 Interview with 17S, Appendix in Chapter 5, Table 2, March 22, 2018.
38 Interview with 6NGO; interview with 1S, Appendix in Chapter 5, Table 2, January 28, 2018; interview with 13S, Appendix in Chapter 5, Table 2, March 22, 2018.
39 Interview with 13S.
40 *Navin A/L Moorthy v Ketua Pengarah Pendaftaran Negara, Malaysia & Ors Malaysia* (Unreported, High Court of Malaya, Originating Summons No: 24NCvC-2011-12/2013) (Malaysia); Ida Lim, "After 17 Years, Stateless Teen Finally Recognised As Malaysian," *Malaysia Mail Online*, April 6, 2016. http://www.themalaymailonline.com/malaysia/article/after-17-years-stateless-teen-finally-recognised-as-malaysian. See also interview with 3L, Appendix Table 2, January 22, 2018.
41 Interview with 6NGO.
42 Interview with 1L.
43 Madhuvita Janjara Augustin (Suing through Next Friend Margeret Louisa Tan) v Augustin A/L Lourdsamy & Ors, [2018] 1 MJL 307 (Court of Appeal) (Malaysia) [Madhuvita,Louisa Tan]; Lim Jen Hsian & Anor v Ketua Penegarah Jabatan Pendaltaran Negara & Ors [2017] 8 MLJ 122 (Asmabi Mohmad J) (High Court of Malaya) (Malaysia); Interview with 2S, Appendix Table 2, January 28, 2018
44 Interview with 4S.
45 Interview with 13S.
46 Interview with 13S; interview with 18S, March 23, 2018; *Madhuvita, Louisa Tan*, [2018] 1 MJL 307; interview with 4L, Appendix Table 2, January 23, 2018; interview with 2L, Appendix Table 2, XX.
47 Interview with 11S, Appendix in Chapter 5, Table 2, March 22, 2018.
48 Interview with 12S, Appendix in Chapter 5, Table 2, March 22, 2018.
49 Interview with 2PL, Appendix in Chapter 5, Table 2, March 20, 2018.
50 See generally Azizah Kassim, "Filipino Refugees in Sabah: State Responses, Public Stereotypes and the Dilemma over Their Future," *The Southeast Asian Studies* 47, 1 (2009): 52–88; Helen Brunt, "Statelessness at Sea" in *The World's Stateless Children*, eds. Laura van Waas and Amal de Chickera, (Oisterwijk: Wolf Legal 2017) 290–94; Asia Pacific Refugee Rights Network, "The Vulnerability of Bajau Laut (Sama Dilaut) Children in Sabah," (Position Paper, March 2015) http://www.aprrn.info/1/images/PDF/Bajau_Laut_position_paper_FINAL.pdf; Camilla Olson, "Malaysia: Undocumented Children in Sabah Vulnerable to Statelessness," *Refugees International Bulletin*, June 13, 2007. https://www.refworld.org/docid/47a6ee98d.html.
51 See Greg Constantine, "Malaysia: Held in the Shadow of the Sunrise," *Nowhere People Stories* (Online Exhibition, 2015). http://www.nowherepeople.org/new-page/.
52 Allerton, "Contested Statelessness in Sabah," 254–55; Kassim, "Filipino Refugees in Sabah," 57–58.
53 Interview with 7S, Appendix in Chapter 5, Table 2, March 20, 2018.
54 Interview with 8S, Appendix in Chapter 5, Table 2, March 20, 2018.
55 See Equal Rights Trust, *Confined Spaces: Legal Protections for Rohingya in Bangladesh, Malaysia and Thailand*, (Equal Rights Trust, 2016). https://www.equalrightstrust.org/ertdocumentbank/Confined%20Spaces_0.pdf.
56 Adam Bemma, "Malaysia: A Rohingya Safe Haven?" *Aljazeera*, November 23, 2017. https://www.aljazeera.com/news/2017/11/malaysia-rohingya-safe-hav-

en-171122190637814.html; interview with 2L, Appendix in Chapter 5, Table 2, February 5, 2018.
57 Interview with 9NGO, Appendix in Chapter 5, Table 2, February 28, 2018.
58 Interview with 11NGO, Appendix in Chapter 5, Table 2, February 28, 2018.
59 *Federal Constitution of Malaysia*, article 19.
60 Allerton, "Contested Statelessness in Sabah," 261; Mayuko Tani, "ASEAN Aims to Express 'Concern' on Rohingya Crisis for First Time," *Nikkei Asian Review,* November 13, 2018, https://asia.nikkei.com/Politics/International-relations/ASEAN-aims-to-express-concern-on-Rohingya-crisis-for-first-time; RF Dorall, "Muslim Refugees in Southeast Asia, the Malaysian Response," *Asian Migration* 1, 3 (1988).
61 Stephen Dziedzic, "ASEAN: Malaysian PM condemns inaction of Aung San Suu Kyi over Rohingya 'Suffering,'" *ABC News*, March 18, 2018. http://www.abc.net.au/news/2018-03-18/asean-malaysia-pm-confronts-aung-san-suu-kyi/9560112.
62 "Roundtable on Rohingya in Malaysia: Bridging the Gap Between Aid and Resettlement," *Monash University Malaysia, Centre for Public Policy Studies*, March 6, 2018. https://www.monash.edu.my/news-and-events/pages/latest/articles/2018/a-roundtable-on-the-rohingya-in-malaysia.
63 Interview with 16S, Appendix in Chapter 5, Table 2, March 21, 2018; interview with 5L, January 29, 2018 also provided a salient example.
64 Interview with 12NGO, Appendix in Chapter 5, Table 2, February 6, 2018.
65 See Kristy Belton, *Statelessness in the Caribbean* (Philadelphia: University of Pennsylvania Press, 2017); Gábor Gyulai, "Statelessness in the EU Framework for International Protection," *European Journal of Migration and Law* 14, 3 (2012): 279–95; Manly, "UNHCR's Mandate and Activities"; Laura Van Waas and Monica Neal, "Statelessness and the Role of National Human Rights Institutions" (Legal Studies Research Paper Series No 022/2013, Tilburg Law School, October 2013).
66 Geneva Conclusions, 23.
67 *Case No A/18* [1984] 75 ILR 176 (Iran–United States Claims Tribunal), 173 para 5; "Claims of Dual Nationals in the Modern Era: The Iran–United States Claims Tribunal," *Michigan Law Review* 83, 3 (1984): 601; Kannoff, "Dueling Nationalities,"1390–1. See also Charles N. Brower and Jason D. Brueschke, *The Iran–United States Claims Tribunal* (The Hague, Boston, London: Martinus Nijhoff 1998): 321.
68 HRC, "CCPR General Comment No 27: Article 12 (Freedom of Movement), CCPR/C/21/Rev.1/Add.9 (2 November 1999).
69 Gyulai, "The Determination of Statelessness," 119; HRC, "CCPR General Comment No 27: Article 12 (Freedom of Movement), CCPR/C/21/Rev.1/Add.9 (2 November 1999), para 20.
70 See for example, Yasmin Soysal, *Limits of Citizenship Migrants and Postnational Membership in Europe* (Chicago: University of Chicago Press, 1994); Seyla Benhabib, *Transformations of Citizenship: Dilemmas of the Nation State in the Era of Globalization* (Assen: Koninklijke Van Gorcum, 2001).
71 Interview with 1L.
72 Interview with 3L, Appendix Table 2, January 22, 2018.
73 Ayelet Shachar, *The Birthright Lottery: Citizenship and Global Inequality* (Harvard University Press, 2009), 171–174.
74 Shachar, *The Birthright Lottery*, 171-174.
75 Shachar, *The Birthright Lottery*, 171-174.
76 Shachar, *The Birthright Lottery*, 171-174.

77 Harold Cardinal and Walter Hildebrandt, *Treaty Elders of Saskatchewan: Our Dream is that Our Peoples Will One Day be Clearly Recognized as Nations* (Calgary: University of Calgary Press, 2000); Sylvia McAdam (Saysewahum), *Nationhood Interrupted: Revitalizing nêhiyaw Legal Systems* (Vancouver: UBC Press, 2015); Sylvia McAdam, *Cultural Teachings, First Nations Protocols and Methodologies* (Saskatoon: Saskatchewan Indian Cultural Centre, 2009).

78 For example, Franz Benda-Beckman, Keebet Benda-Beckman, eds. *Between Kinship and the State: Social Security and Law in Developing Countries* (Foris Publications, 1988); Faterneh Ebtehaj, Bridget Lindley, and Martin Richards, eds. *Kinship Matters* (Hart Publishing, 2006); Cecilia Ayón, Eugene Aisenberg, and Andrea Cimino, "Latino Families in the Nexus of Child Welfare, Welfare Reform and Immigration Policies: Is Kinship Care a Lost Opportunity?" *Social Work* 58, 1 (2013): 91.

79 For example, Megan Gaucher, *A Family Matter: Citizenship, Conjugal Relationships and Canadian Immigration Policy* (Vancouver: UBC Press, 2018); Catherine Lee, *Fictive Kinship: Family Reunification and the Meaning of Race and Nation in American Immigration* (Russell Sage Foundation, 2013).

80 For example, Marilyn Strathem, *Kinship, Law and the Unexpected: Relatives are Always a Surprise* (Cambridge University Press, 2005); James Faubion, *The Ethics of Kinship: Ethnographic Inquiries* (Rowman & Littlefield Publishers, Inc, 2001); Courtney Megan Cahill, "Regulating at the Margins: Non-Traditional Kinship and the Legal Regulation of Intimate and Family Life," *Arizona Law Review* 45 (2012): 43.

CHAPTER 6

1 In a works-in-progress workshop in June 2020, Dr. Luna Vives, in one of her working pieces on migration of unaccompanied migrant children across the Mediterranean border referred to "administrative death" and I borrow this term from her. See Luna Vives and Kira Williams, "Closing the Gap: Official Statistics on the Migration of Unaccompanied Migrant Children Across the Mediterranean" in *Research Handbook on the Law and Politics of Migration*, ed Catherine Dauvergne (Cheltenham: Edward Elgar Publishing Ltd, 2021).

2 Kate Hepworth, "Encounters with the Clandestine and the Nomad: The Emplaced and Embodied Constitution of Non-Citizenship," *Citizenship Studies* 18, 1 (2014) 2.

3 Lars Tummers and Victor Bekkers, "Policy Implementation, Street-Level Bureaucracy, and the Importance of Discretion," *Public Management Review* 16, 4 (2014): 528.

4 Laura Pottie and Lorne Sossin, "Demystifying the Boundaries of Public Law: Policy, Discretion, and Social Welfare" *UBC Law Review* 38, 1 (2005): 307.

5 Michael Lipsky, *Street-Level Bureaucracy: Dilemmas of the Individual in Public Services* (New York: Russell Sage Foundation, 1980), 14; Tony Evans and Peter Hupe, eds. *Discretion and the Quest for Controlled Freedom* (Cham: Palgrave, MacMillan, 2020), 75; Steven Maynard-Moody and Michael Musheno, *Cops, Teachers, Counselors: Stories from the Front Lines of Public Service* (University of Michigan Press, 2003); Vic Satzewich, *Points of Entry: How Canada's Immigration Officers Decide Who Gets In* (Vancouver: UBC Press, 2015); Michael Adler, "Understanding and Analysing Administrative Justice" in *Administrative Justice in Context*,

ed. Michael Adler (London: Hart Publishing, 2010); Marc Hertogh, "Through the Eyes of Bureaucrats: How Front-Line Officials Understand Administrative Justice" in *Administrative Justice in Context,* ed. Michael Adler (London: Hart Publishing, 2010), 204; Laura Pottie and Lorne Sossin, "Demystifying the Boundaries of Public Law"; Jennifer Raso, "Unity in the Eye of the Beholder? Reasons for Decision in Theory and Practice in the Ontario Works Program" *University of Toronto Law Journal* 70, 1 (2020): 1; Patrick Scott, "Assessing Determinants of Bureaucratic Discretion: An Experiment in Street-Level Decision Making," *Journal of Public Administration Research and Theory* 1 (1997): 35.

6 See Evans and Hupe, *Discretion and the Quest for Controlled Freedom*, 75; Maynard-Moody and Musheno, *Cops, Teachers, Counselors*; Satzewich, *Points of Entry*; Adler, "Understanding and Analysing Administrative Justice"; Hertogh, "Through the Eyes of Bureaucrats," 204; Pottie and Sossin, "Demystifying the Boundaries of Public Law"; Lipsky, *Street-Level Bureaucracy*; Raso, "Unity in the Eye of the Beholder?"; Scott, "Assessing Determinants of Bureaucratic Discretion," 35; Jennifer Elrick, *Making Middle-Class Multiculturalism: Immigration Bureaucrats and Policymaking in Postwar Canada* (University of Toronto Press, 2021).

7 Droit Gassner and Anat Gofen, "Street-Level Management: A Clientele-Agent Perspective on Implementation," *Journal of Public Administration Research and Theory* 28, 4 (2018): 551.

8 Lipsky, *Street-Level Bureaucracy*, 14.

9 Pottie and Sossin, "Demystifying the Boundaries of Public Law," 147; See also Mahabir Prashad Jain, "Administrative Law of Malaysia and Singapore," *Journal of the Indian Law Institute* 22, 4 (1980): 594; Gan Ching Chuan, "Malaysian Administrative Law at the Crossroads: *Quo Vadis?*" *Jurnal Undang-Undang* 36 (2009): 13; Wan Azlan Ahmad and Nik Ahmad Kamal Nik Mahmod, *Administrative Law in Malaysia* (Malaysia: Sweet & Maxwell Asia, 2006).

10 Pottie and Sossin, "Demystifying the Boundaries of Public Law," 147; see also Gan Chee Keong, Ahmad Azam Mohd Shariff, Ramalinggam, and Nazura Abdul Manap, "An Overview on the Public Interest Litigation in Malaysia: Development and Dilemma Under Provision of Remedies for Enforcement of Fundamental Rights," *Mediterranean Journal of Social Sciences* 7, 2 (2016): 114.

11 Genevra Richardson, "The Legal Regulation of Process" in *Administrative Law and Government Action*, eds. Genevra Richardson and Hazel Genn (Oxford: Clarendon Press, 1984), 105, quoted in Adler, *Administrative Justice in Context*, 129, 131.

12 Richard Lempert, "Discretion in a Behavioural Perspective: The Case of a Public Housing Eviction Board" in *The Uses of Discretion*, ed. Keith Hawkins (Oxford: Clarendon Paperbacks, 1994): 186.

13 Lipsky, *Street-Level Bureaucracy*, 14.

14 Evans and Hupe, *Discretion and the Quest for Controlled Freedom*, 75; Maynard-Moody and Musheno, *Cops, Teachers, Counselors*; Satzewich, *Points of Entry* (Vancouver: UBC Press, 2015); Adler, "Understanding and Analysing Administrative Justice"; Hertogh, "Through the Eyes of Bureaucrats," 204; Pottie and Sossin, "Demystifying the Boundaries of Public Law"; Lipsky, *Street-Level Bureaucracy*; Raso, "Unity in the Eye of the Beholder?"; Scott, "Assessing Determinants of Bureaucratic Discretion."

15 Hertogh, "Through the Eyes of Bureaucrats," 220.

16 Hertogh, "Through the Eyes of Bureaucrats," 220.

17 Graham Allison, *Essence of Decision: Explaining the Cuban Missile Crisis* (Boston, MA: Little Bron, 1971), quoted by Brodkin, "Policy Work," i258.

18 Keith Hawkins, ed, *The Uses of Discretion* (Oxford: Clarendon Paperbacks, 1994), 11.
19 See Genevieve Cartier, "Administrative Discretion and the Spirit of Legality: From Theory to Practice," *Canadian Journal of Law and Society* 24, 3 (2009): 313. In the article, Cartier explains the "dual conceptions of discretion" citing A.V. Dicey, *Introduction to the Study of the Law of the Constitution,* tenth edition, (London: Macmillan, 1959), 188; see also Hawkins, *The Uses of Discretion,* 13.
20 Hawkins, *The Uses of Discretion,* 14 referring to Ronald Dworkin and Denis Galligan.
21 Hawkins, *The Uses of Discretion,* 22. See also John Willis, "The McRuer Report: Lawyers' Values and Civil Servants' Values," *University of Toronto Law Journal* 17 (1968).
22 Hawkins, *The Uses of Discretion,* 24.
23 Hendrik Wagenaar, "'Knowing' the Rules: Administrative Work as Practice," *Public Administration Review* 64, 6 (2004): 643.
24 Mary Pat Baumgartner, "Social Limits to Discretion: An Organizational Perspective" in *The Uses of Discretion,* ed. Keith Hawkins (Oxford: Clarendon Paperbacks, 1994), 129–30.
25 Baumgartner, "Social Limits to Discretion," 136; Lempert, "Discretion in a Behavioural Perspective," 227; Scott, "Assessing Determinants of Bureaucratic Discretion," 51–52.
26 Those espousing the view that frontline workers work for the benefit of those they serve are as follows: citing Evelyn Brodkin, "Policy Work: Street-Level Organizations Under New Managerialism," *Journal of Public Administration Research and Theory* 21 (2011): 253 cited by Eva Thomann, Nadine van Engen, and Lars Tummers, "The Necessity of Discretion: A Behavioural Evaluation of Bottom-Up Implementation Theory" *Journal of Public Administration Research and Theory* 28, 4 (2018): 584; Lael Keiser, "State Bureaucratic Discretion and the Administration of Social Welfare Programs: The Case of Social Security Disability," *Journal of Public Administration Research and Theory* 9, 1(1999): 87–106; Steven Maynard-Moody and Shannon Portillo, "Street-Level Bureaucracy Theory" in *Oxford Handbook of American Bureaucracy,* ed. Robert McGregor Douglas (Oxford, Oxford University Press, 2010); Eva Thomann, "Is Output Performance All About the Resources? A Fuzzy-Set Qualitative Comparative Analysis of Street-Level Bureaucrats in Switzerland," *Public Administration* 93 (2015): 177–194; Tummers and Bekkers, "Policy Implementation, Street-Level Bureaucracy."
27 Scott, "Assessing Determinants of Bureaucratic Discretion," 51–52; Evelyn Brodkin, "Discretion in the Welfare State" in *Discretion and the Quest for Controlled Freedom,* eds. Tony Evans and Peter Hupe (Cham, Switzerland: Palgrave MacMillan, 2020), 75.
28 Anna Pratt and Lorne Sossin, "A Brief Introduction of the Puzzle of Discretion," *Canadian Journal of Law and Society* 24, 3 (2009): 301; see also Peter Mascini, "Discretion from a Legal Perspective" in *Discretion and the Quest for Controlled Freedom,* eds. Tony Evans and Peter Hupe (Cham, Switzerland: Palgrave MacMillan, 2020): 75
29 Elrick, *Making Middle-Class Multiculturalism.*
30 Kenneth Culp Davis, *Discretionary Justice: A Preliminary Inquiry* (Baton Rouge, LA: Louisiana State University Press, 1969); Hawkins, *The Uses of Discretion,* 30;

Peter Manning, "'Big Bang' Decisions: Notes on a Naturalistic Approach" in *The Uses of Discretion*, ed. Keith Hawkins (Oxford: Clarendon Paperbacks, 1994), 250.

31   Nicola Lacey, "The Jurisprudence of Discretion: Escaping the Legal Paradigm" in *The Uses of Discretion*, ed. Keith Hawkins (Oxford: Clarendon Paperbacks, 1994), 372; Pratt and Sossin, "Discretion in the Welfare State," 306; Peter Fitzpatrick, *The Mythology of Modern Law* (London: Routledge, 1992).

32   Pratt and Sossin, "Discretion in the Welfare State," 303; see also Adler, *Administrative Justice in Context*; Roncarelli v Duplessis, [1959] SCR 121; Robert Kagan, "The Organization of Administrative Justice Systems: The Role of Political Mistrust" in *Administrative Justice in Context*, ed. Michael Adler (London: Hart Publishing, 2010), 161. Adler writes: "Administrative officials are squeezed between public expectations for 'total justice' and, on the other side, by never-fully-adequate funding and the inevitable pathologies of bureaucracy" (129). Adler also says that, "When political parties, interest groups, legal experts or political leaders distrust the competence, political neutrality, and fairness of bureaucrats, they are inclined to demand stricter control of administrative discretion through detailed rules, rights to participate in administrative decision-making processes, more formal and adversarial legal procedures, and searching judicial review of administrative decisions" (179-180). See also Joel Handler, "Discretion: Power, Quiescence and Trust," in *The Uses of Discretion*, ed. Keith Hawkins (Oxford: Oxford University Press, 1994).

33   Pratt and Sossin, "Discretion in the Welfare State," 304; see also Nicola Lacey, "The Path Not Taken: HLA Hart's Harvard Essay on Discretion," *Harvard Law Review* 127, 2 (2013): 636; Davis, *Discretionary Justice*.

34   Elizabeth Emens, *Life Admin: How I Learned to Do Less, Do Better, and Live More* (Houghton Mifflin Harcourt, 2019), 3

35   Emens, *Life Admin*, 3–4.

36   Emens, *Life Admin*, 8.

37   Emens, *Life Admin*, 8–9.

38   Emens, *Life Admin*, 13.

39   Emens, *Life Admin*, 12.

40   Interview with 1S, Appendix in Chapter 5, Table 2, January 25, 2017; interview with 2S, Appendix in Chapter 5, Table 2, January 28, 2018; interview with 3S, Appendix in Chapter 5, Table 2, March 6, 2018; interview with 4S, Appendix in Chapter 5, Table 2, January 28, 2018; interview with 5S, Appendix in Chapter 5, Table 2, March 5, 2018; interview with 9S, Appendix in Chapter 5, Table 2, March 20, 2018; interview with 10S, Appendix in Chapter 5, Table 2, March 22, 2018; interview with 11S, Appendix in Chapter 5, Table 2, March 22, 2018; interview with 12S, Appendix in Chapter 5, Table 2, March 22, 2018; interview with 13S, Appendix in Chapter 5, Table 2, March 22, 2018; interview with 14S, Appendix in Chapter 5, Table 2, March 21, 2018; interview with 19S, Appendix in Chapter 5, Table 2, March 23, 2018.

41   Interviews with 6S, Appendix in Chapter 5, Table 2, March 20, 2018; interview with 7S, Appendix in Chapter 5, Table 2, March 20, 2018; interview with 8S, Appendix in Chapter 5, Table 2, March 20, 2018.

42   Interview with 10S.

43   Interview with 2L, Appendix in Chapter 5, Table 2, February 5, 2018.

44   Interview with 6L, Appendix in Chapter 5, Table 2, January 30, 2018.

45 Interview with 2S.
46 Interview with 2S.
47 Interview with 8S.
48 Interview with 5NGO, Appendix in Chapter 5, Table 2, January 30, 2018; interview with 12NGO, in Chapter 5, Appendix Table 2, February 6, 2018
49 Interview with 3A, Appendix in Chapter 5, Table 2, January 25, 2018; interview with 11NGO, Appendix in Chapter 5, Table 2, March 8, 2018.
50 Interview with 3A; interview with 12NGO.
51 Interview with 10NGO, Appendix in Chapter 5, Table 2, March 16, 2018.
52 Interview with 3A.
53 Interview with 3A.
54 Interview with 2S; interview with 2NGO, Appendix in Chapter 5, Table 2, January 23, 2018; interview with 12NGO.
55 Interview with 2S; interview with 2NGO; interview with 12NGO; interview with 3A.
56 Interview with 2S; interview 7S.
57 Interview with 1NGO, Appendix in Chapter 5, Table 2, January 17, 2018.
58 Interview with 1NGO.
59 Interview with 4S; interview with 5S; interview with 6S; interview with 7S; interview with 8S; interview with 9S; interview with 10S; interview with 11S; interview with 12S; interview with 13S; interview with 17S, Appendix in Chapter 5, Table 2, March 22, 2017; interview with 18S, Appendix in Chapter 5, Table 2, March 23, 2018.
60 Interview with 5S; interview with 17S.
61 Interview with 3PL, Appendix in Chapter 5, Table 2, February 12, 2018.
62 Interview with 3A.
63 Interview with 1PL, Appendix in Chapter 5, Table 2, January 28, 2018.
64 Interview with 2PL, Appendix in Chapter 5, Table 2, March 20, 2018.
65 Interview with 1L, Appendix in Chapter 5, Table 2, January 9, 2018.
66 Interview with 3A.
67 Interview with 6L.
68 Interview with 3A.
69 Interview with 3A.
70 Interview with 1S; Interview with 3S; Interview with 6S.
71 Interview with 1S.
72 Interview with 6S.
73 Interview with 12NGO.
74 For example, interview with 4NGO, January 17, 2018; interview with 5NGO; interview with 12NGO.
75 Interview with 12NGO.
76 Interviews with 2S; interview with 3S; interview with 6S; interview with 7S; interview with 8S; interview with 9S; interview with 11S; interview with 12S; interview with 13S; interview with 14S; interview with 15S, Appendix in Chapter 5, Table 2, March 21, 2018; interview with 16S, Appendix in Chapter 5, Table 2, March 21, 2018.
77 Interview with 1S; interview with 2S; interview with 3S; interview with 4S; interview with 5S; interview 9S; interview with 15S; interview with 16S; interview with 17S.

78 Interview with 3NGO, Appendix in Chapter 5, Table 2, January 18, 2018; interview with 8NGO, Appendix in Chapter 5, Table 2, February 26, 2018; interview with 12NGO.
79 Interview with 3NGO.
80 Interview with 4NGO; interview with 7NGO, Appendix in Chapter 5, Table 2, January 28, 2018.
81 Interview with 10NGO.
82 Interview with 1NGO.
83 Interview with 1NGO.
84 Interview with 3A.
85 Interview with 6NGO, Appendix in Chapter 5, Table 2, January 30, 2018.
86 Interview with 6NGO.
87 Interview with 2NGO; interview with 6NGO.
88 Interview with 8S.
89 Interview with 9S.
90 Interview with 12S; interview with 3A; interview with 2NGO.
91 Interview with 3A.
92 Interview with 6S.
93 Interview with 1PL.
94 Interview with 1PL; interview with 2PL.
95 Interviews with 9NGO, Appendix in Chapter 5, Table 2, February 28, 2018; interview with 11NGO.
96 Interview with 3S.
97 Interview with 15S.
98 Interview with 3A.
99 Interview with 14S.
100 Interview with 6NGO; Interview with 2PL
101 Interview with 2PL
102 Interview with 1PL; Interview with 5L, Appendix in Chapter 5, Table 2, January 29, 2018; interview with 2NGO
103 Interview with 2NGO.
104 Interview with 2NGO.
105 Interview with 1L.
106 Interview with 2L.
107 Interviews with 8S.
108 Interview with 8S.
109 Interview with 12NGO.
110 Interview with 1NGO; interview with 2NGO; interview with 6NGO.
111 Interview with 4S; interview with 12S.
112 Interview with 10S.
113 Interview with 11S.
114 Interview with 18S.
115 Interview with 9S.
116 Interview with 8NGO; interview with 6NGO.
117 Interview with 3A. Confirmed by 8NGO.
118 Interview with 5NGO.

119 Interview with 5NGO; interview with 2NGO.
120 Interviews with 2NGO; interview with 3A; interview with 13NGO, Appendix in Chapter 5, Table 3, April 9, 2018.
121 Interview with 3A.
122 Interview with 2NGO.
123 Interview with 8NGO.
124 Interview with 2L.
125 Interview with 5NGO.
126 Interview with 1L.
127 Interview with 1L.
128 Interview with 5L.
129 Interview with 5L.
130 Interview with 3L, Appendix in Chapter 5, Table 2, January 22, 2018.
131 Interview with 3L.
132 Interview with 2NGO.
133 Interview with 5NGO.
134 Interview with 6NGO.
135 Interview with 1NGO.
136 Interview with 2PL; interview with 1NGO.
137 Interview with 2PL; interview with 1NGO.
138 Interview with 3A.
139 Interview with 8NGO.
140 Interview with 8NGO.
141 Interview with 2NGO; interview with 11NGO.
142 Interview with 2NGO.
143 Interviews with 6NGO; interview with 3A.
144 Interview with 5S.
145 Interview with 2L.
146 Interview with 10S.
147 Interview with 4S; interview with 11S.
148 Interview with 4S.
149 Interview with 4S.
150 Interview with 6L.
151 Interview with 12NGO.
152 Interview with 12NGO.
153 Interview with 1S, interview with 4S. In both cases, a friend introduced the person to a paralegal.
154 Interview with 2S.
155 Interview with 2S; interview with 3S. 3S met the paralegal through a teacher at school. Interview with 4S; interview with 15S; interview with 16S; interview with 2NGO; interview with 5NGO; interview with 6NGO; interview with 7NGO; interview with 8NGO; interview with 9NGO; interview with 10NGO; interview with 11NGO; interview with 12NGO; interview with 13NGO.
156 Interview with 17S.
157 Interviews with 7S; interview with 8S; interview with 9S; interview with 10S; interview with 11S; interview with 12S; interview 13S; interview with 18S.
158 Interview with 12NGO; interview with 3A.

159 Interview with 5L; interview with 7L, Appendix in Chapter 5, Table 2, March 17, 2018, also confirmed this. 7L was working in the same firm.
160 Interview with 3L.
161 Interview with 1L, 2L, 3L, 8L.
162 Interview with 1NGO.
163 Interview with 19S.
164 Interview with 1PL.
165 Interview with 1L.
166 Interviews with 1S; interview with 2S; interview with 3S; interview 4S; interview with 5S; interview with 6S; interview with 8S; interview with 9S; interview with 11S; interview with 12S; interview with 13S; interview with 18S.
167 Interview with 3A.
168 Interview with 6NGO.
169 Interview with 2NGO.
170 Interview with 10NGO.
171 Interview with 12NGO.
172 Interview with 9NGO.
173 Interview with 10NGO.
174 Interview with 6NGO.
175 Ho Kit Yen, "Rectify SOPs to Allow Adopted Children Citizenship, Rights Group Tells Govt" March 16, 2023, https://www.freemalaysiatoday.com/category/nation/2023/03/16/rectify-sops-to-allow-adopted-children-citizenship-rights-group-tells-govt/.
176 Interview with 4S; interview with 9S.
177 Interview with 4S.
178 Interview with 4S.
179 Interview with 8S.
180 Interview with 9S.
181 Interview with 1NGO.
182 Interview with 6NGO.
183 Interview with 4S.
184 Interview with 12S; interview with 13S.
185 Interview with 12S.
186 Interview with 12S.
187 Interview with 11S.
188 Interview with 11S.
189 Interview with 11S.
190 Interviews with 1S; interview with 2S; interview with 5S; interview with 6S; interview with 17S; interview with 1PL; interview with 2PL; interview with 3A; interview with 1NGO; interview with 2NGO; interview with 5NGO; interview with 6NGO; interview with 7NGO; interview with 8NGO; interview with 9NGO; interview with 10NGO; interview with 11NGO; interview with 12NGO; interview with 13NGO.
191 Interview with 1S.
192 Interview with 3S.
193 Interview with 4S.
194 Interview with 6S; interview with 9S.
195 Interview with 10NGO.

Endnotes 233

196 Interview with 8L.
197 Interview with 3S; interview with 7S.
198 Interviews with 1S; interview with 3S; interview with 4S; interview with 7S; interview with 9S; interview with 14S; interview with 2NGO.
199 Interviews with 1L; interview with 8L; interview with 1PL; interview with 3PL; interview with 1NGO; interview with 6NGO; interview with 10NGO.
200 Interview with 3S.
201 Interview with 1PL.
202 Interview with 6NGO.
203 Lew Yee Hong, [2020] 1 CLJ 419: para 9.
204 Registration Rally Observation (January 26, 2018); interview with 9S.
205 Interview with 1L.
206 Interview with 8L.
207 For example, Nandita Sharma, *Home Economics: Nationalism and the Making of 'Migrant Workers' in Canada* (Toronto: University of Toronto Press, 2005); Gabriel Chin, "Regulating Race: Asian Exclusion and the Administrative State," *Harvard Civil Rights-Civil Liberties Law Review* 37 (2002): 1–64; Susan Sterett, Nicole DuPuis, and Faith Gibson Hubbard, "Administrative Law and Service Learning: Clients, Repetition, and Race," *Administration & Society* 49, 5 (2017): 679; Patrick Weil, "Races at the Gate: A Century of Racial Distinctions in American Immigration Policy (1865–1965)," *Georgetown Immigration Law Journal* 15 (2001): 625; Kristin Collins, "Illegitimate Borders: Jus Sanguinis Citizenship and the Legal Construction of Family, Race and Nation," *Yale Law Journal* 123 (2014): 2134; Carrie Arnold, "Racial Profiling in Immigration Enforcement: State and Local Agreements to Enforce Federal Immigration Law," *Arizona Law Review* 49 (2007): 113; Mae Ngai, "The Architecture of Race in American Immigration Law: A Reexamination of the Immigration Act of 1924," *Journal of American History* 86, 1 (1999): 67; Constance Backhouse, "Fairness in Immigration Law: Baker, 1999" in *Clair L'Heureux-Dubé: A Life* (Vancouver: UBC Press, 2017); Yasmeen Abu-Laban, "Keeping 'em Out: Gender, Race and Class Biases in Canadian Immigration Policy" in *Painting the Maple: Essays on Race, Gender and the Construction of Canada*, ed. Veronica Strong-Boag (Vancouver: UBC Press, 1998); Suzanne Shanahan, "Different Standard Differences: Contemporary Citizenship and Immigration Debates," *Theory and Society* 26, 4 (1997): 421.
208 Celeste Watkins-Hayes, "Race, Respect, and Red Tape: Inside the Black Box of Racially Representative Bureaucracies," *Journal of Public Administration Research and Theory* 21, supp 2 (2011): 233.
209 Interview with 5NGO.
210 Interview with 3S; interview with 5S; interview with 10S; interview with 19S.
211 Interview with 5S.
212 Interview with 3S.
213 Lim Kai Lin, [2018] 1 LNS 1828: para 2.
214 Interview with 5L.
215 Interview with 12NGO.
216 Interview with 2NGO.
217 Interview with 2NGO.
218 Interview with 3A.
219 Interview with 3A.

220 Interview with 10NGO.
221 Interview with 5NGO.
222 Interview with 6NGO.
223 Interview with 6NGO.
224 Interview with 8L, Appendix Table 2, March 23, 2018.
225 Interview with 6NGO, Appendix Table 2, January 30, 2018.
226 Interview with 3A.
227 Interview with 8L.
228 Interview with 19S.
229 Interview with 1PL.
230 Interview with 1PL.
231 Interview with 3L.
232 Juliet Pietsch and Marshall Clark, "Citizenship Rights in Malaysia: the experience of social and institutional discrimination among ethnic minorities," *Citizenship Studies* 18, 2 (2014): 309.
233 Sin Yee Koh, "How and Why Race Matters: Malaysian-Chinese Transnational Migrants Interpreting and Practicing Bumiputera-Differentiated Citizenship," *Journal of Ethnic and Migration Studies* 41, 3 (2015): 543.
234 Interview with 5NGO.
235 Interview with 5L.
236 Interview with 5L.
237 Interview with 2NGO.
238 Interview with 8L.
239 Interview with 8L; Interview with 1L.
240 Interview with 6L.
241 Interview with 2NGO.
242 Interview with 6NGO.
243 Interview with 6NGO.
244 Interviews with 1S; interview with 2S; interview with 3S; interview with 4S; interview with 5S; interview with 9S; interview with 11S, March 22, 2018. See Appendix Table 2; interview with 14S; interview with 1L; interview with 3L; interview with 1NGO; interview with 10NGO
245 Interview with 2S; interview with 14S.
246 Interview with 1NGO.
247 Interview with 6NGO.
248 Raso, "Unity in the Eye of the Beholder?" 1.
249 Interview with 1NGO.
250 Interview with 6NGO.
251 Interview with 1L.
252 Interview with 1PL.
253 Interview with 2L.
254 Interview with 2NGO.
255 Interview with 8L.
256 Interview with 1L.
257 Interview with 8L.
258 Interview with 10NGO.
259 Emens, *Life Admin*, 18–28.

260 Elizabeth Cohen, *The Political Economy of Time* (New York: Cambridge University Press, 2019), 3.
261 Cohen, *The Political Economy of Time*, 4–11.
262 Interview with 8NGO.
263 Interview with 3A.
264 Interviews with 1S; interview with 2S; interview with 3S; interview with 4S; interview with 5S; interview with 6S; interview with 9S; interview with 11S; interview with 12S; interview with 13S; interview with 14S; interview with 15S; interview with 16S; interview with 17S; interview with 18S. See also Ahmad Mustakim Zulkifli, "30 Years of Waiting for Citizenship" March 22, 2023, https://www.malaysianow.com/news/2023/03/23/30-years-of-waiting-for-citizenship.
265 Interviews with 3S; interview with 16S.
266 Interviews with 1S; interview with 2S; interview with 6S.
267 Interviews with 4S; interview with 5S; interview with 9S; interview with 11S; interview with 12S; interview with 13S; interview with 14S; interview with 18S.
268 Interviews with 15S; interview with 17S.
269 Interview with 3PL.
270 Interview with 3L.
271 Interviews with 6L; interview with 10NGO.
272 Interview with 1NGO. See also 10NGO.
273 Interviews with 1NGO; interview with 2NGO; interview with 6NGO; interview with 8NGO; interview with 12NGO.
274 Interview with 1PL.
275 Interview with 2L.
276 Interviews with 3L; interview with 8L; interview with 12S; interview with 18S; interview with 10 NGO .
277 Interview with 1L.
278 Interviews with 1S; interview with 2S; interview with 3S; interview with 4S; interview with 5S; interview with 9S; interview with 11S; interview with 12S; interview with 13S; interview with 14S; interview with 15S; interview with 18S.
279 Interviews with 1S; interview with 4S; interview with 5S; interview with 9S; interview with 12S; interview with 13S; interview with 14S; interview with 18S.
280 Interview with 18S.
281 Interview with 2S.
282 Interviews with 3S; interview with 11S; interview with 15S.
283 Interviews with 1PL; interview with 2A, Appendix in Chapter 5, Table 2, April 9, 2018; interview with 1L; interview with 3L; interview with 6L; interview with 3A; interview with 1NGO; interview with 6NGO; interview with 8NGO; interview with 10NGO.
284 Interview with 10NGO.
285 Interview with 3L.
286 Interview with 4L, Appendix in Chapter 5, Table 2, January 23, 2018.
287 Interview with 6L.
288 Interview with 5L.
289 Interview with 8NGO; interview with 10NGO.
290 Interview with 12NGO.
291 Interview with 8L.

292 Interview with 1NGO.
293 Interview with 8NGO.
294 Lipsky, *Street-Level Bureaucracy*.
295 Interview with 2S.
296 Interview with 4S.
297 Interview with 10S.
298 Interview with 5L.
299 Interview with 2L; interview with 3L.
300 Peter A. Gall, "Problems with a Faith Based Approach to Judicial Review," *Supreme Court Law Review* 66, 2(d) (2014): 222–31.
301 Adler, *Administrative Justice in Context*, 145.
302 Patrick Birkinshaw, "Grievances, Remedies and the State — Revisited and Re-appraised" in *Administrative Justice in Context*, ed. Michael Adler (London: Hart Publishing, 2010), 353–82; Tom Mullen, "A Holistic Approach to Administrative Justice?" in *Administrative Justice in Context*, ed. Michael Adler (London: Hart Publishing, 2010), 383–420; Lipsky, *Street-Level Bureaucracy*; Patrick Dunleavy, Simon Bastow, Jane Tinkler, Sofia Goldchluck, and Ed Towers, "Joining Up Citizen Redress in UK Central Government" in *Administrative Justice in* Context, ed. Michael Adler (London: Hart Publishing, 2010), 421–56.
303 Shamsul A. B., "A History of Identity, an Identity of a History," *Journal of Southeast Asian Studies* 32, 3 (2001): 359.
304 Shamsul A. B., "Nations-of-Intent in Malaysia" in *Asian Forms of the Nation*, eds. Stein Tonnesson and Han Antlov (London: Curzon, 1996), 325.
305 Shamsul A. B., "Nations-of-Intent in Malaysia," 330.
306 UN Economic and Social Council, "Comments Received from Governments on the Subject of the Draft Protocol relating to the Status of Stateless Persons: Belgium" (27 February 1953) UN Doc E/2373.
307 Ad Hoc Committee on Statelessness and Related Problems, "Summary Record of the Fourth Meeting" (26 January 1950) UN Doc E/AC.32/SR.4, para 3.
308 Susan Parker, "Esther Duflo Explains Why She Believes Randomized Controlled Trials Are So Vital" (Centre for Effective Philanthropy, June 23, 2011).
309 See for example, Jessica Ball, Harriot Beazley, Natasha Fox, and Leslie Butt, "Advancing Research on 'Stateless Children': Family Decision Making and Birth Registration among Transnational Migrants in the Asia-Pacific Region" *Migration & Mobility,* Paper No. MMP 2014-02 (2014); Leslie Butt and Jessica Ball, "Birth Registration in Southeast Asia: A Child's Foundation Right?" *Asian Population Studies* 13, 3 (2017): 223; Shuzhuo Li, "Birth Registration in China: Practices, Problems and Policies" *Population Research and Policy Review* 29 (2010): 297; Joshua Amo-Adjei and Samuel Kobina Annim, "Socioeconomic Determinants of Birth Registration in Ghana" *BMC International Health and Human Rights* 15 (2015): 14; Imke Harbers, "Legal Identity For All? Gender Inequality in the Timing of Birth Registration in Mexico" *World Development* 128 (2020); Simon Szreter, "The Right of Registration: Development, Identity Registration, and Social Security — A Historical Perspective" *World Development* 35, 1 (January 2007): 67.
310 Interview with 3A.
311 Claudia Cappa and T. Wardlaw, *Every Child's Birth Right: Inequities and Trends in Birth Registration* (Washington: UNICEF, 2013); UNICEF, *The 'Rights' Start to Life: A Statistical Analysis of Birth Registration* (Washington: UNICEF, 2005); Jonathan

Todres, "Birth Registration: An Essential First Step toward Ensuring the Rights of All Children," *Human Rights Brief* 10, 3 (2003): 32; Casey Dunning, Alan Gelb, and Sneha Raghavan, *Birth Registration, Legal Identity, and the Post 2015 Agenda* (Centre for Global Development, September 2014); Sally Sheldon, "From 'Absent Object of Blame' to 'Fathers Who Want to Take Responsibility': Reforming Birth Registration Law," *Journal of Social Welfare and Family Law* 31, 4 (2009): 373–89; Keith Breckenridge and Simon Szreter, eds. *Registration and Recognition: Documenting the Person in World History* (London: British Academy, 2012); Brad Blitz, Kara Apland, Mary Laga ay, Elizabeth Yarrow, et al., *Birth Registration and Children's Rights: A Complex Story* (Dublin: Plan International, 2014); Conklin, *Statelessness*, 141.

312 Sara Ahmed, *Willful Subjects* (London: Duke University Press, 2014), 7.

313 Kaitlyn Greenidge, "The Dread of Taxes That Even Beyoncé Can't Fix," *New York Times*, April 8, 2017, http://www.nytimes.com/2017/04/08/opinion/sunday/the-dread-of-taxes-that-even-beyonce-cant-fix.html. See a Canadian example involving an Indigenous person seeking services at a bank: Angela Sterritt, "Indigenous Grandfather and 12-Year-Old Handcuffed in Front of Vancouver Bank After Trying to Open an Account," *CBC News*, January 9, 2020, https://www.cbc.ca/news/canada/british-columbia/indigenous-girl-grandfather-handcuffed-bank-1.5419519?__vfz=medium%3Dsharebar.

314 Interview with 3PL; interview with 5L; interview with 17S; interview with 10S.

315 Interview with 2S; interview with 3S; interview with 4S; interview with 5S; interview with 10S; interview with 11S; interview with 12S; interview with 17S.

316 Jennifer Nedelsky, *Law's Relations: A Relational Theory of Self, Autonomy, and Law* (Oxford University Press, 2011), 14.

317 Cartier, "Administrative Discretion," 381–406.

CHAPTER 7

1 To listen to a conversation I had with Roisah, listen to *Migration Conversations* podcast episode titled, "Roisah's Statelessness" available on Apple Podcasts, Spotify, and Google Podcasts.

2 To listen to a conversation I had with my father, listen to *Migration Conversations* podcast episode titled, "A Father's Dream" available on Apple Podcasts, Spotify, and Google Podcasts.

3 Sara Ahmed, *Willful Subjects* (Durham, NC: Duke University Press 2014), 7; Teresa Brennan, *The Transmission of Affect* (Ithaca, New York: Cornell University Press, 2004), 56.

4 Stellan Vinthagen and Anna Johansson, "'Everyday Resistance': Exploration of a Concept and its Theories" *Resistance Studies Magazine* (2013): 1.

5 Judith Butler, *Undoing Gender* (London: Routledge, 2004).

6 Shompa Lahiri, "Performing Identity: Colonial Migrants, Passing and Mimicry Between the Wars," *Cultural Geographies* 10 (2003): 409.

7 Engin Isin, "Performative Citizenship" in *The Oxford Handbook of Citizenship*, eds. Ayelet Shachar, Rainer Bauböck, Irene Bloemraad, and Martin Vink, (London: Oxford University Press, 2018); Daiva Stasiulis and Abigail Bakan, "Negotiating Citizenship: The Case of Foreign Domestic Workers in Canada," *Citizenship: Pushing the Boundaries* 57 (1997): 112.

8 See for example Jabatan Pendaftaran Negara v MEMK, [2020] 1 LNS 199.

9 Gift of Citizenship for Stateless Top Student," *The Sun Daily*, March 28, 2019,

https://www.thesundaily.my/local/gift-of-citizenship-for-stateless-top-student-BX734366.

10   Interviews with 3A, Appendix in Chapter 5, Table 3, January 25, 2018; 5NGO, Appendix in Chapter 5, Table 3, January 30, 2018; interview with 1L, Appendix in Chapter 5, Table 2, January 9, 2018; interview with 8L, Appendix in Chapter 5, Table 2, March 23, 2018.

11   Sara Ahmed, *On Being Included: Racism and Diversity in Institutional Life* (Durham, NC: Duke University Press, 2012), 116.

12   Ahmed, *On Being Included*, 117.

13   Hashini Kavishtr Kannan, "Stateless Top Scorer Finally Gets Her Citizenship" *New Straits Times,* March 28, 2019.

14   "Gift of Citizenship for Stateless Top Student," *The Sun Daily,* March 28, 2019, https://www.thesundaily.my/local/gift-of-citizenship-for-stateless-top-student-BX734366.

15   "DNA Paternity Test Enables Yanesha to Become a Malaysian Citizen," International Biosciences, https://www.ibdna.com.my/dna-paternity-test-yanesha-malaysian-citizenship/. See also Ketua Pengarah Pendaftaran Negara, Malaysia et al v Navin Moorthy, Order dated 29 July 2015 (No K/P 730520-10-5805): para 29 where the court notes that "The fact that the plaintiff's father has succeeded in bringing up the plaintiff well is reflected in the many awards and academic achievements of the plaintiff."

16   Azzman Abdul Jamal, "Good Grades But Not Citizenship Leaves Young Girl in the Lurch" (April 1, 2023), https://www.malaysianow.com/news/2023/04/02/good-grades-but-no-citizenship-leaves-young-girl-in-the-lurch; Ahmad Mustakim Zulkifli, "Without Citizenship, Youth Dreams of Musical Career" March 24, 2023, https://www.malaysianow.com/news/2023/03/25/without-citizenship-youth-dreams-of-musical-career.

17   Freida Wong and Richard Halgin, "The 'Model Minority': Bane or Blessing for Asian Americans?" *Journal of Multicultural Counseling and Development* 34 (2006): 38, 41 and 43; see also Stacey J. Lee, "Behind the Model-Minority Stereotype: Voices of High- and Low-Achieving Asian American Students," *Anthropology & Education Quarterly* 25 (1994): 413–29; Paul Wong, Chienping Faith Lai, Richard Nagasawa, and Tieming Lin, "Asian Americans as a Model Minority: Self Perceptions and Perception by Other Racial Groups," *Sociological Perspectives* 41 (1998): 95–118; Elizabeth S. W. Toupin and Linda Son, "Preliminary Findings on Asian Americans: The Model Minority in a Small Private East Coast College," *Journal of Cross-Cultural Psychology* 22 (1991): 403–17; Cliff Cheng, "Are Asian American Employees a Model Minority or Just a Minority?" *Journal of Applied Behavioural Science* 33, 3 (1997): 277–90; Thomas K. Nakayama, "'Model Minority' and the Media: Discourse on Asian America," *Journal of Communication Inquiry* 12, 1 (1988): 65–73; Keith Osajima, "Asian American as the Model Minority" in Min Zhou and James V. Gatewood, eds *Contemporary Asian America: A Multidisciplinary Reader* (New York: New York University Press, 2000), 215–25; Ronald Takaki, *Strangers from a Different Shore: A History of Asian Americans* (New York: Penguin Books, 1989); Lucie Cheng and Philip Q. Yang, "Asians: The 'Model Minority' Deconstructed" in *Ethnic Los Angeles,* eds. Mehdi Bozorgmehr and Roger Waldinger, (New York: Russell Sage Foundation, 1996), 305–44.

18   Yuko Kawai, "Stereotyping Asian Americans: The Dialectic of the Model Minority and the Yellow Peril," *The Howard Journal of Communications* 16 (2005): 109–10;

See also N Gotanda, "Re-Producing the Model Minority Stereotype: Judge Joyce Karlin's Sentencing Colloquy in *People v Soon Ja Du*" in *Reviewing Asian America: Locating Diversity*, eds. Wendy L. Ng, Soo-Young Chin, James S. Moy, and Gary Y. Okihiro (Washington: Washington State University Press, 1995); Frank H. Wu, *Yellow: Race in America Beyond Black and White* (New York: Basic Books, 2002), 67; Nazli Kibria, *Becoming Asian American: Second-Generation Chinese and Korean American Identities* (Baltimore: John Hopkins University Press, 2002); Kawai, "Stereotyping Asian Americans," 113; Claire Jean Kim, "The Racial Triangulation of Asian Americans," *Politics & Society* 27, 1 (1999): 17; Gary Y. Okihiro, *Margins and Mainstreams: Asians in American History and Culture* (Seattle: University of Washington Press, 1994); Ellen Wu, *The Color of Success: Asian Americans and the Origins of the Model Minority* (Princeton University Press, 2013): 8–9.
19 Wu, *The Color of Success*, 3.
20 Wu, *The Color of Success*, 3–7; Kawai, "Stereotyping Asian Americans," 110; Kim, "The Racial Triangulation of Asian Americans"; Homi K. Bhabha, "The Other Question" in *Contemporary Postcolonial Theory: A Reader*, ed. Padmini Mongia (London: Arnold, 1996).
21 Kawai, "Stereotyping Asian Americans," 114; Osajima, "Asian American as the Model Minority," 451.
22 Okihiro, *Margins and Mainstreams*, 142.
23 Kawai, "Stereotyping Asian Americans," 118.
24 Richard Dyer, "The Role of Stereotypes" in *Media Studies: A Reader*, eds. Paul Marris and Sue Thornham (New York: New York University Press, 2002), 249.
25 Lahiri, "Performing identity," 416.
26 Butler, *Undoing Gender*, 224.
27 Isin, "Performative Citizenship," 507.
28 Butler, *Undoing Gender*, 350–77.
29 Isin, "Performative Citizenship," 515 (original emphasis).
30 Angela Garcia, "Hidden in Plain Sight: How Unauthorized Migrants Strategically Assimilate in Restrictive Localities in California," *Journal of Ethnic and Migration Studies* 40, 12 (2014): 1895.
31 Garcia, "Hidden in Plain Sight," 1896.
32 Chan Kwok-Bun and Caroline Pluss, "Modeling Migrant Adaptation: Coping With Social Strain, Assimilation and Non-Integration," *International Sociology* 28, 1 (2013): 49; Alastair Ager and Alison Strang, "Understanding Integration: A Conceptual Framework," *Refugee Studies* 21, 2 (2008): 166–91; Garcia, "Hidden in Plain Sight," 1895; See also Roger Brubaker, "The Return of Assimilation? Changing Perspectives on Immigration and its Sequels in France, Germany and the United States," *Ethnic and Racial Studies* 24 (2001): 531–48; Nathan Glazer, "Is Assimilation Dead?" *Annals of the American Academy of Political and Social Science* 530, 1 (1993): 122–36; Richard Alba and Victor Nee, *Remaking the American Mainstream: Assimilation and Contemporary Immigration* (Boston: Harvard University Press, 2003); Ruben Rubaut, "Assimilation and its Discontents: Between Rhetoric and Reality," *International Migration Review* 31 (1997): 923–60; Alejandro Portes and Min Zhou, "The New Second Generation: Segmented Assimilation and its Variants," *Annals of the American Academy of Political and Social Sciences* 530, 1 (1993): 74–96; Herbert Gans, "Second Generation Decline: Scenarios for the Economic and Ethnic Futures of the Post-1965 American Immigrants," *Ethnic and Racial Studies* 15, 2 (1992): 173–92; Tomas Jiminez and David Fitzgerald,

"Mexican Assimilation: A Temporal and Spatial Reorientation," *Du Bois Review* 4 (2007): 337–54.

33 Garcia, "Hidden in Plain Sight," 1895.
34 Kwok-Bun and Pluss, "Modeling Migrant Adaptation," 60.
35 Homi K. Bhabha, *The Location of Culture* (London: Routledge, 1994): 128.
36 Elaine Ginsberg, "The Politics of Passing" in *Passing and the Fictions of Identity*, ed. Elaine Ginsberg (Durham, NC: Duke University Press, 1996), 3
37 Ginsberg, "The Politics of Passing," 2–3.
38 Lahiri, "Performing identity," 413.
39 Lahiri, "Performing identity," 415.
40 Ginsberg, "The Politics of Passing," 6.
41 Lahiri, "Performing identity," 416.
42 Nurfadzilah Yahaya, *Fluid Jurisdictions: Colonial Law and Arabs in Southeast Asia* (Ithaca, New York: Cornell University Press, 2020).
43 Isin, "Performative Citizenship," 515.
44 "Gift of Citizenship for Stateless Top Student," *The Sun Daily*, March 28, 2019. https://www.thesundaily.my/local/gift-of-citizenship-for-stateless-top-student-BX734366.
45 Ida Lim, "Top-Scoring Roisah Stateless No More With Early Birthday Gift of Citizenship," *Malay Mail*, March 28, 2019. https://www.malaymail.com/news/malaysia/2019/03/28/top-scoring-roisah-stateless-no-more-with-early-birthday-gift-of-citizenshi/1737285.
46 Hashini Kavishtr Kannan, "Stateless Top Scorer Finally Gets Her Citizenship," *New Straits Times*, March 28, 2019. https://www.nst.com.my/news/nation/2019/03/473723/stateless-top-scorer-finally-gets-her-citizenship.
47 Kannan, "Stateless Top Scorer."
48 "Gift of Citizenship."
49 Interview with 1NGO, Appendix in Chapter 5, Table 2, January 17, 2018; interview with 6NGO, Appendix in Chapter 5, Table 2, January 30, 2018; interview with 8L, Appendix in Chapter 5, Table 2, March 23, 2018; interview with 1L, Appendix in Chapter 5, Table 2, January 9, 2018; interview with 1PL, Appendix in Chapter 5, Table 2, January 28, 2018; interview with 2L, Appendix in Chapter 5, Table 2, February 5, 2018; interview with 2NGO, Appendix in Chapter 5, Table 2, January 23, 2018; interview with 3A, Appendix in Chapter 5, Table 2, January 25, 2018; interview with 10NGO, Appendix in Chapter 5, Table 2, March 16, 2018; interview with 3L, Appendix in Chapter 5, Table 2, January 22, 2018.
50 Interview with 1L.
51 Interview with 8L, Appendix in Chapter 5, Table 2, March 23, 2018.
52 Interview with 6NGO.
53 Interview with 8NGO, Appendix in Chapter 5, Table 2, February 28, 2018.
54 Interview with 5NGO, Appendix in Chapter 5, Table 2, January 30, 2018.
55 Interview with 6NGO.
56 Interview with 10NGO.
57 Interview with 10NGO.
58 "Formerly Stateless Girls Ace SPM Despite Issues," *The Star Online*, March 29, 2019. https://www.thestar.com.my/news/nation/2019/03/29/formerly-stateless-girls-ace-spm-despite-issues/.

59 "Home Ministry Irresponsible for Blaming Parents of Stateless Children," *New Straits Times*, March 26, 2019, https://www.nst.com.my/news/nation/2019/03/473046/home-ministry-irresponsible-blaming-parents-stateless-children.

60 "Unconstitutional to Blame Parents for Stateless Kids, says LFL," *Malaysiakini*, March 25, 2019. https://www.malaysiakini.com/news/469567.

61 UN, "Sustainable Development Goals Agenda," *United Nations*, 2020. https://www.un.org/sustainabledevelopment/development-agenda/; Marion Fourcade and Kieran Healy, "Classification Situations: Life-Chances in the Neoliberal Era," *Accounting, Organizations and Society* 38 (2013): 559–72.

62 "Family Support Group for Stateless Malaysian Children," *Facebook*, https://www.facebook.com/statelesschildrenmy/.

63 Ethel Tungohan, "From the Politics of Everyday Resistance to the Politics From Below: Migrant Care Worker Activism in Canada" Dissertation (University of Toronto, 2014): 4.

64 See for example Michele Ford and Nicola Piper, "Southern Sites of Female Agency: Informal Regimes and Female Migrant Labour Resistance in East and Southeast Asia" in *Everyday Politics of the World Economy*, eds. John Hobson and Leonard Seabrooke (Cambridge University Press, 2007), 63–80; Ligaya Lindio-McGovern, *Filipino Peasant Women: Exploitation and Resistance* (University of Pennsylvania Press, 1997); Ethel Tungohan, *Care Activism: Migrant Domiestic Workers, Movement-Building, and Communities of Care* (Champaign, Illinois: University of Illinois Press, 2023)..

CHAPTER 8

1 Interview with 6NGO.
2 Interview with 8NGO.
3 Interview with 8NGO.
4 Stanley Cohen, *States of Denial: Knowing about Atrocities and Suffering* (New York: John Wiley & Sons, 2013).
5 Bruna Seu, "Knowing and Not Knowing: Implicatory Denial and Defence Mechanisms in Response to Human Rights Abuses" in *Psychosocial Imaginaries*, ed. Stephen Frosh (London: Palgrave MacMillan, 2013).
6 Phillip Cole, "Insider Theory and the Construction of Statelessness" in *Understanding Statelessness*, eds. Tendayi Bloom, Katherine Tonkiss, and Philip Cole (New York: Routledge, 2017), 255–67.
7 Cole, "Insider theory," 255; Ayelet Shachar, *The Birthright Lottery: Citizenship and Global Inequality* (Cambridge, MA: Harvard University Press, 2009); See Joseph Carens, "In Defence of Birthright Citizenship" in *Migration in Political Theory: The Ethics of Movement and Membership*, eds. Sarah Fine and Lea Ypi (Oxford University Press, 2016): 222 for Carens's rebuttal to Ayelet Shachar.
8 Neil Walker, "The Place of Territory in Citizenship" in *The Oxford Handbook of Citizenship*, eds. Ayelet Shachar, Rainer Bauböck, Irene Bloemraad, and Martin Vink, (London: Oxford University Press, 2017): 554.
9 Rainer Baubock, "Changing the Boundaries of Citizenship: The Inclusion of Immigrants in Democratic Politics," in *From Aliens to Citizens: Redefining the Status of Immigration in Europe*, ed. Rainer Baubock (Vienna: Avery, 1994), 199–232.
10 Sarah Song, "The Significance of Territorial Presence and the Rights of Immi-

grants" in *Migration in Political Theory: The Ethics of Movement and Membership*, eds. Sarah Fine and Lea Ypi (Oxford: Oxford University Press, 2016).

11 Lindsey Kingston, *Fully Human: Personhood, Citizenship, and Rights* (Oxford: Oxford University Press, 2019): 67 (original emphasis).

12 Charles Mills, "Race and Global Justice" in *Domination and Global Political Justice: Conceptual, Historical, and Institutional Perspectives*, eds. Barbara Buckinx, Jonathan Trejo-Mathys, and Timothy Waligore (New York: Routledge, 2015): 196.

13 Tendayi Bloom, *Noncitizenism: Recognizing Noncitizen Capabilities in a World of Citizens* (London: Routledge, 2018): 32.

14 Kamal Sadiq, "Postcolonial Citizenship" in *The Oxford Handbook of Citizenship*, eds. Ayelet Shachar, Rainer Bauböck, Irene Bloemraad, and Martin Vink, (London: Oxford University Press, 2017): 178–79.

15 Sadiq, "Postcolonial Citizenship," 179–80.

16 Jennifer Nedelsky, *Law's Relations: A Relational Theory of Self, Autonomy, and Law* (Oxford University Press, 2011), 3.

17 Nedelsky, *Law's Relations*, 3.

18 Hadley Freidland, *Reclaiming the Language of Law: The Contemporary Articulation and Application of Cree Legal Principles in Canada* (PhD dissertation, University of Alberta Faculty of Law, 2016), 165.

19 Val Napoleon, *Thinking About Indigenous Legal Orders* (Research Paper, National Centre for First Nations Governance, 2007), 19.

20 Zainab Amadahy, "Community, 'Relationship Framework,' and Implications for Activism," *Rabble*, July 13, 2010. http://rabble.ca/news/2010/07/community-%E2%80%98relationship-framework%E2580%99-and-implications-activisim.

21 Catherine Dauvergne, *Making People Illegal: What Globalization Means for Migration and Law* (Cambridge: Cambridge University Press, 2008); Bloom, *Noncitizenism*.

22 Darcy Lindberg, "kihcitwâw kîkway meskocipayiwin (Sacred Changes): Transforming Gendered Protocols in Cree Ceremonies through Cree law" (Master's thesis, University of Victoria, 2017), 53–54.

INDEX

adopted children,
    burden of proof on, 76–8, 144
    judicial considerations for, 69, 75–6, 84
    out-of-court case resolution, 74, 89, 91, 159
    parental strategies for, 73–6, 90–1, 131
    processes for, 125–6, 133–4, 136, 145–6
    revocation or denial of citizenship, 73–6, 79–80, 121–3, 166–8
    rights for, 50, 69, 74
    stories of stateless, 99, 103–4, 114, 156–8, 177–9, 183–91
    see also birth certificates; mother's citizenship; remedies for statelessness
Adoption Act (Malaysia, 1952), 65, 121
    narrow interpretation of, 75–6, 78
administrative law, 90
    statelessness through, 12, 111, 159
Adrian, Yuen Ben Lee, 1–2
advocacy for stateless persons, 5, 7, 183
    challenges in, 69, 74, 127–8, 172
    legal, 58–9, 65, 87–92, 174
    processes in, 117, 122–4, 126, 148, 187
    self-, 3, 115
    stories of, 96, 101, 108, 137, 165–7
    strategies of, 82, 131, 136, 159, 169, 189–90
    vibrant community, 20, 22, 49
Ahmed, Sara, 139, 151
Allerton, Catherine, 21
Anak Negeri, 24, 28, 35–6
Anderson, Benedict, 28
Arendt, Hannah, 15–16
Asia,
    European imperialism in, 32
    statelessness in, 12, 16, 51
Asian Americans, 153
Asian culture,
    notions of, 27, 34
    Western versus, 14–16
Assam (India), Bengali Muslims in, 12, 18, 171

assimilation,
    immigrant efforts at, 141–2, 152, 155–6
    process of, 155–6
    resistance to, 40, 156
    state strategy of, 38, 152–3, 155
Association of Southeast Asian Nations (ASEAN), 12
    convention ratification, 51–2
    human rights, approaches to, 52, 103

Bajau Laut, 21, 36, 41
bank accounts, barriers to accessing, 5–6, 157, 237n313
Batchelor, Carol, 48
Bauböck, Rainer, 14
Benhabib, Seyla, 15
Bhagwati, Prafullachandra, 58
Bhatia, Amar, 14
birth certificates, 137, 176
    challenges obtaining, 118–21, 145, 178
    confiscation of, 70, 72–4, 128, 144, 154, 181
    fraudulent, 121, 128, 144, 181, 186
    ghost citizen creation via, 70–4, 78, 98–100, 121, 180–4
    normative understandings of, 67, 71–2, 88–9
    revocation of citizenship via, 70–2, 74–5, 130–1, 136, 190
birth registration,
    challenges in, 75, 79, 114–16, 120–2, 131
    denial of citizenship, 86, 139, 144, 178–80, 190
    lack of documentation, 72–4, 97–100, 116, 118, 187
    late, 79–80, 103, 119–21, 181
    legal provision for, 50, 66–9, 80
    other country, 71, 183
    process of, 80, 131, 147–9
birthright citizenship, 50–1, 171
    examples of, 9, 47, 53
    exceptions to, 9, 60, 82, 106–7, 173
Bloemraad, Irene, 14

Bloom, Tendayi, 14–15, 172
borders,
    citizenship theorization and, 14, 16–18, 41, 107, 190
    statelessness within, 41, 61–2
    state control and, 8, 16–17, 105, 174–5
Bosniak, Linda, 42
British colonization,
    citizenship laws, shaping, 3, 6, 10, 27, 31–2
    independence from, 12, 28–30, 37, 66–7
    legacies of, 17–18, 27, 166
    racial categorization in, 30–2, 40, 166, 168
    statelessness and, 3, 24, 97
    see also colonization, European; racial categorization
Brunei, 20, 29, 52
    River, 19, 165
Budlakoti v Canada, 60
Bumiputera,
    demographics of, 35–6, 41
    meaning of, 33–5, 37
    non-Bumiputera versus, 34–7, 39, 43
    recognition of status, 33–6, 38–9
Butler, Judith, 143, 151, 154
Byrd, Jodi, 11

Calvin, Robert, 9
Canepa v Canada, 58
censuses, 17, 30, 32, 34
Chan Tai Ern case, 83
Cheong, Amanda, 139, 160–1
children, stateless,
    adopted, see adopted children
    familial hardship from, 114–15, 119, 134, 137–9, 168
    as "illegitimate," 67, 75–81, 103, 120–2, 166
    proportion of, 6, 73–4, 79–80, 113, 176
    rights of, 50, 65, 88–9
    state work against recognition, 21, 76–7, 82–6, 136–7
    stories of, 23, 70–2, 80–4, 96–102, 143–7, 179–90
    systemic denial of, 65, 70, 122, 163
    see also birth registration; birthright citizenship

Chinese,
    descent, 34–9, 101, 128
    family members, 100–1, 141, 163, 180
    identity, colonial, 32–3
    immigration to Malaysia, 30, 37
    intermarriage with, 130, 178–81, 183–4
    Malaysian trade with, 29–30
    statelessness among, 19–20, 98, 128
    stereotypes of, 31, 128–9
Chin Kooi Nah case, 77, 86
Chung, Erin Aeran, 15
citizenship, 54, 146
    absence of, see citizenship status, being without
    automatic (operation of law), 66–9, 74–80, 85–7, 97, 161
    birthright, see birthright citizenship
    colonial impacts on, 9, 15, 17, 31–9, 42, 166–8
    competing claims on, 15, 35–9, 42–3, 56, 58, 158
    concepts of, 3, 8–9, 14–15, 39–41, 171–4
    denial of, 4–6, 28, 60–2, 86–8, 106–7, 168–72
    discretionary (by registration), 68, 85–7, 127, 135, 161
    dual, 83
    ghost, see ghost citizenship
    feminist critiques of, 13
    jus nexi, 95, 105–7
    jus sanguinis (blood based), 52, 76–81, 108, 173
    jus soli (birthright), see birthright citizenship
    Malaysian notions of, 33–4, 39, 42, 54, 146, 168
    model citizen construction and, 150–4, 156
    via naturalization, 46–7, 53–4, 66, 69, 103, 133
    need for proof of, 72–3, 77, 84, 115–16, 138, 147
    performing, 142–3, 151, 153–9, 172
    politicization of conferral, 121, 125, 132–3, 140, 157
    postcolonial, see postcolonial citizenship

Index   245

removal of, 61, 70-1, 82, 157, 171
republican versus liberal models, 13, 196n56
second-class, 39, 42
stateless persons' belief in, 3-4, 23-4, 43, 104
temporal limitations of, 77, 80-1, 83, 85-6, 121, 133
universalist notions of, 13, 15
citizenship law,
    barriers in, 23, 48-9, 52-3, 84, 122
    British impacts on, 3, 6, 10, 27, 31-2
    differentiating identities and, 35-7, 100, 107-8, 115
    in Malaysia, 65-9, 71-2, 80-2, 100, 143
    research on, 21, 54
    state discretion in, 47, 51-3, 69-70, 110-12, 125, 157-9
citizenship status, being without,
    barriers to citizen benefits, 3, 5-7, 51, 118
    research on, 54, 143
Clark, Marshall, 33, 130
class(ed) relations,
    citizenship and, 30, 39, 42, 112, 143, 156
    racialized scholars and, 20-1
Cole, Phillip, 14, 171
colonization, European, 175
    international legal order in, 8-9, 15, 27, 192n15
    legacies of, 27-8, 31-2, 156
    see also British colonization
Conklin, William, 47-8, 53
Constitution of Malaysia, 13, 22, 161
    citizenship rights in, 41, 65-9, 74, 97
    discriminatory application of, 69-72, 76-83, 86
    Malay privileges in, 32-5, 38-9, 102
    racial categorization in, 10, 97, 168
    stipulations in, 29, 75, 136, 143-5
Convention against Torture, 24, 65
Convention on the Reduction of Statelessness (1961), 47
    signatories to, 45-6, 51-2, 65
Convention Relating to the Status of Stateless Persons (1954), 45
    normative views of, 46-7

rights in, 49-51, 92
signatories to, 45-6, 51-2, 64-5
Convention on the Rights of the Child (CRC), 52
    obligations under, 50-1, 64-5
criminalization, stateless persons', 3, 6, 56-7, 60-2
critical race theory, 142, 175

Daniels, Timothy, 31, 33, 203n25
Daud, Nursyahirah Mohd, 160-1
decolonial practices, 25
deportation,
    citizenship shielding from, 3
    fear/risk of, 6, 12, 95, 114, 165
    persons facing, 56-8, 60, 188
detention, immigration,
    children in, 88, 190
    fear of, 6, 95, 114, 165
    research on, 13, 98, 177
    stateless persons in, 79-80, 88, 98, 117, 188-90
deviance, stateless persons', 6, 17-18, 63, 142, 168-9
Dhamoon, Rita Kaur, 10, 23
DNA tests, 90, 98, 119-20, 122, 177, 183-6
documentation, 18, 88
    administrative labour of, 84-5, 93, 123, 145, 151, 182
    application challenges, 109, 115-17, 120-4, 132, 177
    assistance with, 123-4, 159-63
    black market and scams for, 122
    discrimination regarding, 118-19, 128-9, 131-3, 157, 174-5
    exclusion of stateless persons through, 18, 68-9, 72-3, 152, 189-90
    imagined communities and, 18, 35
    importance of, 70, 92, 99, 113-14, 183
    lack of stateless persons', 4-5, 13, 24, 46, 96-100, 117, 187
    loss of government, 5, 99, 103, 120-2, 136-7, 178-83
    nation-state building and, 18, 32, 101-2
    systems of, 17-18, 71, 80, 174-5
    as technical problem, 18, 48, 163, 170

see also birth certificates; birth registration
Duraisingh, Samuel, case, 77

East Malaysia, 29, 207n124
  Indigenous persons of, 41
education, 33
  barriers to, 3, 97, 103, 118–19, 144, 165
  rights to, 12, 46
  statelessness persons' lack of, 6, 18, 21, 115, 156
employment, 6, 46, 55
  barriers to, 3, 97, 165
ethnicity, 50–1, 181
  community links via, 4, 15, 30, 38
  disunity, 41–2, 155–6
  Malay versus non-Malay, 33–9, 41, 128–30
  statelessness and, 42, 101, 152
  use of term, 24, 28
ethnographic analysis, use of, 22, 25, 65
exclusion, structural, 6, 13–14, 154–5
  in citizenship framework, 37, 42, 62, 74, 172
  in research, 12, 53

federal government, 182
  citizenship and Malayness, 33–9, 42
  duties of, 68
  positions in, 29, 66
folklore, Malaysian and Asian, 1–2
Foo Toon Aik case, 75–6
foreignness, stateless persons',
  children's, 71, 79–80, 122–3, 168, 176
  contestation of, 3, 17–18, 22, 89, 158
  lack of evidence for, 4, 56, 84–5, 104–6
  mothers', 79–83, 100–1, 168, 180
  negative repercussions of, 6, 12, 150–1, 167, 174
  racial categorization and, 10, 23, 36, 130–1, 171–2
  state/legal narratives of, 6–8, 13, 21 42–9, 63, 92–5
  subjective interpretations of, 59–60, 69–70, 132–4, 137
foundlings, 47, 99

Gabriel, Sharmani Patricia, 33, 36–8
gender(ed) relations, 143
  discrimination, 100, 128
  racialized scholars and, 20–1
Geneva Conclusions, 92–3
genuine and effective links,
  denial of ghost citizens', 7, 21, 42–3, 71, 82, 92–3, 171–2
  home country, 3–4, 12–14, 58, 84, 104–7, 166
  interpretations of, 53–5, 60–3, 67–8, 77–80
  lack of documentation on, 13, 96–100, 169
  research on, 92, 99, 102, 108, 153
ghost citizens,
  concept of, 3–4, 42–3
  denial of, 4–6, 28, 45, 60–3, 86–8, 106–7, 168–72
  as haunting, 2, 6–7, 176
  legal development of, 45, 51–3, 69–84, 110–12, 125, 157–9
  see also stateless persons
ghost citizenship, 3–4
  adoption and, 73–6, 79–80, 121–3, 166–8
  birth certificates and, 70–4, 78, 98–100, 121, 180–4
  conferral of, 72–4, 86, 139, 144, 178–80, 190
  "illegitimate" children and, 67, 76, 79–84, 120, 103, 143
  Malaysian citizenship application processes, 68–9, 109, 115–17, 120–4, 132, 177
  state assumptions with, 51, 65–9, 71–2, 78–82, 100, 143
ghosting, by states, 5, 47
  international law permitting, 51, 62–3, 69
  in Malaysia, 68–70, 78–9, 132
ghost stories, 1, 176; *see also* Pontianak
Ginsberg, Elaine, 155–6
Gowayed, Heba, 20–1
Gyulai, Gàbor, 92–3, 95

Haja Mohideen MK Abdul Rahman case, 68, 70, 80
health care, 165
  barriers to accessing, 3, 6, 12, 103, 157

Hirschman, Charles, 31–2
Hoang, Kimberly Kay, 20–1
Home Minister, 69, 87, 132–3, 158, 162–3, 166
  meeting with 146–7, 154
home state,
  genuine and effective links to, *see* genuine and effective links
  ghosting by, 4–6
human rights,
  administrative dilution of, 16–17, 55, 174
  attempts to resolve statelessness via, 12, 14, 92, 174
  international legal instruments for, 16, 49–53, 64–5
  state narratives of, 45–6, 64–5
  state reservations with, 20, 52, 65, 171
Human Rights Committee (United Nations), decisions, 55–8, 60

identities,
  colonial impacts on, 17, 31–8, 166
  contestation of, 27–9, 95, 106
  indigenous, 30–1, 39–40
  "Malay," 27, 30–4, 37–9, 42, 152
  national, 6, 13–15, 17, 39, 42–3, 50, 138
  parental, 77, 82
  racial categorizations and, 17–18, 23, 31–4, 39, 127
  shedding, 155–6
  stateless persons', 17–18, 42, 46, 70–2, 88–9, 154, 168
  terms describing, 28–9
identity documents, 18–19
  applications, 99, 101, 113–14, 128, 182
  loss of, 178, 181
  revocation of citizenship, 70, 72, 74, 174
illegality, 129
  narratives of statelessness and, 3, 17–18, 84, 158, 169
Ilyasov v Kazakhstan, 58–9
imagined communities, 18
  nations as, 28, 42
immigrants, 129, 155
  colonial notions of, 33, 36–8, 43

immigration, 141, 169
  controls, 41, 116
  detention, 13, 88, 98, 190
  law, 56, 58, 197
  waves of regional, 30, 37
imperialism,
  British, 24, 30
  racialized citizenship under, 15, 32, 36, 173
Indians,
  identity, colonial, 31–3, 128
  immigration to Malaysia, 30, 34, 36–8, 180–9
  Tamil, 97, 99, 178, 191
indigeneity,
  conceptions of, 12, 39–40, 173
  statelessness and, 24–5, 30–1
Indigenous law, 107, 140, 173–4
Indigenous persons,
  as bumiputera, *see* Bumiputera
  identity, colonial, 32–5, 37–8, 172–3
  kinship notions of, 107–8, 129, 140
  "Malayness" of, 30–3, 37–9, 43
  settler colonial hierarchies versus, 11, 30–1, 39–40
  statelessness and, 24–5, 30–1, 101–2, 129, 177–8, 188
  use of term, 24, 28
Indonesia, 29, 52, 79
  migrants from, 41, 71, 97, 101–2, 116, 188
  family members from, 30, 123, 178–9, 181, 184–6
International Convention on the Elimination of All Forms of Racial Discrimination (ICERD), 51, 53, 65
International Court of Justice (ICJ), 11–12, 54
International Covenant on Civil and Political Rights (ICCPR), 65
  interpretations of nationality, 50, 52, 60–1
  statelessness vis-à-vis, 55–6
International Covenant on Economic, Social and Cultural Rights (ICCPR), 50
international law, 8
  rights to nationality under, 50–1, 54–5, 61–3, 104

statelessness in, 44, 46–8, 62, 69, 85, 170
state prerogatives versus, 52–3, 58, 62–3, 170–1
Iran-US Claims Tribunal, 54–5
Islam, 40, 64
"Malayness" of, 30, 32–4, 38, 41, 152, 156
see also Muslims

judicial decisions,
burden of documentation for, 71, 73, 79
discretionary approaches to, 91, 125, 135–7
racial categories in, 10
on statelessness, 7, 75–6, 82, 86–92, 186
judicial notice, 71, 167, 170
concept of, 84–5
jus nexi citizenship, 95, 105–7
jus sanguinis (blood based) citizenship, 52, 76–81, 108, 173
jus soli (birthright) citizenship, *see* birthright citizenship

Kamaruddin, Zuraida binti, 146, 148–9
Kampong Ayer, 19, 165
Kingston, Lindsey, 14, 172
kinship, 3, 28, 69, 95, 167
Indigenous legal traditions of, 107–8, 140
need for recognition of, 4, 7, 41–2, 153–5, 158, 176
Koya, Latheefa, 148–50

law-as-text,
assumptions with, 45, 63, 80, 112
deference to, 45, 106, 174
limitations of, 62, 112, 174
Lee Chin Pon case, 75–6
legal processes,
barriers in, 123–5
assistance and advocacy in, 117, 122–4, 126, 148, 187
citizenship, 68–9, 109, 115–17, 120–4, 132, 177
fees in, 91, 109, 119–20, 124, 144
stateless persons' ghosting, 68–70, 78–9, 91, 132

legal reform, statelessness, 81–2
implementation problems, 12, 17, 44–5, 112, 159
Legitimacy Act (Malaysia, 1961), 65
Lew Yee Hong case, 127
liberalism, citizenship under, 13–15, 28, 172
Liechtenstein v Guatemala, *see* Nottebohm case
Lim Jen Hsian case, 81, 83
Lim Kai Lin case, 70, 86, 128
Lindberg, Darcy, 174–5

Madafferi v Australia, 58
Madhuvita case, 70, 81
Malacca, port of, 30
Malay persons,
becoming, 30, 38, 41–3, 97, 152–7, 168
privileges versus non-Malays, 32–4, 36–41, 128–31
see also Bumiputera; Indigenous persons
Malaysia,
airline slogan, 27
citizenship acquisition in, 33–4, 39, 42, 54, 66–70, 146, 168
colonial history of, 3, 17–20, 27–8, 31–2, 138, 156
constitution of, see Constitution of Malaysia
demographics of, 34–5, 41, 129
formation of Federation of, 10, 17–18, 29–30
human rights instruments, signing, 20, 51–2, 64–5, 171
statelessness in, 3, 20–2, 29, 65–6, 131, 144, 154
see also East Malaysia; Peninsular Malaysia
Malaysia Day, citizenship and, 66–7, 97–8
Malaysians,
assumptions about, 33, 37–8, 157, 166
demographics, 34–5, 41, 129
Indigenous persons versus, *see* Indigenous persons
stateless identification as, 22, 131, 144, 154

Western thought system interference, 28, 32
see also Malay persons
Manickam, Sandra, 32
Manly, Mark, 44
marriage, 12
   after stateless child's birth, 71, 75–8, 96, 100–1, 179–81, 184
   certificates, 98, 118, 120, 124–5, 130
   importance in citizenship, 79, 81–3, 101–2, 117, 176, 182
   lack of legal, 67, 130, 143, 166, 177–8, 183–5, 189
   "mixed," 100–1, 177, 186–7, 189
   registration, 97, 118, 123, 125–6, 163, 181
masuk Melayu (becoming Malay), 30, 38, 41–3, 97, 152–7, 168
   three pillars of, 34, 152, 156
Mawani, Renisa, 24
membership, state,
   assumptions of, 14–15, 33, 172–3
   different notions of, 11, 33, 107, 171
   Western state notions of, 9, 17–18, 27, 49
migrants, 11
   challenges facing, 116, 129, 188
   children of, 98, 102–3, 179
   lack of rights for, 16, 98
   narratives about, 17, 36, 40–1, 156, 158, 167, 170
   research on, 13, 21, 30, 178, 190
   use of term, 23–4
Mills, Charles, 172
mine workers, 30, 37, 203n25
Ministry of Home Affairs, 145, 166
   meetings at, 22, 147
model citizen narratives, 150–4, 156
Mohamed Sadik Mohamed Ali case, 80
mothers' citizenship, 176
   as foreign, 6–7, 79–83, 100–1, 168, 180, 188
   importance for children's, 70–1, 77, 81, 178
   Malaysian fathers versus, 70–1, 77–82, 100, 120, 131, 188
Muslims, 152, 181, 184, 190
   in Assam, India, 12, 18
   dakwah (missionaries), 40

   investment in Malay Muslim state, 41–2, 52, 130
   refugees, 102–3
   treatment of non-Muslims versus, 100, 130, 143, 188
   see also Islam
Myanmar, genocide against Rohingya, 12, 18, 52, 102, 171

Nah, Alice, 29–30, 32, 37–40
Nalaln Kunji Kanan case, 72
nationalism, 13, 28
   ethnic, 33, 173
nationality, 29, 42, 100, 174
   dominant and effective test, 48, 54, 78, 105
   international legal instruments on, 49–53, 55
   lack of, 93, 95, 138
   "one's own country" and, *see* "one's own country"
   Statelessness Conventions on, 45–9
   state prerogative on, 48–9, 58, 61–2, 69
   variable rights to, 44–52, 57, 83
nation building,
   colonial impacts on, 31–3, 173
   racialized identities and, 42, 168, 175
   strategies of, 42–3, 112
Nedelsky, Jennifer, 140, 173
Neuman, Gerald, 58–9
noncitizenship, 14–15
Nottebohm case, 53–5
Nystrom v Australia, 59

"one's own country," 192n5
   Human Rights Committee cases, 55–60
   state-individual power imbalance, 58, 60–1
   stateless persons' links to, 3–5, 11, 60–1, 77, 104–5, 108
Ong Boon Hua case, 72–3
ontology of statelessness, 5, 7, 14, 17, 169–70
Orang Asli, 36, 40
   indigeneity of, 24, 28, 33, 39–41
   major groups of, 34–5, 39–40
Orang Ulu, 24, 28, 36, 41

250 GHOST CITIZENS

Othering, 82, 134, 153
    stateless persons', 4, 17–18, 23, 42, 158, 167–72
out-of-court case resolution, 74, 91

Pang Wee See case, 86
Papua New Guineans, 71–2, 79, 185, 188
parental links, citizenship, 4, 55–6, 66–7, 89, 122
parents, 60, 118
    biological versus adoptive, 73–4, 77–8, 90
    burden of citizenship proof, 72, 76–8, 82–3, 98–9, 163
    foreign mothers, *see* mothers' citizenship
    racial categorization and, 131, 152, 166
    statelessness and, 67, 70, 75, 98–103, 139, 178–81
    see also adopted children; marriage
Peninsular Malaysia, 21, 29–30
    Indigenous persons of, 34–5, 39
Philippines, the, 51, 79, 144, 184
    immigration from, 41, 101–2, 188–90
Pietsch, Julie, 33, 130
plantation workers and children, 98, 103, 115, 123, 203n25
    pre-independence, 30, 37, 97, 188, 204n42
Pontianak, 3, 5, 142
    about, 1–2, 6–8, 176
    sightings of, 2, 7
postcolonial citizenship, 64, 143, 156, 168
    research on, 15, 18, 171–2
postcolonial states, 12
    citizenship law in, 15, 27, 95, 143
    kinship in, 107
    racial identification in, 10, 24, 39, 43, 156
poverty, 34
    stateless persons', 6, 18, 115, 139
purgatory, 61, 168
    ghost citizens in, 6–8, 20, 165, 167, 176

race, 4, 180
    international legal instruments on, 49–50
    Malaysian understandings of, 28, 32, 35
    use of term, 28–9
racial categorization,
    colonialism legacies of, 10, 18, 31–4, 96, 138, 166–8
    exclusion through, 18, 32, 35–7, 107, 153, 171–3
    policy making and, 38–9, 43, 112, 130, 172
    statelessness and, 23–4, 27–8, 42, 71, 143, 176
    stereotypes of, 31, 55, 127–30, 143, 153–5
racialized communities,
    administrative exclusion of, 127–8, 138
    colonization, impacts of, 10, 17–18
    national narratives and, 42, 153–4, 175
racism, 3, 6, 11
    government officials', 73, 127–31, 168
Ramanoojum case, 80
registration, 10
    assistance with, 123–4, 159–63
    birth, *see* birth registration
    citizenship, 12, 68, 85–7, 127, 135, 161
    challenges, 109, 115–17, 120–4, 132, 177
    marriage, 97, 118, 123, 125–6, 163, 181
    rallies, 22, 127, 130, 141, 159–62, 181
    systems, 17–18, 71, 80, 174–5
Refugee Convention, 24, 103
    limited protection for statelessness, 49–50, 65, 138
refugees, 44, 184
    research on, 13, 188
    state denial of, 7, 103, 189
    terminology of, 24
remedies for statelessness, 88–91
rights, 12, 15–16, 46
    adopted children's, 50, 69, 74
    human, *see* human rights
    Malaysian citizenship, 41, 65–9, 74, 97
    stateless children, 50, 64–5, 88–9
    state sovereignty versus, 16–17

Rohingya, genocide by Myanmar, 12, 18, 52, 102, 171
Roisah bin Abdullah, story of, 141–59

Sabah, 29, 116, 191
　Indigenous communities in, 33–6, 41
　statelessness in, 21, 72, 97–8, 102–3, 187, 189
Sadiq, Kamal, 15, 34, 36, 41, 172–3
Sarawak, 22, 29, 182
　Indigenous communities in, 33–6, 41
　statelessness in, 72, 101–2, 116
Schachar, Ayelet, 106–7
self-governance, 13, 105
Shamsul Amri Baharuddin, 31–2, 35, 138
social services, barriers to accessing, 3, 6
sovereignty, territorial, 47, 58
　European colonization, 8–9, 14, 36, 192n15
　human rights versus, 16–17, 28, 38
speculation on citizenship, 61, 82, 84–5, 106, 167, 170
Spiro, Peter, 53–4
statelessness,
　condition of, 3–4, 11–14, 114, 153–4
　construction of, 7–8, 28, 43, 63, 70, 168
　de jure, 23, 48
　denial of, 4–6, 45, 60–3, 86–8, 106–7, 168–72
　in situ, 5, 23, 54–5, 94–5, 104–5, 170–2, 175
　as legal problem, 12, 44, 48
　Malaysia's creation of, 3, 20–2, 29, 65–6, 69–72, 131, 144
　rights regime versus, 15–16, 50, 64–5, 88–9
　state thinning of, 85, 92
stateless persons, 41, 84, 97
　barriers facing, 3–7, 21, 48–53, 113–19, 122, 157
　burden of proof by, 71–3, 77–9, 92–3, 98–9, 163
　categories of, 97–103
　concept of, 3–4, 23–4, 114
　gaslighting of, 4–7, 62, 85, 166–7
　identity of, 17–18, 42, 46, 70–2, 88–9, 154, 168
　narratives about, 6–8, 13, 21, 42–9, 63, 84, 92–5, 115

　numbers of Malaysian, 94, 97–9
　recognition of, 5–6, 21, 76–7, 82–6, 114–15, 136–7
　survival work of, 6–7, 114, 158, 172, 191
　see also ghost citizens
states,
　assumptions about, 16–17, 33, 48–9, 62–3, 80, 112
　as benevolent, 152, 156–9
　border protection, 8–9, 16–17, 105, 174–5
　citizenship conferral by, *see* citizenship
　colonial violence of, 8–12, 24, 30
　concept of, 9–11
　(dis)loyalty to, 6, 23, 42, 168
　emergence of, 8–9
　focus on recognition by, 14, 16, 62–3, 93
　obligations of, 7, 16, 50–1, 53, 62, 69
　prerogative power of, *see* states' prerogative power
states' prerogative power, 106, 175
　inegalitarian practices and, 16–17, 47–8, 69, 174
　legal infrastructure prioritizing, 50, 52–3, 58, 62–3, 85–6
Stewart v Canada, 56–8
Subramanium, Yogeswaran, 33, 36, 40

Tamils, 99, 178, 191
　in Peninsular Malasia, 21, 97, 115
Tan Lee case, 71
Thailand, 83, 102, 130
　family members from, 75–6, 79, 81, 101, 179–84, 187
Than Siew Beng case, 65, 74, 77–8, 82–3
"time of birth" limits, cases of, 77, 79–81, 83, 182
transparency, lack of, 20, 88, 132, 138, 157, 175

United Nations High Commissioner for Refugees (UNHCR), 48, 184, 189, 191
　guidelines for stateless persons, 24, 44–5, 92
　refugee registration, 97, 102–3

see also Convention against Torture;
    Refugee Convention
Universal Declaration of Human Rights,
    16, 50, 64

Van Waas, Laura, 44, 46–8

Walia, Harsha, 18
Warsame v Canada, 59
watching briefs, 92
Western culture,
    non-Western versus, 14–15
    rights regime in, 15–16, 198n93
    values of, 14–15, 174
whiteness, 20, 31

Yong Lee Hua case, 72–3
Yosof, Rohana, 76